THE WITCHES OF S

An emotive, haunting story of a community torn apart, the Essex witch accusations and trial of 1581–1582 are, taken together, one of the pivotal instances of that malign and destructive wave of misogynistic persecution that periodically broke over early modern England. Yet, for all their importance in the overall study of witchcraft, the so-called witches of St Osyth have largely been overlooked by scholars. Marion Gibson now sets right that neglect. Using fresh archival sources – and investigating not just the village itself, but also its neighbouring Elizabethan hamlets and habitations – the author offers revelatory new insights into the sixteen women and one man accused of sorcery, while also asking wider, provocative questions about the way history is recollected and interpreted. Combining landscape detective work, a reconstruction of lost spaces and authoritative readings of crucial documents, Gibson skilfully unlocks the poignant personal histories of those denied the chance to speak for themselves.

MARION GIBSON is Professor of Renaissance and Magical Literatures at the University of Exeter and a Fellow of the Royal Historical Society. Fascinated by witches' stories for nearly thirty years, she is the author of *Reading Witchcraft* (1999), *Early Modern Witches* (2000), *Witchcraft and Society* (2003), *Witchcraft Myths in American Culture* (2007), *Imagining the Pagan Past* (2013), *Rediscovering Renaissance Witchcraft* (2017) and *Witchcraft: The Basics* (2018). In addition she serves as general editor of the Cambridge University Press series *Elements in Magic*.

'This terrific book is that of a historian at the top of her game, bringing all her knowledge, research skills and writing ability to the task. In so doing, Marion Gibson has made an important addition to our knowledge of Elizabethan witchcraft. But the text is also written for a more general audience and is engagingly written with that audience in mind too. Thus, the book has all the virtues of a "crossover" study that will appeal both to the academic specialist and the more general reader. It demonstrates that good history writing can be erudite as well as entertaining.'

– Philip Almond, Professor Emeritus of the Study of Religion, University of Queensland, author of The Lancashire Witches: A Chronicle of Sorcery and Death on Pendle Hill

'Marion Gibson is a very well-established and respected scholar with a particular reputation for expertise in the kind of sources she uses so effectively in this book. She is able to combine here first-rate academic research with a popular and accessible literary style. The book takes a very famous English witchcraft case and supplies genuinely new material by which that case may be understood, both by a close rereading of the celebrated text and by a contextualisation of it in a range of hitherto completely untapped local records.'

– Ronald Hutton, Professor of History, University of Bristol, author of The Witch: A History of Fear, from Ancient Times to the Present

'An excellent monograph and contribution to the field of witchcraft studies.'

– Diane Purkiss, Professor of English Literature, University of Oxford, author of The Witch in History: Early Modern and Twentieth-Century Representations

THE WITCHES
OF ST OSYTH

PERSECUTION, BETRAYAL AND
MURDER IN ELIZABETHAN
ENGLAND

MARION GIBSON

University of Exeter

CAMBRIDGE
UNIVERSITY PRESS

Shaftesbury Road, Cambridge CB2 8EA, United Kingdom

One Liberty Plaza, 20th Floor, New York, NY 10006, USA

477 Williamstown Road, Port Melbourne, VIC 3207, Australia

314–321, 3rd Floor, Plot 3, Splendor Forum, Jasola District Centre, New Delhi – 110025, India

103 Penang Road, #05–06/07, Visioncrest Commercial, Singapore 238467

Cambridge University Press is part of Cambridge University Press & Assessment, a department of the University of Cambridge.

We share the University's mission to contribute to society through the pursuit of education, learning and research at the highest international levels of excellence.

www.cambridge.org
Information on this title: www.cambridge.org/9781108796842

DOI: 10.1017/9781108859608

First published 2022
First paperback edition 2024

A catalogue record for this publication is available from the British Library

Library of Congress Cataloging-in-Publication data
NAMES: Gibson, Marion, 1970– author.
TITLE: The witches of St Osyth : persecution, betrayal and murder in Elizabethan England / Marion Gibson, University of Exeter.
DESCRIPTION: Cambridge, United Kingdom ; New York, NY, USA : Cambridge University Press, 2022. | Includes bibliographical references and index.
IDENTIFIERS: LCCN 2022024927 | ISBN 9781108494670 (hardback) | ISBN 9781108859608 (ebook)
SUBJECTS: LCSH: Witch hunting – England – St. Osyth – History. | Witchcraft – England – St. Osyth – History. | Trials (Witchcraft) – England – St. Osyth – History.
CLASSIFICATION: LCC BF1581 .G5356 2022 |
DDC 133.4/3094267–dc23/eng/20220729
LC record available at https://lccn.loc.gov/2022024927

ISBN   978-1-108-49467-0   Hardback
ISBN   978-1-108-79684-2   Paperback

CONTENTS

A colour plate section will be found between pages 168 and 169.

v

FIGURES

ACKNOWLEDGEMENTS

Thanks to: Alex Wright at Cambridge University Press for giving me the opportunity to write this book and Katie Idle, Bethany Johnson and Santhamurthy Ramamoorthy for assistance with its production; Carol Bailey for detailed and sensitive indexing; Tim Sargeant of St Osyth Priory for kindly giving me a tour of the Priory estate, the Sargeant family, and Helen Pollintine for facilitating my visit; the Clarke family at Lee Wick for hospitality; the brilliantly helpful and friendly staff of Essex Record Office, especially Vanda Jeffrey and Neil Wiffen, and thanks to Neil for reading the book in manuscript; the staff at the National Archives Kew, London Metropolitan Archives, Cambridge University Library, Suffolk Record Office, Ipswich Branch and Cheshire Archives; Chris Thornton for generously sharing his Victoria County History work and reading the book in manuscript; Jonathan Durrant for reading the book in manuscript; Jake Millar for sharing his local knowledge; John Worland for sharing his film and discussing his findings; Tracey Norman, Mark Norman and Circle of Spears for *Witch*; Syd Moore for her commitment to Essex witches; Simon Coxall for discussing howeland gallows; the University of Exeter, particularly Emily Selove, for their contributions to magical studies at the university; Ronald Hutton, Owen Davies, Diane Purkiss, Philip Almond, Jay Johnston, Will Pooley, Poppy Corbett, Anna Kisby-Compton, Tabitha

Stanmore, Nicola Whyte, Kate Hext, Richard Noakes, Jo Esra, Lucy Hilliar, Dorka Tamas and Anna Milon for encouragement and reflection on history, landscape, witches and magic; my professional services colleagues for their work through the pandemic, especially Tim Seelig and Poppy Smith; my agents Joanna Swainson and Sarah Levitt; the booksellers, postwomen, postmen and delivery drivers who brought me books; most of all Harry for suggesting in 2018 that I go back to the St Osyth witches and have another look; mum, Hoppy and Buster, the Cricket Club/vaccine centre, Derriford Hospital NHS Trust, and our neighbours and their dogs for keeping us sane.

WHO'S WHO

ALDUST, JOHN – a wealthy farmer of Little Oakley and Ramsey, churchwarden of Ramsey. Cousin of John and Elizabeth Herd, John is asked by Annis Herd to intercede for her at the church court, to which she has been presented by John Wade and Thomas Cartwrite

ANWICK, ROBERT AND JOANE WELD ANWICK – moderately well-off farmers of Little Oakley. Joane, daughter of Richard and Anne Weld, and cousin of Godlife Weld Osborne and Anne Weld West, is walking with Annis Herd when she is accused by Richard Harrison

BARNES, 'MOTHER' – a St Osyth woman held to be a witch and cunning woman, died 12 February 1582

BARRENGER, PHILIP (also known as Cowper) – a labourer aged twenty-three, son of Joan Pechey of St Osyth and accused of incest with her

BAXTER, ALES – maidservant to Richard and Alice Rosse at Little Clacton, and by implication accuser of the Selles family

BENNETT, ELIZABETH – a farmer of Wellwick, St Osyth, the wife of John Bennett. Elizabeth is accused of killing her neighbours William and Joan Byet and several others

BRASYER, JOHN – the Brasyers are wealthy farmers of Walton le Soken, and tenants of Walton Hall. John accuses Joan Robinson of witchcraft

BRETT, JOHANE AND WILLIAM – small-holding tenants of Little Oakley. Johane cared for Anne Harrison during her final illness and William is a churchwarden of Beaumont

BUTLER, JOHN – wealthy tenant of Lee Wick, St Osyth, farmer and landlord with interests in milling and fishing. John is said to have been bewitched by Ales Newman or Elizabeth Bennett

BYET, WILLIAM AND JOAN – next-door neighbours of Elizabeth Bennett, said to have been killed by her

CARTER, JOHN – a small farmer of Thorpe le Soken who accuses Margaret Grevell of bewitching his brewing

CARTER, MARGERY – the wife of farmer William and part of the Carter family of Thorpe le Soken and Walton le Soken. Margery accuses Joan Robinson

CARTWRITE, THOMAS AND CECILY THURLETHORPE BLOSSE CARTWRITE – wealthy farmers of Great and Little Oakley, related to the Marven and Blosse families and having dealings with the Wades. Thomas is a churchwarden of Little Oakley, who will present Annis Herd to the church court with John Wade and accuses her of bewitching his cattle

CHESTON, JOAN – a wealthy farmer and widow of Robert Cheston of Thorpe le Soken and Walton le Soken. Joan accuses Ales Manfield and Margaret Grevell, whom she charges with harming her cattle and killing Robert

COCK'S WIFE – a cunning woman of Weeley, consulted by Ursley Kempe

CROSSE, THOMAS – a farmer of Thorpe le Soken, who accused Margaret Ewstace of witchcraft and died in about 1579. Thomas was the husband of Felice Okey and brother-in-law of Robert Sannever

DARCY, BRIAN – magistrate, at St Clere's Hall, St Osyth. The son of Thomas Darcy of Tolleshunt Darcy (died 1557) and his wife Elizabeth, Brian attended Lincoln's Inn in the 1560s. He is married to Bridget Corbett. Brian holds property at Tiptree, Witham and elsewhere, and appeared at Quarter Sessions in 1576–1577 represented by William Whetcrofte to defend claims on his large estate

DARCY, JOHN AND FRANCES RICH DARCY – second Lord Darcy and Lady Darcy; John died in 1581. They were the parents of Thomas, third Lord Darcy

DARCY, THOMAS – third Lord Darcy, succeeds to his title in 1581 and marries Mary Kitson

DARCY THOMAS AND CAMILLA GUICCIARDINI DARCY – the eldest brother and sister-in-law of Brian Darcy, of Tolleshunt Darcy

DARCY, THOMAS AND ELIZABETH DE VERE DARCY – first Lord Darcy and Lady Darcy, whose children were Robert (died 1569), Thomasine and John (their heir)

DEATH, THOMAS AND AGNES – a mariner and his wife of Great Clacton, the parents of Marie Death (born 1564) who accuses Cisley Selles of bewitching her, and of John (born 1576), whom they accuse Cisley of killing

DOWSING, ANNIS – a child witness and the daughter of accused witch Annis Herd and William Dowsing, born 1575

DOWSING, WILLIAM – the father of Annis Dowsing, husband of Susan Orris (died 1578) and Anne Smyth (died before 1582)

DUCKE, ALLEN – a farmer of Walton le Soken, who accuses Joan Robinson

DURRANT, HENRY – a butcher of St Osyth and father of Rebecca Durrant, whom he accuses Ales Hunt of killing. Henry also consults Ursley Kempe about witchcraft events when she is imprisoned in Colchester Castle

EWSTACE, ELIZABETH – a farmer of Thorpe le Soken with lands at Eustac and Hopkin Eustac on Hamford Water, the mother of Margaret Ewstace. Elizabeth was born in about 1529; she provided ointment to Ales Manfield, who accuses her, and she is also accused by Robert Sannever

EWSTACE, MARGARET – the daughter of Elizabeth Ewstace, servant to Robert Sannever in the mid-1560s. After sacking Margaret, Robert accused her and her mother of killing his child and his brother-in-law Thomas Crosse and she is also accused by Ales Manfield

GLASCOCK, ANNIS – the wife of the sawyer John Glascock of St Osyth, and a lodging-house keeper. Annis is accused by Ursley Kempe of bewitching children in the families of Michael Stevens and William Page

GREVELL, MARGARET – a widow of Thorpe le Soken, born about 1527. Margaret is accused by Ales Manfield, Joan Cheston and Nicholas Strickland of the murder of Robert Cheston, attacks on brewing and baking and killing her own husband

HARRISON, ANNE SPENCER – the wife of Richard Harrison, Rector of Beaumont, and widow of Hugh Spencer. The Harrisons were married in 1568, had five children and lived at Little Oakley as well as at Beaumont. In summer 1580, Anne quarrelled with Annis Herd and with the final words before her death before Christmas 1581, she accused Annis of killing her

HARRISON, RICHARD – Rector of Beaumont, widower of Anne Spencer Harrison. They were the parents of Richard, Mary, Thomas, James and Anne. Richard senior was in London when his wife quarrelled with Annis Herd and subsequently accuses Annis himself of theft and witchcraft. He and his son Richard would later face their own accusations

HAYWARD, WILLIAM AND MARGARET – moderately wealthy farmers of Frowick, St Osyth, and neighbours to Elizabeth Bennett. Ales Hunt, one of whose children Margaret had christened, is accused by Ursley Kempe of killing William's cattle

HERD, ANNIS – a poor but well-connected woman from Little Oakley, with multiple lovers. The daughter of Robert and Charity Herd, Annis is the unmarried mother of Annis Dowsing (whose father William was her lover at least from 1573 to 1575) and a boy. She has been presented to the church court for immorality and witchcraft, and is accused by John Wade, Thomas Cartwrite, Bennet Lane, Andrew and Anne Weld West, Richard and Anne Harrison and Godlife Weld Osborne; subsequently she is also accused of killing William Dowsing's wives

HERD, JOHN – a wealthy farmer from Little Oakley, active in the 1570s and 1580s when his children were baptised. John has business dealings with Robert Anwick, John Aldust (his cousin), John Wade and the Marven family, and the Herd family hold extensive lands across Little Oakley and Ramsey

HEWET, JOAN – maidservant to Joan Robinson at Walton le Soken. The Hewet family hold lands in the Soken manors, especially at Thorpe le Soken and Skighawe

HOOKE, WILLIAM – a painter of St Osyth, next-door neighbour of Ales Newman, whom he accuses of witchcraft

HUNT, ALES BARNES – the wife of William Hunt, under-employed mason of St Osyth. Ales is the daughter of 'Mother' Barnes, sister of Margerie Barnes Sammon and mother of Febey Hunt. Ales is accused by Ursley Kempe of killing William Hayward's cattle and Henry Durrant's daughter, and herself accuses Joan Pechey – her mother-in-law Widow Hunt's next-door neighbour in Nether Hoo – of witchcraft

HUNT, FEBEY – a child witness, the daughter of Ales and William Hunt, born about 1574

JOHNSON, JOHN – Collector for the Poor in St Osyth, in which capacity he gave food donations to Joan Pechey and denied money to Ales Newman. John and his wife died suddenly in 1581 and his death was attributed to both women's witchcraft

KEMPE, LAWRENCE – of Thorpe le Soken, brother of Ursley Kempe. Lawrence alleges that his wife died after a fight with Ursley

KEMPE, URSLEY GREY – of St Osyth, cunning woman, midwife-nurse and unmarried mother of Thomas Rabbet. Ursley is Lawrence Kempe's sister. She lives near her friend Ales Newman, whom she accuses of sharing in her witchcraft. Ursley also accuses Elizabeth Bennett, Ales Hunt and Annis Glascock. She is herself accused by Grace Thurlowe of killing her daughter Joan, by Annis Letherdall of killing her daughter Elizabeth, by her brother of killing his wife, of causing various illnesses and of killing Edena Stratton. Ursley will be imprisoned at Colchester Castle, and questioned there by villagers and magistrates about the death of John, second Lord Darcy

LANE, BENNET RUSHE AND WILLIAM LANE – of Little Oakley, married in 1581. Bennet was the widow of William Rushe and William the widower of Anne or Agnes Lane. The Lanes were poor people with two children – Bennet's step-children – and little property. Bennet accuses Annis Herd of witchcraft

LETHERDALL, ANNIS AND RICHARD – the parents of two children and a baby (Elizabeth), whom Annis accuses Ursley Kempe of bewitching. Annis will help to search the bodies of Ursley and possibly other accused women for witches' teats

MANFIELD, ALES – of Thorpe le Soken, born about 1519. Ales accuses Margaret Grevell, Elizabeth and Margaret Ewstace, Cisley Selles, Ursley Kempe, 'Mother' Turner, Ales Barnes Hunt and Margerie Barnes Sammon and is herself accused by Joan Cheston of bewitching her animals and by Richard Rosse of arson

MILES, ALES – a farmer of Walton le Soken; she accuses Joan Robinson

NEWMAN, ALES – of St Osyth, wife of William Newman (although he dies during 1582), friend of Ursley Kempe and godmother to her son Thomas Rabbet, and neighbour of William Hooke. Ursley accuses Ales of sharing in her witchcraft against Elizabeth Letherdall, Joan Thurlowe and Edena Stratton, and killing John Johnson and his wife

OKEY, FELICE CROSSE – widow of Thorpe le Soken, who accuses Elizabeth Ewstace of killing her former husband Thomas Crosse. Felice is the sister of Robert Sannever

OSBORNE, GODLIFE WELD AND EDMUND OSBORNE – of Little Oakley, small farmers married in 1575, and the parents of Edmund (died 1577) and Susan. Godlife was born in 1558, the daughter of John Weld and sister of Anne Weld West, Dorothy Weld Cressie (died 1573) and Richard Weld (died 1572). Joane Weld Anwick is her cousin

PAGE, WILLIAM – a gardener of St Osyth Priory, father of Charity Page and foster-father of a nurse-child, both of whom he accuses Annis Glascock of killing. His wife may have consulted Ursley Kempe as a cunning woman

PECHEY, JOAN – of St Osyth, where she has lived for forty years. Friend of 'Mother' Barnes and mother of Philip Barrenger (or Cowper), Joan lives in Nether Hoo as the neighbour of Widow Hunt. She is accused by Ales Hunt, and suspected of killing John Johnson from whom she received food donations

STRATTON, JOHN AND EDENA – John accuses Ursley Kempe of killing his wife Edena in 1582. Their relative Robert Stratton is a servant of John Butler

STRICKLAND, NICHOLAS – a butcher and farmer, of Thorpe le Soken and Kirby le Soken. He accuses Margaret Grevell of witchcraft

TENDERING, JOHN – a wealthy merchant of St Osyth and the Sokens who confirms the story of William Byet's evidence against Elizabeth Bennett

THURLOWE, GRACE AND JOHN – of St Osyth, where Grace is a servant of the Darcy family. Grace and John are the parents of Davy and Joan, whom Ursley Kempe is accused by Grace of attacking in 1581, killing baby Joan

UPCHER, EDWARD   a farmer of Walton le Soken, who accuses Joan Robinson of witchcraft after going to Colchester Castle to consult Ursley Kempe

WADE, JOHN – a wealthy farmer, of Little Oakley where he tenants the Hall farm; he also has lands in Tendring (where many of his children were baptised) and Moze. John is churchwarden in Moze parish. He accuses Annis Herd of bewitching his animals after he presents her to the church court with Thomas Cartwrite. John is connected to the wealthy Marvens and Herds, is bailiff of Little Oakley manor and employs several servants

WALTER, ALES – a moderately wealthy farmer, of Walton le Soken, who is connected to a wider Walter family with lands across the Sokens and Clactons. She accuses Joan Robinson of bewitching her animals

WELD, JOHN AND MARGARET – the parents of Anne Weld West, Godlife Weld Osborne, Richard Weld junior (died 1572) and Dorothie Weld Cressie (died 1573). John was a mariner and small farmer who died in 1571, holding land in Little Oakley and Ramsey

WELD, RICHARD SENIOR AND ANNE – the parents of Joane Weld Anwick and Dorothie Weld Wood. Richard shares the tenancy of Gardelers in Little Oakley with Hugh Spencer and his wife Anne, later Anne Spencer Harrison

WEST, ANDREW AND ANNE WELD WEST – the brother-in-law and sister of Godlife Osborne, cousins of Joane Weld Anwick, guardians of Richard Weld junior and parents of multiple children. Small farmers, the Wests accuse Annis Herd of harming their animals

WHETCROFTE, WILLIAM JUNIOR – son of the lawyer and town clerk William Whetcrofte of Ipswich, Wherstead and Witnesham and his wife Alice, William junior is a clerk and pamphleteer

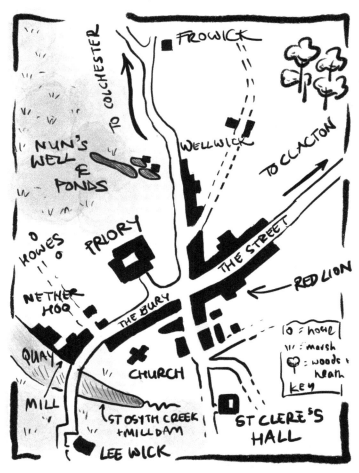

MAP 1 Map of St Osyth. (Source: author.)

MAP 2   Map of eastern Essex. (Source: Joe LeMonnier.)

ABBREVIATIONS

ATAJR   *A True and just Recorde* (London, 1582)

CRO   Cheshire Record Office

CUL   Cambridge University Library

ERO   Essex Record Office, Chelmsford

LMA   London Metropolitan Archives

SRO   Suffolk Record Office, Ipswich Branch

TNA   The National Archives, Kew, formerly Public
        Record Office (PRO)

Introduction

Welcome to St Osyth

~

St Osyth village clusters where four lanes meet, on a foreland between the pebbly North Sea beaches and the mudbanks of the River Colne. From its low hill you can look west in the direction of London and east towards the Netherlands across the sea. In past times the village's chandleries and sail-lofts equipped barges trading between the Thames Valley, the east coast of England and Holland. St Osyth's fields and fisheries supplied big markets, most notably London. Ships of up to thirty tons could navigate – carefully – up the silty little creek to the village wharf and they shipped out cargo after cargo: tiles, bricks, gravel, wood, wool, vegetables, fish, oysters and cheese. St Osyth was a lively hub, although now it is a quiet corner: it hardly feels like the setting for the panicked whirl of activity that spreads a witch-hunt across the map, from home to home, village to village. Yet that is what St Osyth and its surrounding villages became in the winter of 1582: witchland.

In Elizabethan times the quayside rang with the hammering, singing and swearing of shipwrights and sawyers, rope slapping on sea-bleached wood, sails cracking as they filled with wind. Smells of pitch and resin fragranced the air. On Mill Street, which led from the quay to the Priory, inns catered to hungry mariners as well as to carriers bringing produce to and from the ships. Landladies made malty Essex ale and beer, and served mutton, from marsh-fed sheep, and rabbit pie: there was a warren in the Little Park next to Mill Street. Deals were done and trade disputes argued out in the market square and guild halls, one of which was a former monastic hospital. It stood on Mill Street too, in the section called The Bury outside the Priory gate, and was flanked by the fine houses of gentry and merchants facing onto the Priory grounds. A large community of farmers, craftspeople and specialist traders – painters, victuallers, dyers, wheelwrights, oyster dredgers, blacksmiths, spinners, clothiers, saltmakers, shoemakers, glovers, caulkers – served the town, its traders and sailors.[1]

Before reclamation and drainage extended its fields and firmed its paths, the village must have felt even more maritime than it does now: the end of the Essex earth and the beginning of the water. Estuarine Essex was flooded more deeply then, and was wilder. Hills that now look down on flat green fields were once islets standing above pools and reed beds, and where the land rose above the tideline it did so as heathland and scrub. Essex maps still bear names that tell this story: Causeway End, Marsh Road, Heath Farm. Early field names frequently included the suffix 'marsh' and some were called 'wadings' or 'swamp'. Villages were linked in Elizabethan times by fragile bridges, wooden walkways and earthen banks that repeatedly required repair but seldom received it. Even in

---

[1] Cheshire Archives DCH/o/17; Valerie Scott and Libby Brown, *St Osyth: Conservation Area Appraisal and Management Plan* (Tendring: Tendring District Council, 2010) *passim*; Christopher Thornton and Herbert Eiden, eds., *The History of the County of Essex* vol. 12 (London and Woodbridge: Institute of Historical Research /Boydell and Brewer, 2020) 133–40, 147–9.

FIGURE I.I   The Mill, St Osyth. (Source: Chronicle / Alamy Stock
Photo.)
Note: A black and white version of this figure will appear in some
formats. For the colour version, please refer to the plate section.

modern times, the Essex coast has the feel of a land very
close to becoming sea, 'a series of gently swelling ridges,
green rollers of smooth grassland, about half a mile from
wave to wave'.[2]

St Osyth went right down to sea level at the creek –
which was also known as 'the fleet' – but it had areas
of higher ground too: the village sits on the crown of
a mound, and Beacon Hill is nearby. The main area of
settlement on the mound was connected to the coastal
marshes by a narrow causeway that dammed the creek
to form a tidal mill pool (Figure I.1). Until this causeway
was widened and straightened in 1936, large vehicles such

[2] E.g. ERO D/DHw T99; D/DZl 18; D/DCr M1; Donald Maxwell, *A
Detective in Essex* (London: John Lane, 1933) 18.

3

as buses could not venture across it. They had to turn around at the end of Mill Street, unable to go out onto the flat marshlands.[3]

By then, the coast was dotted with chalets, bungalows and caravan parks, but in Elizabethan times it was empty except for a few farmhouses and their sheep and cattle. Parts of it often flooded, south of the fleet and along its length, despite sea walls. Even in recent times a tidal surge could pour up to a mile inland in Essex, as it did disastrously in the 'Great Flood' of 1953. On that January night, the St Osyth mill dam was under five feet of debris-swollen water and at Lee Wick to the south the water depth reached ten feet.[4]

In calmer seasons, the marsh along this stretch of the Essex coast was a lonely, still place. Swans, ducks, gulls and wading birds – curlews and oystercatchers – picked over the flats for worms and shellfish, sand eels, refuse and flies. When it was hot, the creeks ponged at low tide of decaying sea weed and discarded waste from fish-gutting that had been tipped in near the quay. Further out, there were flocks of dunlin, turnstones and plovers trotting across silvery mud, and herons stabbing salty pools. Humans were rarer creatures than birds. Banked paths

---

[3] Geraldine Craig, *St Osyth* (Clacton-on-Sea and St Osyth: Guild Press and St Osyth Historical Society, 2003) 13, 15; Thornton and Eiden, *The History of the County of Essex* 145–147.

[4] Phyllis Hendy, *St Osyth Parish Council: The First 100 Years* (Clacton-on-Sea: Campwood Press, 1993) 46–7; Thornton and Eiden, *The History of the County of Essex* 67 – two people drowned in the floods at St Osyth (Point Clear) in 1953; see also Hilda Grieve, *The Great Tide* (Chelmsford: Essex County Council, 1959) *passim* and *Essex and the Sea* (Chelmsford: Essex County Council, 1970) 1–6; Craig et al., *St Osyth* 71.

and, where these ran out, oval wooden boards strapped to the feet kept oystermen, bait-diggers and wild-fowlers from the ooze. Whiting, cod and gurnard could be caught offshore, and there were flatfish, shellfish and mullet in the creeks. Oyster pits riddled the foreshores. The sea provided villagers in this corner of the county with both food and salt but, although there was plenty of saline water, long, dry summers could easily cause drought: eastern Essex is the least rainy part of England. This was one of many challenges for farmers. In summer, wheat and barley fields could bake and crack, but during storms the waves pounded sea walls and river cliffs, and spray soused all the coastal lands.[5]

Farm-folk in the coastal villages and all over the district of Tendring Hundred raised pigs, cattle and sheep, many of whom fed on the marshes where they ate a coarse hay. Farmers' wives and their maids churned butter and pressed curds into vast quantities of cheese made from milk from both cows and sheep. The local cheeses were famous for their size: huge wheels of hard sheep's cheese were shipped out of St Osyth from the quay to be sold in local markets along the coast and in London. The cheese-making farmers also kept geese, ducks and some chickens and sold their meat, eggs and feathery down. Raising and selling chicks was a profitable business. Where they could, people also planted plum and apple trees or kept bees on the heaths to supplement their diet and income. In the hedgerows were fat blackberries, free

---

[5] Thornton and Eiden, *The History of the County of Essex* 151–2; see Hervey Benham, *Essex Gold: The Fortunes of the Essex Oysterman* (Chelmsford: Essex Record Office, 1993).

FIGURE I.2 Old houses in Stone Alley, St Osyth. (Source: Rodger
Tamblyn / Alamy Stock Photo.)
Note: A black and white version of this figure will appear in some
formats. For the colour version, please refer to the plate section.

food but with a short season at the end of summer, and
likewise there were hips and nuts. But in general there
were few large trees outside of the copses. At St Osyth
these copses were Riddles Wood and Hartley Wood,
both of which were inland and north of the village. There
was also little shelter from hedgerows, so crops and creatures alike shivered in the legendarily sharp east wind.

That bitter wind meant that St Osyth's medieval clap-
board houses could be draughty, and when wet they rotted
and leaked. In summer, mosquitos whined in and spread
fever among those whom they bit. Some homes were of
thatch and cob or clay construction with earthen walls,
warm in winter but vulnerable to heavy rain (Figure I.2).
So were many of the barns that kept grain and animal

fodder dry. Mould and mice whittled away carefully hoarded stores. If trade was bad, St Osyth's poorer people had limited food to fall back upon. They could apply to the Collector for the Poor, a charitable parish office filled by a clothmaker in the early 1580s: John Johnson, whose wealth came from the wooltrade. Wool dominated the economy of the women and many of the men of the village, so John would interact with them almost daily as his agents distributed wool to clean, spin and dye. As Collector, he would give them a little money or a little beef and bread from the charitable funding he had collected. Some folk flourished, but it was not a forgiving time or place to be poor.

Before the Augustinian canons had closed their doors at St Osyth some fifty years before, things had been different, at least in the memories of older people. Trade was brisker, and the canons had a straightforward religious duty to give alms. They appointed a dedicated almoner to do so, and he held Amperswick Farm in the village. Older memories of wealth and charitable piety were associated with a seventh-century foundation, after whose first abbess – Lady Osgith or Osyth, a Mercian princess and martyr – the village was renamed. Its original name, Cicc or Chiche, remained in legal documents but most people called the place 'Saint Oses' or, more briefly, 'Toosey'. When Osyth's successors, the canons, left and their foundation was closed, asset-stripped and privatised in 1539, ancient patterns of trade and charity both ceased. They were replaced piecemeal under the direction of the land's new owners: the Darcy family. The Darcys renamed the site 'the Priory' and they held other formerly religious property in the village and beyond.

7

The Tolleshunt branch of the family owned St Clere's Hall, a few hundred yards from the Priory, and the wider family held lands across Essex through Little and Great Clacton out to Walton le Soken on the east coast and also in many parishes inland. In fact, it must have seemed that Darcy men owned almost all the rights to everything in the area. Just about everyone was a tenant, partner or debtor of theirs in some way, and this fact will matter later in the story of the witches of 1582.

The Darcys gave gifts to the Elizabethan-style food bank maintained by the Collector, and they would have fed their poorer neighbours on religious holidays and during the peak seasons of agricultural work.[6] But still people went hungry and sometimes they were understandably ungrateful for the scraps they were given from the loaded Priory tables. Some looked back to earlier times with nostalgia, others had welcomed the religious changes of the Reformation and felt they should have gone further. Across the Darcy lands and beyond, people met in unlicensed assemblies to hear radical preachers or debate shocking ideas of religious autonomy. Even the suspicion of such activities prompted sharp questions from ecclesiastical authorities. Meantime, international

---

[6] Jake Millar, email 2 February 2021; Craig, et al., *St Osyth* 62, 64–5; Thornton and Eiden, *The History of the County of Essex* 135, 139–40; F. G. Emmison, *Elizabethan Life: Home, Work and Land* (Chelmsford: Essex County Council, 1976) 8; ERO D/DGh M45/16; Philip Morant, *The History and Antiquities of the County of Essex*, vol. 1 (London, 1748) 456; Hendy, *St Osyth Parish Council* 6; F. G. Emmison, *Tudor Food and Pastimes* (London: Ernest Benn, 1964) 46–53; on poverty and charity see Marjorie Keniston McIntosh, *Poor Relief in England 1350–1600* (Cambridge: Cambridge University Press, 2012) especially 252–69.

religious links and trading relationships had changed, as had the practices and markets that sustained the villagers. The overseas wool trade that had flourished in eastern England in medieval times because of its proximity to Flanders and Holland faltered, and nothing could replace the wealth it had brought to St Osyth and the wider Tendring district.

It was in this context – of economic and religious change, of the tense relationship between the villagers of Tendring Hundred and the Darcys and in the middle of a bitter, hungry winter – that the first witchcraft accusations were made in St Osyth in February 1582. This book explores those accusations and their consequences. While the story of the Essex witches of 1582 is indeed a story about St Osyth, it is also a story of Weeley, Little Clacton, Thorpe le Soken, Little Oakley, Beaumont, Moze, Walton le Soken and the other villages and manors of the Darcy estates, as well as their wider connections across eastern England. But it all starts in St Osyth, with two women whose anger grew to engulf not just their own but also the surrounding villages, and with the man whose assumptions framed their quarrel, encouraged and spread it to serve his own ends. Let's start at the hearth, the heart of the home of the first accuser: Grace Thurlowe.

I

St Osyth

Grace, Ursley, Annis and Ales

~

In the winter of 1581 the son of Grace Thurlowe, a servant at St Osyth Priory, began to be tormented by a peculiar illness. The boy Davy was 'strangely taken', his mother said: there was no ready explanation for his symptoms. Horribly, 'the palms of the child's hands were turned where the backs should be, and the back in the place of the palms'. Some strangely taken people suffered fits or convulsions and this kind of muscle spasm might have been afflicting Davy.[1] Whatever was wrong, he was in sufficient pain that he was unable to sleep and Grace put him to bed in the chimney corner, a quiet hearthside nook that would keep him warm. She and the boy's father, her husband John Thurlowe, were alarmed. As ordinary villagers, they had no access to a physician – costly and distant doctors. The Thurlowes did not 'live in' at St Osyth Priory, where Grace worked, and even if they had done they would have been very lucky indeed if her employer Lord Darcy would pay for medical help. Instead, they did what most villagers would do: they asked a neighbour who had a reputation for knowing about medical matters to take a look at Davy.

[1] For several examples see Marion Gibson, *Early Modern Witches* (London and New York: Routledge, 2000) especially chapters 1, 5, 9, 12 and 13, Gibson, ed., *Early English Trial Pamphlets* vol. 2 (London: Pickering and Chatto, 2003) and *Possession, Puritanism and Print* (London: Pickering and Chatto, 2006).

Their visitor, Ursley Kempe, had been practicing as a healer, a 'cunning body', for about a decade. She used herbs and magical rituals in her work, and she claimed to have a particular expertise with cases of bewitchment.[2] The fact that Ursley was asked to visit Davy suggests that because his illness was so strange, his parents suspected he was under a malignant spell. Ursley's remedy can only have confirmed that suspicion. When she came to the Thurlowes's cottage, she went to the boy's bedside, took him by the hand and said 'Ah good child, how art thou loden!' after which she went out of the house door. This she did three times, each time repeating the phrase 'Ah good child, how art thou loden!' The words, and her exiting of the property three times, suggest that she was acknowledging the 'load' of the illness on Davy, and attempting to transfer it to herself and carry it away, out of the Thurlowes's home. This was a classic treatment for bewitchment, aimed at removing the spell and casting it out of doors. Sometimes a spell might even be projected onto another person or a passing animal in order to get rid of it.[3] And Ursley's magical treatment did seem to work on Davy. That night he slept well, which he had not done for a long time. His exhausted mother Grace was relieved, and as she walked from her house down Mill Street towards St Osyth tidemill the next day she met Ursley and told her that Davy had slept normally. 'God be thanked!' Grace remarked piously. But Ursley's

---

[2] *A True and just Recorde (ATAJR)* 2A–2Av, 2A7–2A8.
[3] *ATAJR* 2A; e.g. Lawrence Normand and Gareth Roberts, eds., *Witchcraft in Early Modern Scotland* (Edinburgh: Edinburgh University Press, 2000) 242.

response suggests that she felt it was not just God who should be thanked for the patient's condition. 'Aye, aye' she nodded, telling Grace 'I warrant thee, it [the child or her cure] shall do well'. Ursley's 'warrant' or promise that Davy would flourish suggests that she felt her own powers were now engaged in ensuring his further recovery. What happened next indicates that she was also thinking ahead to other medical services that she could perform for the Thurlowe family.

At the time of Davy's illness, Grace was about six months pregnant with her next child, and she was beginning to suffer with lameness as well. Hurrying heavily down the road towards the fleet, she presented Ursley with a valuable opportunity. As they neared the time of their delivery, sixteenth-century women who could afford it paid a female 'keeper' to look after them as their lives became restricted by custom and necessity. In rich families, a number of women would divide 'keeping' tasks: several to care for, amuse and pray with the mother in her confinement, a midwife or midwives to attend the birth with male doctors to advise, a professional wet nurse to suckle the child while the mother recovered and the child grew towards being able to eat solid food, and other nurses, minders and educators to shape the young lord, lady or prince's behaviour and mind. But for a servant like Grace, a single keeper would have to do, someone to ease the strain on her bad legs, assist at the birth and help her with the tasks of motherhood. Ursley wanted that job.[4]

---

[4] *ATAJR* 2Av–2A2; the tidemill's site dates from the thirteenth century. Most recently, an eighteenth-century building survived as a working mill until 1929, but was demolished in 1963 when it was derelict (Craig et al., *St Osyth* 13); Emmison, *Tudor Food* 28–29.

However, something interfered in Ursley's plan to extend her relationship with Grace. Perhaps some incident happened that made Grace choose another keeper, or perhaps she had never intended to choose Ursley at all. Perhaps she was concerned about Ursley's magical reputation, a mixed blessing. The ability to do magic was a dangerous gift, and those who employed cunning bodies sometimes feared that the magic that helped them one day might harm them the next. Further, it was one thing to come to a private arrangement with a cunning body to cure a single illness, but another to formally employ that person over a longer period of time. Grace's own employers might have thought her impious, since the relationship between cunning magic and Christian trust in God's will was confusing. That uncertainty can be seen in the spiky little exchange that Grace and Ursley had on Mill Street, Grace being keen to show that she credited God with Davy's improvement, Ursley emphasising the role her knowledge and skill had in it, whether God willed it or no.

But there was another fact about Ursley that would make a godfearing woman flinch from employing her formally: Ursley had a 'base' or 'bastard' child, born out of wedlock in defiance of Christian teachings, the sermons she heard at St Peter and St Paul whenever she attended St Osyth's parish church (Figure 1.1). This boy, Thomas Rabbet, was about seven years old at the time of Davy Thurlowe's illness. No other children of Ursley's are mentioned: perhaps Thomas and his mother lived alone together. Thomas's father was presumably surnamed Rabbet and Ursley was known as Ursley Gray as well as Ursley Kempe so we can imagine

FIGURE I.I The Church of St Peter and St Paul in
St Osyth. (Source: Author's photo.)
Note: A black and white version of this figure will appear in some
formats. For the colour version, please refer to the plate section.

her as a woman who had had at least two partners in
her life. Perhaps she had been married to a man named
Gray – she mentions healing a woman named 'Gray's
wife' at some time in the last decade, perhaps a relation
by marriage, and there were Grays in St Osyth's seafaring community. The will of Charles Graye in 1583
mentions his house in Mill Street called Birdes, and his
ketch the *Anne Graye*.⁵ Ursley had a brother, Lawrence
Kempe, confirming that Kempe was her birth name.
But her brother and his wife did not get on with Ursley,

---

⁵ *ATAJR* 2A3v, 2A, 2A7v; will of Charles Graye 29 September 1583,
  F. G. Emmison, *Essex Wills: The Bishop of London's Commissary Court
  1578–1588* (Chelmsford: Essex Record Office with Friends of Historic
  Essex, 1995) 82.

and he lived in a different village, Thorpe le Soken. This family rift would also have suggested difficulties to a potential employer like Grace.

Before her sister-in-law, Lawrence Kempe's wife, died she and Ursley had even had a physical fight, when they met by chance on Eliot's Heath north of St Osyth, near Clay Street and the tile kiln. Lawrence said that his wife later told him that she had attacked Ursley, pulled up her skirts and beaten her about the hips, calling her names. Ursley said that one of those names was 'witch' but the other one was 'whore'. If Grace needed reasons not to employ Ursley as her keeper she did not have far to go to find them: Ursley had an illegitimate child and her own sister-in-law regarded her as little better than a prostitute. Perhaps Ursley actually did earn money from sex work: she later tells us that she took in wool to clean, dye and spin, and we have seen that she earned money through healing, but she may have had a third source of income too since her main job in the wool industry was not well paid. Either way, respectable Grace wouldn't want to be closely associated with her, and she chose another woman as her keeper.[6]

So when she began her period of confinement, or lying in, awaiting her labour, Grace's awkward relationship with Ursley came to a crisis. Not content with silently envying the rival keeper, Ursley visited the Thurlowes's house 'and seemed to be very angry for that she had not the keeping in of ... Grace'. This was an intimidating development: no-one wanted an angry cunning body in their

---

[6] ERO D/DCr M1; *AJATR* 2A8, E4v–E5, 2A3–2A3v.

bedroom, especially during late pregnancy, a vulnerable time. And either Grace had already started to become suspicious of Ursley's magic, or the unexpected incursion into her home frightened her, because she reacted with something close to an accusation of witchcraft. Grace said to Ursley that 'if she should continue lame as she had done before, she would find the means to know how it came, and ... she would creep upon her knees to complain of them to have justice done upon them'. She was coming to believe, in other words, that her lameness was not a natural condition. Instead, it might be caused by witchcraft. Specifically, Grace thought it might be caused by *Ursley's* witchcraft.

At first, Ursley tried to parry the implicit accusation. She said that a complaint to the magistrate about someone causing lameness would be 'a good turn'. But Grace pressed on. 'Take heed', she warned her uninvited guest, 'Ursley, thou hast a naughty name'. This was a decisive moment. A naughty name was a good deal worse than it sounds today, when 'naughty' means something a little self-indulgent: eating a cream cake instead of a crispbread. In the sixteenth century naughty meant thoroughly wicked, without goodness, reprobate. Grace had made her ambiguous reference to witchcraft personal and Ursley could not pretend to misunderstand. She retorted at once that 'though she could unwitch, she could not witch', meaning that although she could heal she could not harm. And she quickly made Grace an offer. If Grace 'would send her keeper away', Ursley would show her a valuable magic trick: 'how to unwitch herself or any other at any time'. Grace did not take Ursley up on her offer, although later we do learn the secret that Ursley would have shared with her, because Ursley told it to someone else. All that, however, is still to come.

Grace and John Thurlowe's baby, Joan, was born in early summer 1581 and soon after the birth, as Grace said later, Ursley 'fell out with her' again. She was still pursuing her old claim to be the family's carer, this time arguing that Grace ought to have let her 'have the nursing of' the baby 'at such times as she ... continued in work at the Lord Darcy's place'.[7] The fact that Grace did not trust Ursley with her daughter or, perhaps more importantly, allow her to make money as her babysitter further damaged the ties between the two women. And then a tragedy struck the Thurlowe family. Only a few months after her birth, Joan fell out of her cradle and injured herself badly. She died three days after the fall. Pause for a moment, reader, to let the shock of the little girl's death sink in. History without empathy is only ever half a story.

How could such a tragic death have occurred? Was the baby the victim of some assault or was her fall an accident – a cradle overturning on an uneven wooden or dirt floor, in a crowded tenement or cottage? Grace does not explain. What she does discuss, however, is Ursley's reaction. Grace recounts bitterly that on hearing the news of Joan's fall, Ursley responded 'it maketh no matter. For she might have suffered me to have the keeping and nursing of it'. This verbal shrug seemed to the grieving mother to be a sign of great evil. Yet despite this provocation she did not immediately approach the magistrate to accuse Ursley of killing Joan. Yes, that is where this story

---

[7] *ATAJR* 2A2–2A2v.

is going: an Assize court indictment for murder. Joan died in early autumn (6 October according to the indictment) but it took Grace until the next February to make a formal accusation against Ursley. This was because Ursley intervened. She came to Grace's door – 'unsent for and without request' Grace notes pointedly – and offered to help alleviate her lameness.

Perhaps Ursley was contrite about her nasty comment. Maybe she was worried Grace would accuse her. She asked twelve pence for her healing services, and Grace agreed to let her help. At last, the employment that Ursley had wanted! Interestingly, though, Grace said later that in agreeing to pay Ursley for her services, she was only 'speaking her fair' – she was playing along.[8] Perhaps in telling her story she was trying to pretend that she had not consulted with, and agreed to employ, someone whom she thought was a sluttish witch: that might lead to awkward questions from pious folk. Some clergymen, like the Maldon minister George Gifford, thought that consulting cunning bodies was as wicked as the act of witchcraft itself because both gained their occult knowledge from probably-demonic sources. He was preaching such ideas just twenty five miles west of Grace's home.[9]

[8] *ATAJR* 2A2–2A2v; J. S. Cockburn, *Calendar of Assize Records: Essex Indictments: Elizabeth I* (London: HMSO, 1978) record 1300.
[9] George Gifford, *A Dialogue Concerning Witches and Witchcraftes* (London, 1593) Hv, etc. Although published a decade after 1582, Gifford was preaching in Maldon in 1582 and it is likely that ideas such as his were known to local churchgoers. Gifford's book suggests acquaintance with *A True and just Recorde*, e.g. the list of witches' activities C2–C2v. See Timothy Scott McGinnis, *George Gifford and the Reformation of the Common Sort* (Philadelphia: Penn State University Press, 2005).

So perhaps Grace was being careful, or perhaps she was still angry with Ursley or intimidated into employing her because she turned up unsolicited on the doorstep. Either way, it appears that Grace did not mean to pay Ursley for any help she offered.

For five weeks, however, under Ursley's care Grace was well. Her lameness disappeared, which seemed to confirm that Ursley did have magical healing powers. Then Ursley came to ask for her bill to be settled and Grace said no. She told Ursley 'that she was a poor and needy woman, and had no money'. Ursley accepted this excuse: the St Osyth villagers knew about poverty and had realistic expectations about being paid in cash. Instead, Ursley asked Grace for a reward in kind, some cheese. But, flatly, Grace said she had none. Either she was telling the truth or she had deliberately chosen to confront Ursley: a dangerous move. Ursley, 'seeing nothing to be had', lost her temper and threatened Grace, telling her that 'she would be even with her'. And immediately, Grace's lameness returned and spread, so that some days she could not even get out of bed or turn over comfortably as she lay. Davy's sickness returned too, as if Ursley had sent it back to him. And after a few months of this double crisis Grace went to the magistrate to complain about Ursley, just as she had promised last spring.[10]

In asking to speak with the magistrate, Grace was taking a risk. Her fears might be dismissed, or she might start something that she had no desire to finish. So it seems likely that before she gave a formal statement on 19

[10] *ATAJR* 2A2v.

19

February 1582, Grace started exploratory conversations about Ursley's magic. There was another factor to consider, too. If at times she could not get out of bed, Grace could not go to Lord Darcy's house to work.

That must have required explaining. Her lameness might have been an arthritic complaint: it was variable from one day to another, and offered no prospect of a simple recovery. Tudor employers had limited patience with a worker whose attendance was unreliable and whose performance was impaired. We do not know what Grace's husband John did for a living, but her own income was certainly threatened by her ill-health. So her accusations may have begun by trying out the story of witchcraft as an excuse for absence. Even Grace's final statement to the magistrate has a tentative quality about it: this likely reflects her earlier attempts to pin down the times and places that she had offended Ursley, and exactly what had followed.

Perhaps her first claims about witchcraft were made to a housekeeper or cook at St Osyth Priory (Figure 1.2), explaining her illness and wondering if, perhaps, it could be ... not a *natural* disease, something *strange*. She might have made reference to fears that she had been 'overlooked', a common term for bewitchment that avoided naming the crime itself, or she might have stated significantly that, of course, she had been on bad terms with that good-for-nothing Ursley Kempe at the time she fell ill. Likely she would have shared her worries with other fellow-servants too – there were probably twenty or thirty to choose from. Grace would have been employed in cleaning, food management and preparation or, more prestigiously, personal care. Her tasks might have

FIGURE 1.2 St Osyth Priory gatehouse.
(Source: ColsTravel / Alamy Stock Photo.)
Note: A black and white version of this figure will appear in some
formats. For the colour version, please refer to the plate section.

included sweeping state rooms, chopping vegetables, washing sheets or maintaining her mistress' clothes. We do not know for sure. But in the months before her complaint to the magistrate she must have received support for her suggestion that the cause of her absences ought to be investigated, because in the end it was.

If Grace had been discussing her ill-health and its possible cause a few winters later, her concerns might have reached the ear of Mary, Lady Darcy, whose role would have included notional responsibility for the female servants of her household. But Thomas, third Baron Darcy, did not marry Mary until April 1583. His father John had died in March 1581 and his mother Frances before that, and at the time of Grace's trouble Thomas and his sister Elizabeth were both unmarried teenagers. There were probably older relatives about – Thomasine, the unmarried and historically near-invisible sister of the second Baron, for example – but they were subordinate the new young lord.[11] So there was an important power vacuum at St Osyth Priory, one that had begun around the time of Davy Thurlowe's illness. The old lord had died, but Thomas was not yet ready to take on all his father's responsibilities and there was no undisputed lady of the house. Who could help Grace get the justice she believed she deserved? Into this gap stepped Thomas's older cousin Brian Darcy.

It's likely that Brian came frequently to St Osyth Priory, perhaps more so since the second Lord Darcy's death. He had a home of his own in the village, as well as properties at Tiptree, Tolleshunt and elsewhere, across well over twenty Essex parishes with further family lands in Suffolk and Norfolk. Why would he base himself in St Osyth if not to make the most of proximity to the Priory and its centre of Darcy power?[12] Extended families gathered at the passing from one generation to another: there were wills to be read, estates to be set in order, mourning customs to be observed, staff to be paid, schooling and guardianships to

[11] Even in 1914, the house had fourteen male staff (Craig et al., *St Osyth* 18); ERO D/DB M160 gives some indication of household inhabitants and dependents in the 1570s and see also Thornton and Eiden, eds., *The History of the County of Essex* 167; for Thomasine see will of Elizabeth Darcy, F. G. Emmison, *Elizabethan Life: Essex Gentry's Wills* (Chelmsford: Essex County Council, 1978) 6–7.

[12] Jonathan Durrant has suggested that the two Darcys' kinship connection is less important than a patronage connection, but the two were felicitously intertwined: Durrant 'A Witch-hunting Magistrate? Brian Darcy and the St Osyth Witchcraft Cases of 1582' *The English Historical Review* 136 (2021) 17.

be arranged and documents to be witnessed. Brian might have played a role in these proceedings. Being based at St Clere's Hall, just half a mile down the road and a five minute canter from the Priory, he constituted an arm of Darcy power in the village and beyond. The authority that his cousin could lend him was potentially massive. And he had his own independent power, too: not only was Brian older than Thomas, experienced in the way of the world and useful in a crisis, he was also apparently religiously conformist, whereas the Barons Darcy were suspiciously traditional in their religion. In the next century they were to become more and more overtly Catholic.

Was Brian also a Catholic? Historians have striven to guess. Alison Rowlands suggests he 'probably held moderate Catholic views' while Peter Elmer places him in a puritan context. Jonathan Durrant suggests that his activities and associations could point towards both Catholicism and puritanical godliness. We just don't know. Brian's will makes a prominent reference to the godly concept of election, a key feature of certain 'hotter' kinds of Protestantism (to use Patrick Collinson's term) including Calvinism. As part of the conventional preamble that opens almost all wills of the period, Brian commends his soul to the hands of God, hoping and trusting that 'I shall amonge others his electe inherit the kingdome of heven.' This certainly looks warmly Protestant. But 'electe' is only one word amongst many, and there is, as Durrant rightly notes, a conflict between this godly buzzword and Brian's known Catholic connections. We do know the Lords Darcy were prominent Catholics and, as we shall see, Brian was perfectly happy to refer to a Catholic demonologist in his magisterial interrogations as well as have his fellow-author dedicate his published pamphlet *A True and just Record* to Brian's Catholic cousin.[13]

English Catholics of the period suffered significant legal disabilities. At every turn after his father's death, powerful as he was, young Thomas would have had questions to answer about religious practice and the future direction of his family allegiances. A tactful Justice of the Peace who was also a relative like Brian could help deflect those questions. And, as it turned out, he could also help Grace Thurlowe. In order to begin her complaint against Ursley Kempe, Grace needed to give a statement, an 'information', to a magistrate, a Justice of the Peace. Her employer Thomas, Lord Darcy, was a Justice but he was young, perhaps not yet ready to deal with his designated role, perhaps not much interested in hearing the complaints of villagers. He seldom attended Assize courts, which he was meant to do and Durrant suggests he was generally disengaged from matters of county administration. Brian Darcy, on the other hand, was an active Justice. He also appears to have been a magistrate looking for a mission. As Rowlands suggests, he set upon the task of questioning suspects with 'unusual zeal'.[14]

---

[13] Patrick Collinson, *The Elizabethan Puritan Movement* (London: Jonathan Cape, 1967) 27; Rowlands wrote the three paragraphs on the St Osyth witches in Thornton and Eiden, eds., *A History of the County of Essex* 218, as their note explains; Peter Elmer, *Witchcraft, Witch-Hunting and Politics in Early Modern England* (Oxford: Oxford University Press, 2016) 30, Durrant 'A Witch-hunting Magistrate?' 17–21 and *passim*.

[14] Cockburn, *Calendar: Essex: Elizabeth*, lists of Justices of the Peace, *passim*; Durrant 'A Witch-hunting Magistrate?' 17, where he explores the savage later assessment of Thomas's character by Harbottle Grimston, as well as his failure to perform local duties.

Helpfully for Brian, Grace Thurlowe was not the only person who was considering complaining about Ursley Kempe in February 1582. Another neighbour, Annis Letherdall, had also fallen out with Ursley. Annis had come to believe that her daughter Elizabeth had fallen victim to witchcraft after a quarrel. In the autumn of 1581, Ursley had sent her son Thomas over to Annis and Richard Letherdall's house to ask if they could spare some scouring sand. Sand, usually ground from sandstone, was used generally for scrubbing: cleaning kitchen tables, shifting stubborn grime from pots and pans. Specifically, in wool-working communities like St Osyth, it was also used for cleaning wool of its grease. Since in return for this cleaning product Ursley offered to dye some clothing for Annis, it is likely that she wanted the sand to carry on her wool work. And that Ursley offered dyeing as a service suggests that she made or at least applied colourings herself, alongside other herbal activities of which we'll read more later.

But there was a problem: Annis was not interested in bartering with Ursley. Like Grace, she knew Ursley had a bad reputation. Speaking to the magistrate later she said plainly that she knew Ursley to be 'a naughtie beast' and so she did not send her any scouring sand. But she did send her elder daughter out to take some sand to another neighbour. Embarrassingly, Ursley saw the girl and also saw what she carried. So Annis wouldn't help her with her vital piecework, but she would help someone she liked better! Annis's daughter said that Ursley 'murmured' something as she passed her, indicating that she made some grumpy comment – or, if you were suspicious enough to think so, that she mumbled a spell. And

FIGURE 1.3 Spinning. (Source: GRANGER / Alamy Stock Photo.)

at once Annis's younger child Elizabeth, a baby only a few months old, fell ill with an unusual swelling around her stomach and bottom.

This swelling continued over the winter and on 10 February, nine days before she spoke to the magistrate, Annis confronted Ursley about it. The long delay in making such an accusation, coupled with what we know of Grace Thurlowe's concurrent suspicions, suggests that tensions had been rising in the village during the long, dark winter and by early February those people who suspected Ursley had gathered the will to act. Accordingly, Annis went to Ursley's house, where she found her spinning wool with another woman (Figure 1.3).

Annis accused Ursley in front of her co-worker, telling her 'that shee had been foorth with a cunning body, which saide … she the said Ursley had bewitched her childe'. It must have been an uncomfortable scene. But Ursley professed disbelief. She not only rejected Annis's accusation, but also said that she knew Annis had not visited a cunning woman. She 'would lay her life', she said, that Annis had not sought any such help. That she felt able to accuse her accuser of lying suggests a strength of character and an aptitude for self-defence that made Ursley a tough neighbour.[15]

However, there was a weakness in her position. Was Ursley saying that she had *magical* insight into what Annis had or had not done? Annis seems to have believed so. Ursley's observation of Annis's life – watching Annis's daughter run errands, for example – suggests that she lived close by and we know from other evidence in *A True and just Recorde* that she also lived between Annis's house and the home of her preferred cunning body. Maybe she just deduced from looking out of the window as she sat spinning that Annis had not visited her advisor. However, Ursley's certainty seemed so suspicious that Annis asked Ursley's guest to bear witness to it. And having claimed that she had visited a cunning body, Annis made good on it. The next day she went to the occult practitioner Mother Ratcliffe, who 'ministered' to the child with her 'skill'. She was pessimistic, though: Annis recounted that Mother Ratcliffe said that 'shee doubted shee shoulde doe it any good'. She was right: little Elizabeth had died by the time of Ursley Kempe's trial. The indictment for her murder states that she was bewitched on 12

---

[15] *ATAJR* 2A3, B.

February – although this is a legal fiction, since it is dated months after her mother had become suspicious – and that she died a fortnight later.[16]

This visit to the cunning woman further confirmed Annis's suspicions of Ursley. As they passed Ursley's cottage going to and from Mother Ratcliffe's, Elizabeth twice pointed at Ursley's window and cried 'wo, wo', seeming to indicate that Ursley was the cause of her woe or suffering. Bewitched children were often thought to possess this kind of diagnostic power, and to be able to finger those attacking them. It was a dispensation from God, a gift of his providence, that otherwise inarticulate infants could speak out to identify Satan's agents. It related to the Bible's statement that truth might be told 'out of the mouth of babes and sucklings' (Psalms 8:2). So, armed with this evidence, and with whatever Mother Ratcliffe might have said, Annis returned to Ursley's house to talk to her again, during which conversation, as she told Brian Darcy later, Ursley 'used suche speeches as moved her to complaine' to him.[17]

Mother Ratcliffe, whose Christian name we do not know, is an important but mysterious figure in Annis Letherdall's story. She may or may not have implicated Ursley Kempe herself, but her 'skill' and authority certainly empowered Annis to make her accusation. Mother Ratcliffe may have used natural remedies, but there is every likelihood that she also used magic in 'ministering' to her patients and deciding who, if anyone, might have harmed them. She was certainly not the only supernatural

<hr>

[16] Cockburn, *Calendar: Essex: Elizabeth* record 1300.   [17] *ATAJR* B, Bv.

agent being consulted by St Osyth villagers in the late sixteenth century, however. Later we will hear about Cock's
wife of Weeley, Herring of Sudbury, and a cunning man
in Ipswich.[18] Another potent figure, Mother Barnes, may
also have been active in St Osyth itself. Mother Barnes
had two daughters, Margery and Ales, whose statements
to Brian Darcy show us just how closely magic and witchcraft were interwoven with every other aspect of life in
the town.

Magic was an everyday matter, a commodity like wool
or bread, something that some people had a gift for and
could do as part of their interactions with other people, or
could learn – for good or ill. And witchcraft power was not
necessarily a bad thing in such a magical culture. When
Ales Barnes, now Ales Hunt, met Brian Darcy later in
his investigations, she stated quite openly that her mother
was a witch. In telling a story about how another woman
had magical knowledge about 'what was saide or done
in any mans house in this towne', Ales unselfconsciously
remarked that in her mother's opinion this woman 'was
skilfull and cunning in witcherie, and could do as much
as the said mother Barnes: this examinats mother, or any
other in this town of St. Osees'.[19] This suggests that multiple people of 'skill' and 'cunning' – loaded words – operated in the area including Mother Barnes and the woman
Ales Barnes Hunt was accusing, Joan Pechey. Whether
they were thought of as 'cunning folk', 'cunning bodies',
people of 'skill' or 'witches' before the outbreak of accusations in 1582, these magical practitioners were drawing

[18] *ATAJR* 2A7, C2, E.   [19] *ATAJR* 2A4v.

on the same pool of occult knowledge and fighting over the same clientele. If Mother Barnes was held to have bewitched a particular villager, then Mother Ratcliffe might fight back on the villager's behalf, and shoot off a volley of curses at Mother Barnes.

It's tempting to speculate that in negotiating such a crowded maze of magical expertise, Ursley Kempe might have triggered some of the antagonism that brought her to the attention of Brian Darcy in February 1582. Ursley's spell for Davy Thurlowe ('Ah good child, how art thou loden!') shows that she used ritual words and actions in her attempts to heal which might have involved throwing negative energies out of the afflicted onto someone or something else. We know too, from her words to Grace, that she also claimed to heal lameness and had been doing so for many years. In this way, she was like Mother Ratcliffe or Mother Barnes: powerful, gifted, wielding occult forces that could potentially bless or curse. She was also, therefore, the professional competitor of other cunning bodies. But stories about Ursley – and we'll hear more of these later – suggest that she did not have the respect that they did. She may have been younger, more marginal, with her small, illegitimate child and her needy demands for cheese and scouring sand. Did Mother Ratcliffe and other skilful persons such as Mother Barnes move against Ursley in the months and weeks leading up to her accusation? Was it one of them who planted the seeds of doubt?

Cunning folk were well known for accusing each other of exercising evil influence: not simply out of malice or professional jealousy, but because it was integral to their work. Diagnosing bewitchment as an ailment meant that someone had to be a witch. And since magical power could be used for good or ill, then – whatever they said about their wholly helpful intentions – healers were prime suspects. Even healing often involved the aggressive redirection of magical energy, in a way that could be harmful. If a patient came to a cunning body complaining of unusual symptoms, the healer might diagnose that they had been bewitched and, through rituals and verbal formulae, lift the spell from them only to throw it back at the person who had supposedly cast it. This blast of returning energy, it was thought, could easily wound or kill.[20] If another 'skilful' body in the neighbourhood fell suddenly ill or died – well, one might conclude that it was their evil rebounding back on them and that they had been a witch as well as an unwitcher.

It's interesting in this context, then, that Mother Barnes died about a week before Ursley Kempe was arrested, on or around 12 February 1582. Was her death thought to be natural? A cluster of deaths of the witches' supposed victims occurred in February 1582: on the 1st, 10th (two deaths), 14th and 26th. It is tempting to suggest as Jonathan Durrant does that there was epidemic disease

---

[20] This reflection is prompted by Jeanne Favret-Saada's observations in *Deadly Words: Witchcraft in the Bocage* (Cambridge and Paris: Cambridge University Press and Fondation de la Maison des Sciences de l'Homme, 1981); see also the classic accounts Owen Davies, *Cunning Folk: Popular Magic in English History* (Oxford: Blackwell, 2007), Davies and Timothy Easton, 'Cunning Folk and the Production of Magical Artefacts' in Ronald Hutton, ed., *Physical Evidence for Ritual Acts, Sorcery and Witchcraft in Christian Britain* (Basingstoke: Palgrave, 2015) 209–231 and Emma Wilby, *Cunning Folk and Familiar Spirits* (Brighton: Sussex Academic Press, 2005).

active in St Osyth which pushed up mortality rates, and when we look in the next chapter at the neighbouring village of Little Clacton we can see some evidence of this. But whatever was going on in the medical world of St Osyth, what was going on in the magical world seems as important. Was Mother Barnes involved in a magical turf war, or a wider disagreement that could be seen as a contest between witches? Later we shall see what happened to the spirits Mother Barnes was said to own, for they went to another witch, or so her daughter Margery Barnes told the magistrate. Meanwhile, as we've seen, just two days before Mother Barnes' death, Annis Letherdall said she had been to see a cunning body who had accused Ursley of bewitching her child, and the day after she certainly went to Mother Ratcliffe, possibly with the same result. Whatever was going on in the winter of 1581–2, Mother Barnes' death surely destabilised the balance of magical power in the village. Perhaps the gossip and suspicion surrounding the death of this 'notorious Witche', as Brian Darcy called Mother Barnes, in some way precipitated the accusation of her less-respected colleague Ursley Kempe?[21]

By the end of 19 February Brian had an earful of suspicious stories about Ursley from both Grace Thurlowe and Annis Letherdall. So the next day he sent for Ursley herself, to put their accusations to her. It was his duty as a magistrate: on receipt of an 'information' about a crime, magistrates like Brian were expected to interrogate the

---

[21] See Durrant 'A Witch-hunting Magistrate?' 26–27 and later; Cockburn, *Calendar: Essex: Elizabeth* records 1300, 1304, 1316; *AJATR* C4.

suspect and record their statement as an 'examination'. But I can imagine – and you may imagine, once you get to know him – that he was immediately engaged by the prospect of questioning a witch. Ursley was arrested and brought to him by St Osyth's constable, one of the village's chief men. He was elected by his fellow-inhabitants or nominated by the magistrate to manage law and order. Constables were well-to-do villagers, a Neighbourhood Watch of unpaid and untrained volunteers: Ursley would have been wary of the constable, and he may well have disapproved of her. Being marched out of her house in front of her neighbours and son, and up the long lane to St Clere's Hall, must have been a sobering experience. Once inside Brian Darcy's home, she would have known that she would be held there and questioned, likely at length.[22]

The Hall would have intimidated a villager used to living in the cramped cottages and tenements of St Osyth. Ursley was in a sprawling, luxurious and yet dangerously intimate space. The house was a timber-framed and brick mansion, richly decorated, warm and comfortable, combining domestic rooms and estate offices. But it also had a moat. It was a home, administrative hub and a fortress, and Ursley was equally a guest, an item of business and a prisoner. This ambiguity of status could cut both ways. In the early 1570s another Essex Justice of the

---

[22] It's not actually certain where the examinations took place. When I first wrote about this in 1999–2000 I assumed Brian used the Priory, but now St Clere's Hall seems much more likely, given the establishment of definite dates for Brian's inheritance of the sub-manor and residence there. This location matches other observers' suggestions – e.g. Craig et al. *St Osyth* 68 and Durrant 'A Witch-hunting Magistrate?' 17.

Peace, Clement Sisley of Barking, had been questioning a suspected witch in his new house Eastbury Hall when she threatened him with revenge and 'he fell on a plaine pavement of free stone ... and strook out the huckle bone of his thigh out of the joynt, so that for three weeks space he could not goe [walk]'. For a long time after the woman's execution he was still using 'stilts' or crutches.[23] The hall-courtroom, the public space where strangers came into the home, was a space where the assertion of power and assessment of risk had consequences for questioner and suspect alike. However, unless she really did possess magical powers, the accused witch was among the most vulnerable of visitors.

The suspect would have been outnumbered, because Brian would have had a secretary with him, a clerkly assistant from his household who performed business and legal tasks in various capacities. Magistrates' clerks' roles varied according to the status of the Justice with whom they worked. Brian would have employed several such managers, agents and personal assistants because his interests ranged across manors, farms, woods, fisheries, roads and bridges, benefices and grants, criminal cases and civil suits. But he may have had other advisors and audience present too, writing or observing: an attorney, clergyman or interested neighbours perhaps. At the end of Ursley's examination appears the phrase 'in the presence of us, whose names bee hereunder subscribed'

---

[23] *The Examination and Confession of a notorious Witch named Mother Arnold* (London, 1595) E3v. Thanks to David Williams for pointing out my house name error in Gibson, *Early Modern Witches* 148; Historic England, 'St Clere's Hall' (1986) https://britishlistedbuildings .co.uk/101309039-st-cleres-hall-st-osyth#.YJvgcNVKjIU

suggesting a number of literate men were there for at least part of the process of examination. Unfortunately the list of names is missing. And no-one recorded Brian's questions to Ursley. After all, no-one would impugn the probity of the magistrate or the truth-status of the record (would they? Occasionally they did, and do, but such assumptions still structure our public records). So we do not know what Ursley was asked and the questioning may have been intense.[24]

Of course, we also do not hear or even read Ursley's words as they came from her, directly. They are mediated by the scribe standing between her and us. He may or may not have recorded what she said correctly, fairly and fully. Ursley's story was complex, easily misunderstood. The scribe's perception of her was also shaped by the situation. He and the magistrate could readily fall into a presumption of guilt: this woman was in trouble with the law, and it is always easy for law-enforcers to think that this is probably deserved. In this case, previous evidence had shown that Ursley had a 'naughty name', which put her further at a disadvantage. Contemporary demonology argued that women were either very good or very wicked, and according to her neighbours Ursley was not very good. Both scribe and magistrate may have had previous knowledge of her: perhaps a public penance by St Osyth's church court for having borne an illegitimate child. Finally, as well as being shaped by pre-existing prejudices, everything Ursley said was shaped by the questioner. All we can do as readers today is to try

---

[24] *ATAJR* 2A8v.

to hear Ursley through the background noise – to admit that this account will not be perfect, but to try to set her words as free as we can from their frame of suspicion and misrepresentation.

We can make some decisions about how to signal this. You will have noticed, for instance, that I refer to all the historical people in this story by their forenames. No-one is labelled only by a surname, as is more conventional in academic writing. Forenames connote many things, but among these are intimacy and vulnerability because in the context of early modern England these are the Christian names that people were given at their baptism. The Christian name of a powerful man in these times and this place was reserved for church, legal and family use, and in society generally it was used by superiors speaking to inferiors. Employers called their employees and dependants 'Grace' or 'John'. In return they were called 'Master Darcy', the title explicitly referencing their control. Labelling our historical subjects with their Christian name, this book makes an attempt to set them on an equal footing by the code of their times, since at the start of their lives – for a few minutes at least – each one was treated equally. This choice also forces us as modern readers to confront their humanity. In most cultures, forenames denote connection. This modern trigger of connective emotion helps us to see and hear better the subjects of history. None is a unit of data or production, none is wholly unknown. It may be possible to write a better history with these thoughts in mind.[25]

---

[25] See also this book's conclusion for further discussion of this.

So: it seems likely that early on in their conversation Brian encouraged Ursley to talk about her healing skills. Perhaps he wanted to know what she had meant when she said to Grace that she could unwitch people but not bewitch them. Like us, he knew that healing and harming were linked. Perhaps he was looking for evidence of the Galenic knowledge that physicians possessed, predicting that he would find only magical rather than medical theory in this woman's methods. It was then that Ursley told Brian the fascinating secret of her spell against lameness, the one she'd once offered to share with Grace Thurlowe. In around 1571 or 1572, she said, she had begun to be troubled herself by 'a lamenes in her bones'. And of course, because she was a poor woman she had gone to a cunning body rather than a physician for help. In this case it was a consultant from Weeley, a village five miles north of St Osyth. This woman was referred to only as Cock's wife, and Ursley explained that she was now dead, which saved Brian sending for her too. The Weeley cunning woman had diagnosed bewitchment, and her prescription was a magical one.

Cock's wife began her treatment unpromisingly: she told Ursley to gather up some hog's dung. After that she was to pick some leaves of chervil, mix them with the dung and hold this so-called 'medicine' in her left hand. In her right hand she was to take a knife, and with it prick the herby dung ball three times. Then she was to throw it into her fire. After that she should use the same knife to make three stabs at the underside of a table, and the knife should be left stuck in the wood. Finally, a more recognisably beneficial activity completed the spell. Ursley should gather three leaves of sage and three of

St John's wort, put them into ale and drink it first thing in the morning and last thing at night. Ursley did as the cunning woman told her, and her lameness was cured. The ingredients used were well-known as part of various remedies. Cecily Arnold – the suspected witch questioned by Clement Sisley at Barking at around the same time – was found to be carrying 'betweene her kercheif and her hat ... wrapped in a linnen cloth swines dung, the herb cherwell dill, red fennel and saint Johns woort' together with a preserved mole's foot. In various combinations and forms, dung, chervil and St John's wort made powerful occult medicine.[26]

The Weeley variant of the spell is probably based on the idea of sympathetic magic. Stabbing the dung and the table suggests an attack on the disease and on the person whose witchcraft was thought to have caused it. Perhaps if the stabbing was effective, the witch would feel pain and have to remove the curse, and perhaps the fact that the knife would stick in the underside of the table, defying gravity, showed that the unwitching was working. Later, we'll see an arrow used in a similar way to unwitch a brewing vat. Likewise burning the dung suggests the cleansing of magical impurities or the malice of an enemy. Later, we'll see fire used again in several unwitching spells. Finally, another element has been grafted onto the charm with the making of the herbal drink. Sage (salvia officinalis) was

---

[26] Cock's wife is untraceable. A Cock family held extensive property across St Osyth including two properties in Mill Street in the mid-seventeenth century (houses known as Warners and Spencers, and the hogfield, ERO D/DCr M1); *The Examination and Confession of ... Mother Arnold*, E3v.

thought to have magical properties to ward off evil, but also to reduce fever and calm nerves – among many other applications, some of which are still in use today. St John's wort (various sorts of hypericum) was thought to be effective against poison and plague, and to cheer and comfort patients. The St Osyth area has its own uncommon form of the herb, Imperforate St John's Wort.[27]

Ever the entrepreneur, Ursley made good use of the herb, dung and ale remedy taught to her by Cock's wife: she began using it to heal others. At least two women, she said, one Gray's wife and one Page's wife, had since sent for her and asked her to heal them of their bewitchment. She had done so, and she confirmed that 'shee knewe them to bee bewitched'.[28] It's not clear how Ursley diagnosed witchcraft as the cause of the two womens' illnesses, but her confidence is important. She had moved in her own mind from being the lame victim of witchcraft to becoming a cunning body herself. She probably used her ritual on Grace Thurlowe, too, because, as we saw, she offered to show Grace how to heal limping caused by witchcraft. And this was exactly what Cock's wife's remedy was designed to cure. So the anti-lameness spell from Weeley came to St Osyth and was in circulation there among the network of cunning bodies and their patients. But by the early 1580s, Ursley's neighbours had also moved on in their opinion of her, and unfortunately some of them now believed her to be a maleficent witch. That was why she was now squirming under Brian's questions.

---

[27] Stanley T. Jermyn, *Flora of Essex* (Fingeringhoe: Essex Naturalists Trust, 1974) 67.
[28] *ATAJR* 2A7v.

Perhaps Ursley hoped that if she explained her magical working to Brian he would see she was just a benign healer. But unfortunately Brian was more likely to have assumed she was guilty: if so, he would have considered it his duty to force her to admit it. He had a particular interest in witchcraft and the extraction of confessions – which may have been why Grace Thurlowe felt empowered to make her accusation, or why it was so well-received. *A True and Just Recorde* shows that Brian and his friends had been reflecting upon a recent work of demonology by a French lawyer. And in this 1580 book, *De la daemonomanie des sorciers (On the demon-mania of witches)*, Jean Bodin had argued that one of the most effective ways to get witches to confess was to lie to them. He believed that it was entirely proper to do so, because they were more than likely to be guilty. He also made several suggestions of ways to get them to confess by deceit:

one must begin with light and humorous matters ... without a court clerk, and conceal one's desire to know all about it ... inquire whether their father and mother practiced this craft ... it is also necessary in order to get the truth from those who are accused or suspected, that judges appear to have pity on them, and tell them it is not they, but the Devil who forced and compelled them to cause peoples' death. So for this reason they are innocent .... One must of necessity admit that it is a virtuous, praiseworthy and necessary thing to lie in order to save an innocent person's life ... so must one do in justice in order to get the truth about hidden wickednesses ...[29]

---

[29] Jean Bodin, *De la Demonomanie des Sorciers* (Paris, 1580) 189r, 191r, 192v, see also Bodin, *Demonomanie* in Randy A. Scott (translator) and Jonathan L. Pearl, eds., *On the Demon-Mania of Witches* (Toronto: Centre for Renaissance and Reformation Studies, 1995) 177–80, 191.

From simple misdirection to outright falsehood, the suspect was to be lulled into an illusory confidence that she could tell her questioner anything.

Brian Darcy copied this strategy. Perhaps he even sent his clerk out of the room: the record shows that someone took notes using the third person ('the said Brian Darcey then promising ...') but at times it could have been Brian himself. He listened patiently to Ursley's talk of healing and then told her that 'if she would deal plainely and confesse the trueth, that shee should have favour'. That means he promised, falsely, that whatever she said would not get her into trouble. He probably said a lot more too since he is described, cynically, as 'giving her faire speeches'. He might have prompted her with leading questions, a tactic he later used with others. I imagine him wheedling, falsely warm. Were there threats, subtle or explicit, mixed with the promises of favour? Whatever happened, *A True and just Recorde* tells us that Ursley's composure dramatically deserted her. 'Bursting out with weeping' she 'fel upon her knees, and confessed that shee had foure spirits'. Two of these were male and killed people. Two were female, and could hurt people, especially by causing lameness, and kill cattle. Triumphant, Brian asked Ursley to elaborate: what were the names and forms of her spirits? She said they were Tyttey, a grey tomcat, Jacke, a black tomcat, Pigin, a black toad, and Tyffin, a white lamb.

These were the sort of spirits that Brian would have expected: the lamb is a surprise but the cats and toad are textbook familiars, supposedly demonic creatures that witches used to project their evil and which they rewarded with food and blood to drink. Where did their names come from, though? *A True and just Recorde* tells us that on 25 February Brian questioned Ursley's son, Thomas Rabbet, and Thomas named his mother's spirits and described their shapes just as she had done. Later on in this story, we'll have reason to suspect that Brian sometimes questioned the children of suspects before he questioned their parents, and then re-dated their evidence. Perhaps this was the case with Thomas and Ursley. Did Ursley break down because Brian told her that her eight-year-old son had confirmed her guilt? Thomas said that his mother 'had foure severall spirites' whom she gave 'beere to drinke and ... a white Lofe or Cake to eate' and that 'in the night time the said spirites will come to his mother, and sucke blood of her upon her armes'. He also told a story about Ursley's friend Ales Newman, whom we'll meet later, and said that she had access to his mother's spirits. They were imagined running errands, pinching, striking and ill-wishing victims, trekking back to the witch with a full report. As Ursley's confession shows, some spirits were imagined as having specialisms, and carrying out expert work and she and her son both described them as 'plaguing' their neighbours to hurt or kill them.[30]

---

[30] *ATAJR* 2A7v–2A8, 2A3v–2A4; See the familiars in *The Examination and Confession of certaine Wytches* (London, 1566) A6; *A Rehearsall both straung and true* (A6, A8v); *The Apprehension and confession of three notorious Witches* (London, 1589, A3, B). E.g. *The Examination and Confession of certaine Wytches* A6–7; *A Rehearsall both straung and true* A5v–A6. On familiars see Wilby, *Cunning Folk* 20 and Victoria Carr, 'Witches and the Dead: The Case for the English Ghost Familiar' Folklore 130:3 (2019) 282–99 and Charlotte Rose Millar, Witchcraft, the Devil and Emotions in Early Moden England (London and New York: Routledge, 2017), also James Sharpe, 'The Witch's Familiar in Elizabethan England' in G. W. Bernard and S. J. Gunn, *Authority and Consent in Tudor England* (Aldershot: Ashgate, 2002) 219–32.

We don't know why Ursley suddenly confessed to keeping demonic spirits but we do know Brian's next question to her, an obvious one. He asked Ursley which spirits she had sent to attack Grace Thurlowe and her family and Annis Letherdall's daughter Elizabeth. Which of her menagerie had done the harm? This was a leading question that assumed Ursley did indeed send spirits to hurt these people, and it elicited the desired answer. Ursley confessed that Tyttey had been sent to punish Grace, whilst Pigin had gone to the Letherdalls' house. Later, Annis Letherdall was called in by Brian to hear Ursley's confession, and Ursley went further with her story. She asked Annis if she had not been terribly afraid on the night when the spirit came to attack her child. Ursley said she herself had been 'in a great swete' about it. After all, it was no small matter to be summoning and sending devils to wreak vengeance on unfriendly neighbours. This imagination of a shared fear and discomfort also suggests that Ursley trying to find some commonality with Annis despite the circumstances: both women had fallen prey to evil forces, it implied.

Once she had started accepting her questioner's premise that she was a wicked witch, and thus confessing what Brian wanted to hear, it appears that Ursley could not stop elaborating. 'Without any asking of her owne free will', Brian or his scribe tells us, she also said that 'shee was the death of her brother Kemps wife'. This was the woman she had fought with on Eliot's Heath, who had called her a whore and witch, and Ursley said she had sent the spirit Jacke to kill her. She had now confessed a wider guilt, and a crime for which she could be executed, and she proceeded to confess another: one of the crimes of which she had first been accused. 'Upon the falling out betweene Thorlowes wife and her', she said, 'shee sent Tyffin the spirite unto her childe, which lay in the Cradle, and willed the same to rock the Cradle over, so as the childe might fall out thereof, and breake the necke of it'.[31] However Grace's baby Joan had in fact died, now it was officially Ursley's fault. Apparently no-one noticed that Ursley had contradicted herself: her she-spirit Tyffin was not able to kill, she had said, but in her final story Tyffin featured as the murderer of the Thurlowes's baby.

Evidently the detail of Ursley's confession was not as important as its general trend. Brian Darcy had got what he wanted, a confession of guilt. Delighted, he went off to eat a hearty supper: life went on for him, surrounded by his family and his servants, while Ursley stewed alone in her fear. She may have been imprisoned in a village lock-up – one on the Colchester Road just a few yards from the Priory wall was in use until the twentieth century – or kept within St Clere's Hall itself. After his meal, Brian recalled Ursley and, careful to consolidate the truth he had uncovered, assembled his other witnesses to hear him go over her evidence with her again. He confronted her with Grace Thurlowe and Annis Letherdall, and Ursley once again wept and knelt, 'and asked forgiveness'. However, while Brian ate Ursley had had time to think over her story, and she introduced a dramatic new refinement into it. Instead of confirming that she had herself sent spirits to harm her neighbours' children, she instead said that 'shee caused Newmans wife to send a

---

[31] *ATAJR* B, 2A8–2A8v.

spirite' to both families. This unexpected change in her story was not a trivial one: it shifted the blame for the witchcraft attacks subtly to someone else, Ursley's former friend Ales Newman.

Ales was a near neighbour of Ursley's and she was mentioned in Ursley's son Thomas's evidence as a friend and his 'Godmother', a woman chosen at a child's baptism as a carer in the event that the mother should die. Ales was a trusted friend of Ursley's, then. She was married, apparently not happily, to a sickly man named William Newman. Their next door neighbour, the painter William Hooke, later told Brian that he had often heard William Newman say to Ales that 'she was the cause of her husband's great miserie and wretched state'. He added that when Ales put food in front of William, they argued, with William repeating 'doest thou not see? Doest thou see?' Perhaps the food had pests on it, or William was hallucinating, since Ales responded 'if thou seest anything, give it some of thy meat' and William cried out to her to 'beate it away'. Their neighbour, listening through the wall, concluded that there were strange creatures at his neighbours' table and that they were making William ill. He was not a good provider and Ales had to visit the longstanding Collector for the Poor, John Johnson, to ask for charity. The Johnson family had premises next to the Guild Hall on The Bury, and it may be here that Ales was overheard asking John for twelvepence because 'her husbande lay sicke'. Like many accused witches, Ales was a poor woman who sought charitable relief.

On this occasion, however, John Johnson refused Ales any help. Although, he said, 'hee woulde gladly helpe her husbande … hee had laide out a great deale more than he

had received'. John was described by another poor villager as 'a very honest man', he was trusted to be witness
to and executor of a will in November 1580 and another in
November 1581, and his statement was entirely plausible.
In 1573, for example, our previous acquaintance the magistrate Clement Sisley complained to the Essex Quarter
Sessions that whilst the Collectors for the Poor in his
area, Barking, were also just and honest men there were
so many poor people that there were insufficient funds
for all of their needs. In 1581 there was an attempt to
present to the court those tax-evaders who were refusing
to pay the amount they owed to the Collectors.³² Faced
with a similar shortfall, John Johnson told Ales Newman
that he himself was 'a pore man, and hee, his wife and
familie, might not want for the helping of her husbande'.
But although times were hard for him as a clothmaker,
Ales likely reflected that he was not as poor as she was.
She 'used some harde speeches unto him' and some suspected that she then caused his sudden death, which had
happened earlier that year. Thomas Rabbet mentioned
this in his evidence, saying that 'he heard her to tel his
mother that she had sent a spirit to plague Johnson to ye
death, and an other to plague his wife'.³³

³² *ATAJR* 2A6v–2A7; wills of Thomas Davy of Clay Street, St Osyth,
  5 November 1581 and Peter Martayne, tailor, 5 November 1580,
  Emmison, *Essex Wills … Commissary Court 1578–1588* 58, 138; John
  Johnson is listed as a collector in LMA DL/B/A/002/MS09537/004 in
  the 1570s; ERO Q/SR 44/27, 78/45.
³³ Or at least Richard Johnson did in 1537: Cheshire Archives
  DCH/o/17; *ATAJR* 2A4v, 2A6v–7, C6. On the Essex cloth industry's
  history, see L. R. Poos, *A Rural Society after the Black Death: Essex
  1350–1525* (Cambridge: Cambridge University Press, 1991).

With this sort of rumour circulating about other women, it is no wonder that Ursley Kempe spent her first night in custody thinking inventively. Was there any way she could escape from the tangled story she had told, perhaps by blaming Ales? Possibly she and Ales actually did believe themselves able to cause harm: either way, she was a useful alternative suspect. The next morning, Ursley asked the constable if she could speak to Brian Darcy again: there was 'one thing … that she had forgotten' to tell him, she claimed. And so back to the magistrate she went on the morning of 21 February, and spilled out a series of accusations against Ales Newman. Some time in late November or December 1581, Ursley said, Ales had come to her house and accused Ursley of witchcraft. She said that 'she woulde take away her witcherie, and carrie the same unto M[aster] Darcey'. Thomas Rabbet told a similar tale (on the 25 or before) and Ales later confirmed some of Ursley's account: in accusing Ursley in the autumn of 1581 she had been, as we know, joining a chorus of suspicion. But Ursley said she thought Ales didn't really mean it. After some sharp argument, therefore, the friends agreed that Ales would take the 'witcherie' – spirits and magical objects? – away. Ales put them in a pot and, compromising, said that she would keep them at her home rather than going to the magistrate with them.

This exchange, carefully related by Ursley to Brian, meant that after the handover of the potful of demons Ales Newman was positioned as the keeper of Ursley's spirits. And so, Ursley continued, when she fell out with Grace Thurlowe around Christmas 1581, she went to Ales with a request. Could Ales please send the spirits to hurt Grace? Ales could. She instructed the grey cat Tyttey to go and attack Grace on whichever part of her body the spirit chose. When Tyttey returned he told Ursley that he had hurt Grace's knee. Ursley provided some blood for Tyttey to suck as a reward, but then the spirit returned to Ales Newman. The same happened when Ursley fell out with John Stratton, she said, naming a new victim who – as far as we know – had not yet formally accused her. Ursley said that John, like a number of other villagers, had called her a whore. His wife had also refused to give Ursley some spices that she wanted. So Ursley asked Ales to send the black cat-spirit Jacke to hurt her and she did. Jacke confirmed he had attacked his victim's back, causing such harm that she would die of it, and Ursley gave him some blood as a reward. Later it would be alleged that she had also bewitched the Strattons' child. Then Jacke went home to Ales, and Ursley said she believed he had had some blood from her too.

Ursley's confession of witchcraft was now very blurred indeed. Whilst she admitted that she had possessed some spirits and fed them, and she had added some new victims to the list of those that the spirits had attacked, it now appeared that the real dirty work of sending the spirits to harm and kill St Osyth villagers was done by Ales Newman. Ursley now reinforced this perception by repeating it as she retold the story of her falling out with Annis Letherdall. On 9 February, she said, she had asked Ales to send a spirit to hurt Annis's baby daughter, and Ales had sent Pigin. It had been difficult to arrange this attack, because William Newman was at home with his wife, and Ursley excluded him from any knowledge of his wife's activities.[34] But it had been done, and Pigin

---

[34] *ATAJR* B, B4v, fold-out table, B2–B2v, 2A4.

had returned victorious. With this triple repeat pattern of stories, Ales Newman now stood accused of all the witchcraft that Ursley had initially accepted as her own responsibility. Of course, Brian sent immediately for Ales to question her about what Ursley had said: like Ursley, this second woman was marched up to St Clere's Hall.

Ales Newman was a rather tougher witness than Ursley Kempe, however. She refused to confess. She admitted that she had visited Ursley's house and told her that 'she knew her to be a witche', but she denied all the other elements of Ursley's story. This created a potentially major problem for Brian: his two key suspects disagreed about the fundamentals of what would become the case for the prosecution. In fact, Ales would not say anything that Brian considered worth recording – his clerk's note of her statement is only a few lines long. So he set himself to break down this awkward resistance by trickery. He judged Ales's character well, too. Noting her obstinacy, Brian told Ales that 'hee woulde sever and part her and her spirits a sunder' and, rising to his tone of challenge, Ales retorted that he would not. 'I wil carry them with me' she asserted. Did she mishear him, or was she referring to some ordinary pets, which he was now calling spirits? Was this sort of flat contradiction her usual mode of communication? Either way, Brian gleefully seized on her words, and pushed her until she was forced to qualify what she had said about taking her spirits away with the rather feeble addendum 'if she have any'.[35] This was enough. Ursley and Ales were now both imprisoned in the village, and committed for trial at the Assizes. Although

---

[35] *ATAJR* B5–B5v.

Ales was Thomas's godmother, there was now no-one to care for the little boy. Where did he go? Ursley must have been desperately worried about how he would fare if she never came home from her Assize trial.

There was another trial to endure first, however. We know from evidence given later, at Little Clacton, that Brian also asked a woman named Margaret Simpson to strip-search the accused at St Osyth. This examination was needed to determine whether their bodies showed any signs of suckling familiars: unusual bloody spots, injuries or teat-like warts, things that other women would supposedly recognise as aberrant. Margaret was described as a woman 'of credite', and was perhaps a relation of the St Osyth curate and former Little Clacton vicar William Simpson. She had Ursley and Ales stripped naked and she – and possibly other women – stared, parted, turned and probed until the accused were thoroughly exposed to her gaze. Margaret concluded that Ursley Kempe at least did have 'sucked spots' on her.[36] Off Ursley and Ales went to confinement, initially in St Osyth, later in Colchester. By then Margaret would have travelled with Brian to Little Clacton to examine witches there and compare their bodily marks with those she had seen at St Osyth: we'll meet her there again later in this book. Far from having finished his enquiries, Brian Darcy was just getting started.

---

[36] *ATAJR* D4; for William Simpson and his wife, left 10 shillings each in April 1582 see Emmison, *Elizabethan Life: Wills of Essex Gentry* 66.

2

The Darcy Lands

Elizabeth, Ales, Margerie and Joan

~

As a result of his enquiries into witchcraft at St Osyth, by 22 February 1582 Brian Darcy had imprisoned Ursley Kempe and Ales Newman and committed them for trial at the next Assizes. The Assizes were the seasonal criminal courts at which suspected felons – those accused of serious crimes – were tried by professional judges. The judges would work with a twelve man jury to decide the fate of the accused. In particular, they would determine whether or not the accused should be convicted of and imprisoned or executed for the crimes alleged against them. Ursley and Ales were now in the hands of these men. However, because the Assizes were held only twice a year, in late spring and late summer, Brian had some time to question his suspects further. So they were not transported immediately to Colchester and then to the town where the next Assize would be held. Or at least Ursley Kempe was not. Instead she continued to be questioned, and she named more women as suspects, which meant that the witch hunt engulfed more people in St Osyth.

This was the first indication that the 'St Osyth' witch trial would spread beyond its immediate area of origin, the few streets around the Priory. It would widen out beyond the town into the surrounding countryside and across some of the many parishes and manors that made up the lands of the Darcy estates. Understanding the scope of the Darcys' lands and the family's hold over the wider area is important for an understanding of the way the St Osyth witchcraft accusations spread. Standing at Bar Corner in St Osyth village, it is impossible not to feel the dominance of the Priory over the surrounding area. Its sheer size made the necessary statement of Darcy wealth, and the whole village literally looked up at the Priory as the home of their lord, to whom they paid rents and fines and whose agents controlled a large part of their everyday activity. From the Priory towers, the wider estate beyond the Little Park begins to be visible. Tucked into a fold of the Priory's immediate field of vision is St Clere Hall, Brian Darcy's home, and beyond that Darcy lands spread west across the river, south and east to the sea and north towards Colchester.

The Darcy estate covered most of the land area from St Osyth outwards some fifteen miles in easterly and northerly directions, the directions that the witch hunt would take. It also included extensive lands at Tolleshunt Darcy in the west and towards Colchester in the north. Other landholdings were scattered across south-east England, but this area of eastern Essex was the heart of the Darcy empire. The estates were run by a tight group of men clustered around their employers: Lord Darcy of Chiche and his immediate family. Some of this group were Darcy cousins and in-laws, like Edmund Pirton of Little Bentley, who served as Bailiff for Weeley among other roles. He was married to Susan, the daughter of Thomas, first Lord Darcy and his wife Elizabeth. As with all the men in the governing group, Edmund was inter- twined with the Darcys and their lands in many ways. As a Justice of the Peace, he worked alongside Thomas, third

Baron, and Brian Darcy. In November 1581, for example, Edmund and Brian made a joint order that an illegitimate child in St Osyth should not be maintained by the townspeople, but should be supported by its supposed father Robert Tasler or Taseleye, a Weeley man, with the sum of sixpence a week until he could prove that this was unjust and he was not the baby's father. He could not prove this and they gaoled him.[1] This kind of social and financial policing by trusted family members and other lieutenants was one way in which the Darcys had established and daily strengthened their hold on the people of their estates. It was not a conscious strategy as such: instead, their dominance was a given basis for life in their 'little commonwealth' as Jonathan Durrant has called it.[2]

Thomas, Lord Darcy, was also lord of many manors beyond St Osyth. Other manorial bailiffs that are known (from the minimal survivals of Darcy estate records of 1574–6), are Philip Cawston of Weeley for the Clactons (where he tenanted Clacton Hall as well as being Keeper of Weeley Park), John Ryvett for Skighawe manor and Little Oakley (where he tenanted the Hall), George Hudson for the Sokens (as tenant of Thorpe Hall), Thomas Glascock for Great Holland, Thomas Wood for Old Hall and New Hall manors in Beaumont, Robert

<hr>

[1] ERO D/DB M160, 161, Q/SR 80/24, Q/SR 80/2, 2a; TNA PROB11/51/388, PROB11/52/474; F. G. Emmison, *Elizabethan Life: Wills of Essex Gentry and Merchants* (Chelmsford: Essex County Council, 1978), 6; F. G. Emmison and Marc Fitch, *Feet of Fines* vol. 5 (Oxford: Leopard's Head, 1991) 206; Cockburn, *Calendar: Essex: Elizabeth* record 766. For Robert Tasler see also ERO D/ACA 7, January 1577.
[2] Durrant 'A Witch-hunting Magistrate?' 18.

Hawkyns for Chiche St Osyth and Richard Badcock for Moze. These men knew well the others who were important in the area: the farmers of large landholdings like Philip Harrys, John Cotton and John Butler in St Osyth, the Brasiers at Walton, gentlemen like the Badghotts at Little and Great Clacton and yeomen like their neighbours the Hubberds of Bovells and the Stubbes of Cann Hall. They were also interconnected with St Osyth merchants like John Tendering and Isaac Grene. This powerful group did not always agree amongst themselves, of course, but they were tightly bound together by family and business. We will see this tightness of local grouping over and over again in the course of this history.

The same names recur in a list of links. Philip Cawston left Edmund Pirton £5 as a goodwill token in his will in 1584, and Edmund witnessed the will with George Hudson. Philip Cawston and Robert Hawkyns were connected by having married into the Marven family of Little Oakley (we will meet them again later in connection with several witch-accusers). Thomas Wood and John Ryvett did a land deal in Moze, Great Oakley and Beaumont in 1571 that was worth £100. Richard Badcock and John Butler put in a recognisance together for two men to keep the peace in 1576, as part of a series of disputes in the early 1570s during which a staggering £17 worth of cheese was (allegedly) stolen from John Tendering by Edward Brasier and his men. In a similar falling out, the St Osyth churchwarden Philip Harrys and Edmund Pirton went to law over the rights to Amperswick farm in St Osyth. Philip did a number of £40 land deals with Isaac Grene there. Isaac witnessed John Butler's will with Philip Harrys and he left a striking gift, 'a deathes heade in goulde', to Francis Harrys. Robert Cawston died at Edward Brasier's house, leaving money and goods to Robert Cotton; the families had a long business and legal history together. Richard Badcock leased land at Little Oakley Hall from John Ryvett, while at the time of his death in 1580, John had loaned £40 to Edmund Pirton. And so on.[3]

The surviving records that tell us about these men are primarily financial, based on dealings in land and legacies.

[3] These are a selection from the records of these men's' lives. ERO D/ DB M160, 161 for all, and: TNA PROB11/68/57, Great Clacton Parish Register 11 December 1570, Weeley Parish Register 23 April 1577, 27 September 1584 (although the registers have ERO classmarks they are listed by name because this how they can be searched digitally); TNA PROB11/127/113, PROB11/68/57 (Cawston); William T. R. Marvin, *The English Ancestry of Reinold and Matthew Marvin of Hartford, CT* (Boston: privately printed, 1900) 56, 64 (Cawston and Hawkins); TNA C2/Eliz/H19/46, PROB11/65/120, ERO T/B 79/1, Emmison and Fitch, *Feet* vol. 5 3, 4, vol. 6 3 and LMA DL/B/A/002/MS09537/004 (Harrys); TNA PROB11/07/205 (Grene); ERO Q/SR 38/6, 7 and 8, 39/114, D/DBm M89, Cockburn, *Calendar: Essex: Elizabeth* records 1887, 2095 (Tendering); TNA PROB11/63/54, 11/69/652, C2/Eliz/R11/55, Emmison and Fitch, *Feet* vol. 5 90, Tendring Parish Register 20 January 1563, 20 February 1564, 18 August 1567, 3 February 1571, 4 March 1577, ERO D/P 388/1/1 Little Oakley Parish Register 29 September 1569, 22 November 1569, ERO D/DEl M76, Cockburn, *Calendar: Essex: Elizabeth* record 696 (Rivett); Emmison and Fitch, *Feet* vol. 5 179, ERO D/DBm M89, Little Clacton Parish Register 25 July 1580, 1 April 1581, TNA PROB11/68/57 (Hudson); Great Clacton Parish Register 15 March 1572, 13 January 1573, 6 January 1575, 15 December 1577, 15 November 1578 (Glascock); Emmison and Fitch, *Feet* vol. 5 156, Little Oakley Parish Register 7 September 1561 (Wood); ERO Q/SR 56/32, 33; TNA PROB11/63/54 (Badcock) TNA PROB11/63/45, Kenneth Walker, *The Story of Little Clacton* (Little Clacton: Little Clacton Parish Council, 1958) at https://littleclacton-pc.org.uk/village-life/local-history/ the-story-of-little-clacton-an-essex-village-1958/, Little Clacton Parish Register 15 August 1564, 3 September 1565 etc (Badghott); TNA PROB/11/34/350 (Stubbes) etc and see later.

There are some records of baptism, marriage and burial. There are a few suggestions of religious orientation: for example, William Hubberd and Robert Cawston both owned copies of Foxe's *Book of Martyrs*. Sometimes there is additional piquant information about characters and relationships. For instance sometime just before 1570, Edmund Pirton's sister Parnell ran up a tailor's bill for seven pounds and eightpence for a gown of fine silk, a pair of damask shoes, pinking ribbon, a gown for her maid, cloth of sarcenet, silk and buckram. William Hubberd left a loquacious seven-page will and a codicil discharging his initial executors. He bequeathed multiple lands, and one hundred pounds to the poor of Little Clacton in 1596. Yet he could not write his own name. But beyond the basic facts what is most noticeable is the web of interconnectivity.[4] These families had carved up the landscape among themselves: its resources, income streams and assets. They owned it through amassing money from 'farming' – not the soil-tilling of the ordinary husbandman but the skimming of taxes and fees. And the men owned it also through marrying women with excellent dowries and legacies, and raising daughters like Parnell Pirton with the same attributes: they were part of their family businesses too.

---

[4] On Essex inventories and wills see the classic F. W. Steer *Farm and Cottage Inventories of Mid-Essex 1635–1749* (Chichester: Phillimore, 1969); Abigail Gomulkiewicz, 'Religious Materiality in Elizabethan Essex (1558–1603)', *Material Religion* 16:3 (July 2020) 275–97 and Erica Fudge, 'Counting Chickens in Early Modern Essex: Writing Animals into Early Modern Wills' in her *Quick Cattle and Dying Wishes: People and their Animals in Early Modern England* (Ithaca, NY: Cornell University Press, 2018) 21–48.

Like the group of bailiffs, other Darcy estate officials were often substantial landowners in their own right. Some were even better connected and had far superior holdings. The estate's Receiver General Thomas Cammock, originally of Layer Marney, had married into the Rich family – like the Darcys – and was cousin to the Earl of Warwick via his wife Frances. Among other land deals, in the early 1570s he and Robert Drury bought from Thomas and Eleanor Tey the manors of Marks Tey, Moyse Hall, Layer de la Haye and Nevendon which comprised over one hundred and fifty houses, two watermills, four dovecotes, two hundred gardens and orchards, seven thousand acres of land, a fishery and ten pounds in rents. George Golding, the Darcys' auditor, was brother-in-law and auditor to the Earl of Oxford, the brother of an MP and also of the translator of Ovid and other Classical authors, Arthur Golding. The Golding family held lands across the Clactons, Weeley and Thorpe, and as far away as Saffron Walden.[5]

The estate's Steward, Geoffrey Nightingale, was a Gray's Inn bencher – a leading and ambitious barrister – and he too had substantial landholdings across Essex. In 1578, for example, he and his wife Katherine sold thirty-two acres of arable land, three of meadow, two of pasture and three of wood in Wimbish and Thunderley, near Saffron Walden, for eighty pounds. In 1590 a man was hanged for stealing three cows worth six pounds from

5 TNA WARD2/58/215/14iii; TNA PROB/11/127/113, 11/121/787, 11/88/189; Emmison and Fitch, *Feet* vol. 5, 164; ERO D/DBm 160; TNA PROB11/59/98, 11/32/177, 11/119/379; ERO D/DRg 2/27; TNA C 54/1039 23 and 54/1095 25, Emmison and Fitch, *Feet* vol. 1, 31; TNA CP 25/2/131/1677/22ElizIEaster 36.

the Nightingales at Newport, where Geoffrey held Pond Cross House. By the 1590s, Geoffrey had bought a large estate in Cambridgeshire and his descendants were baronets by the mid-seventeenth century.[6] As well as nationally important activities, Geoffrey Nightingale had a particularly key hands-on management role in the Darcy estate. He presided over the manorial courts on behalf of Lord Darcy, causing them to be organised by his officials and documented by his clerks, and sitting in judgement himself in each village's manor house or an equivalent space. He would have known the villagers well, sometimes over several generations, as wills were read in court, parcels of land and houses were inherited or exchanged.

Another active agent on the estate was John Barnishe, the Keeper of the Great Park at St Osyth, which stretched north beyond Park Farm to Hartley Wood. Barnishe had the usual connections with other local worthies: for example, he leased tithes at Great Clacton from Gyles Badghott and witnessed his will in 1581, and rented land to John Butler at Lee Wick. Anthony Mannock, meanwhile, was the Keeper of the other St Osyth park, the Little Park which encompassed the Priory itself. His primary lands lay in the Oakleys – the villages of Great and Little Oakley – but he had influence across Essex. It was these park-keepers' job to manage those who watched over the deer herd, organised licensed hunting

[6] Reginald J. Fletcher, ed., *The Pension Book of Gray's Inn* (London: Chiswick Press, 1891) 22, 30, 93; A. W. B. Simpson, 'The Early Constitution of Gray's Inn', *The Cambridge Law Journal* 34:1 (1975) 131–50, 139; Emmison and Fitch, *Feet* vol. 5, 221; Cockburn, *Calendar: Essex: Elizabeth* record 2192; ERO D/DVm 20; G. E. Cokayne, *Complete Baronetage* vol. 2 (Exeter: William Pollard, 1900) 73.

and supplied game for the lord's table and for gifts. They secured the parks within well-maintained fences, usually made of oak palings set on earthen banks, and dealt with poachers. Anthony Mannock's Little Park patch included the rabbit warren, with its warrener undertaking similar tasks, and the network of fishponds by the probable site of the old holy well. Both men also had responsibility for natural resources such as timber, gravel and clay, and for horse pasture. This meant they interacted frequently with local people, in a strong position of authority.

Yet the worldly resources of these men did not mean that they thought themselves immune from attack by those whose lives they were supposed to control. Indeed, some of them thought they had been specifically targeted by witches. One of the accusations that Ursley made against Ales Newman as Brian continued to question her was that she had attacked the cattle farmer John Butler. 'Being at Butlers', Ursley said, Ales had been refused a piece of meat and 'went away mourmuring', a word that usually referred to a spell. Shortly afterwards, Ales sent a spirit to cause John Butler back trouble, with which he was now 'greatly pained'. Later, another suspect, Elizabeth Bennett, was also accused of attacking him – of which more later.[7] John Butler farmed at Lee Wick out on the coastal flats across the fleet and held other property in the village too. The remoteness of Lee Wick suggests that in order to get to 'Butlers', like many of the St Osyth poor

---

[7] Susan Pittman, 'Elizabethan and Jacobean Deer Parks in Kent' unpublished PhD thesis (University of Kent, 2011) 61–2, 64–9, 75, 86–91, 93; ERO D/DB M161; TNA PROB11/88/189, 11/63/45, 11/65/120; see Little Oakley parish register for the Mannocks; *ATAJR* B4v, table.

Ales had walked miles in search of charity, going from farm to shop to mansion across the Darcy estates. From Lee Wick farm to Frowick farm, where further witchcraft accusations were made, is a four mile walk, and we know that the women who trudged the muddy footpaths of St Osyth went to both in search of help. The Darcy tenant farms were of variable size and fertility but to the very poor they represented a cornucopia of resources, sometimes granted and sometimes denied. And the men who owned these farms were surprisingly scared of women who begged at their doors.

John Butler should have felt safe. He was a wealthy yeoman with extensive business interests. He served on Quarter Sessions juries, and was trusted to provide recognisances. At the time of his death in 1583 he held property in Great Clacton, including a fish weir and boat and a ship named the *Peter*, at least six houses in St Osyth which were let to various families, a separate brew house with two coppers and vats, St Osyth mills which he leased from Lord Darcy, and his farm at Lee Wick. When he died, he left to his two daughters Parnell and Agnes one hundred pounds each in marriage portions, along with three pounds to his nephew, forty shillings to his sister, sixty six shillings and eightpence to his four servants, twenty cows, eighty ewes, six rams and a bull, and ten pounds and forty shillings annually to be paid to the poor of St Osyth. To be fair, John Butler does not seem to have formally accused any of the St Osyth women of bewitching him. The only trace of his connection with the trials of 1582 is left in the indictment of Ursley Kempe and Ales Newman for bewitching Edena Stratton on 30 November 1581 so that she died on 14 February 1582. One of John Butler's 'servants' – a term that could mean anything from a farm-hand to an agent or secretary – was Robert Stratton, and John left him twenty shillings in his will. Edena was the wife of John Stratton, rather than Robert, but there is likely a family connection. The Strattons were also friendly with John Butler's business partners the Grenes: William Stratton witnessed Isaac Grene's will in 1606.[8]

Isaac Grene was another businessmen who felt under threat from witches. The Grene family ran a shipping business from St Osyth quay, transporting goods to and from London and along the east coast. Ships of up to thirty tons could reach St Osyth quay, but most were eight to twelve tonnes, flat-bottomed sailing barges, about two metres broad in the beam, and twelve to six-teen metres long. Isaac ran a highly successful shipping line with these craft as his fleet. Yet in 1584 he would accuse at least two St Osyth women, Elizabeth Lumney or Lumley and Alice Boulton, of bewitching six of his hogs worth forty shillings and of murdering his wife Grisell by witchcraft. And there was an even wealthier and nobler victim to give Isaac precedent for his fears. On 9 March 1582 Brian Darcy and his fellow magistrate Thomas Tey went to Colchester to follow up with Ursley Kempe some information that she was said to have given

---

[8] Thornton and Eiden, eds., The History of the County of Essex 80, 139, 146, 151, 155, 168; ERO Q/SR 42/46 (1573), Q/SR 56/32–3 (1576); TNA PROB 11/65/120, PROB11/07/205. John Stratton looks to have remarried: the will of Mary Elliott, singlewoman of St Osyth, written 24 November 1585, leaves much of her estate to her 'father-in-law' (i.e. stepfather) John Streytton, Emmison, *Essex Wills ... Commissary Court 1578–1588* 69 and Emmison, *Elizabethan Life: Wills of Essex Gentry and Yeomen* (Chelmsford: Essex County Council, 1980) 66, will of John Sandon names 'goodwife Butler'.

to visitors to her cell at the Castle. Ursley had been saying an astonishing thing: 'that Tyffyn her white spirit tolde her that Ales Newman had sent a spyrite to plague a noble man'. This man, she told Brian and Thomas, was one 'of whome we (meaning the poore) had all reliefe'. And she had concluded from Tyffyn's intelligence that this noble was 'Lord Darcey'. Ursley did not mean the current Lord Darcy. Although she was reluctant to confirm this to the magistrates now that they were face to face with her asking probing questions, the report they had had of her allegations was that Ales had sent a spirit 'to plague the late Lord Darcey, whereof hee dyed'.[9]

These claims against Ales Newman were not taken up during the legal process against the witches. Perhaps for all the speculation there was simply not enough evidence to proceed. Perhaps the Darcy family recoiled from pursuing the matter further, or were dissuaded from it by others. The suggestion that witches could murder even noblemen, peers of the realm, at will was a terrifying one. It would resurface, be taken to court and apparently proven in 1619 when witches were convicted of killing two of the children of the Earl of Rutland, Lord Roos and his little brother.[10] In that case, though, the accused women had been in regular contact with their supposed

---

[9] Harding, Gibson and Cooke, St Osyth, Essex 34; Cockburn, *Calendar: Essex: Elizabeth* record 1480; neither was convicted of murder, but Alice was found guilty of bewitching Isaac's hogs. There was a property called Lumleys in Mill Street in the mid-seventeenth century, ERO D/DCr M1; *ATAJR* C8.

[10] *The Wonderful Discovery of the Witchcrafts of Margaret and Phillip Flower* (London, 1619); see also Tracy Borman, *Witches* (London: Jonathan Cape, 2013).

victims and one of them was employed in domestic service in the Earl's home at Belvoir Castle. Ales Newman had no such close connection with John, Lord Darcy, as far as we know. His death in 1581 appears to have been attributed to her by Ursley rather than by his immediate family, and there are no further details of the alleged offence. But the very idea that witches had such power – even over men drinking out of golden goblets and sleeping in down beds with velvet hangings – sent a shiver down the Elizabethan spine.

Brian Darcy himself was not a lord, but he was a very powerful man. He had attended Lincoln's Inn from 1562, beginning his studies on 7 February. Thus he was ideally suited to the magistracy and, as we shall see, aspired higher. As well as being learned, he was extremely wealthy. His father Thomas Darcy of Tolleshunt Darcy and Tiptree Priory had died in 1559 and left him – after the death of his mother Elizabeth and the use of his father's executors – the manor of Bentons (lands in Witham, Hatfield Peverell and Wickham), St Clere's Hall and its manorial lands in St Osyth and other lands in the parish, Tolleshunt Major and Tolleshunt Darcy parsonages and associated lands (Garretts, Betts, Prior's Hyde), Estwelches and Westwelches (land in Steeple Stangate, St Lawrence and Halsted), the manor of Wycks (lands in Tolleshunt Major, Mundon, Cold Norton and Bramston), and the manor of Moverons (lands in Brightlingsea, Alresford and Thorrington) as well as an annuity from some of the lands meantime. When Brian died he held four principal manors – St Clere's, Moverons, Tiptree and Bentons – and further lands across south Essex: the Downs in Tolleshunt Major and Tolleshunt Darcy, Donybrookes,

Newlandes, Brightlees and Crooked Crofts (in Witham), lands called Starnes in Wigborough and Tolleshunt Knights, lands at St Clere's Wick, and in addition to the lands already named further acreage in the towns and parishes of Weeley, one of the Clactons, Great and Little Braxted, Fairfield, Faulkbourne, Terling and Inworth.

Brian rented out much of his land to tenant farmers, some of whose names we know in the 1550s and 1580s: Robert Havell at Moverons, John Hickman at Bentons, John Till at the Downs, Thomas Cotesford at Witham, Steven Westwood at Starnes. The wealthiest tenants then sub-let some of their properties to people lower down the social scale, and employed them to plough their land, herd and milk their animals, weed and harvest their crops. Monies flowed upward to the lord of the manor: fees for transactions, duties paid at the time of tenants' deaths and annual rents. The scale of Brian's holdings and thus his income was large: Moverons alone comprised some ten messuages or homes, ten gardens, over a thousand acres of land, two hundred of meadow, eight hundred of pasture, thirty of wood, four hundred of marsh, with a warren in Brightlingsea. Over the years, lands and properties at Maldon, Great Waltham and Hatfield Broad Oak also came into and out of his hands.[11] This was the man who was questioning Ursley Kempe, a woman who owned

---

[11] *Records of the Honorable Society of Lincoln's Inn* vol. 1 (Lincoln's Inn, 1896) 70; Thomas's will TNA PROB11/39/485; Brian's will (Darsie) TNA PROB11/72/295, which is missing a separate indenture drawn up between him and his executors, giving more detail, and inquisition post mortem TNA C142/217/115; ERO Q/SR 39/115, 40/6, 47/12, 58/5, 58/6, 58/81, 59/164, 66/22, 66/81, 74/62, 74/63, 77A/11, 81/18 and others; TNA E201/10292.

virtually nothing, who was routinely rebuffed, sworn at and assaulted. Of course Brian was intimidating and persuasive. Of course his questions caused her to accuse further St Osyth people. These too were women of much lesser status than Brian.

This next group of suspects lived both to the north and the south of St Osyth, and their stories usefully show us the Darcy estate and its landscape through the eyes of its tenants. In Chapter 1 we learned about the network of magical practitioners that operated in the village and now in Chapter 2 we can see how that magic also adhered to certain places in the wider landscape. This chapter offers an experimental map of that spiritual landscape, overlaid on the economic one that we have examined previously. It is tentative, but suggestive. This spiritual mapping starts with a new suspect, Elizabeth Bennett. Brian Darcy began his third round of interrogation of Ursley by asking her a question that was, unusually, documented in *A True and just Recorde*: 'how she knew the said Elizabeth Bennet to have two spirits'. But the phrase 'the said Elizabeth Bennet' also hints that something is missing, because we have not actually heard about Elizabeth before. Perhaps her name came up in an unrecorded questioning session, or was mentioned by Ursley when she was in the lock-up. Whatever the origin of the story about Elizabeth Bennett, Ursley said that in winter 1581 she had gone to Elizabeth's farmhouse to collect some milk that had been promised to her. Elizabeth was not there, however. Ursley had called out 'ho, ho, Mother Bennet are you at home?' and then looked in through a chamber window. Inside, she saw a creature like a ferret exploring a pot covered with a cloth. The creature looked up at Ursley, who – at least in retrospect during her account to the magistrate – concluded that the ferret was a spirit.

Brian Darcy was interested in this observation, although not in questioning Ursley's supernatural assumptions. Why, he asked, did Ursley think the spirit had looked at her? It was hungry, Ursley hazarded. Brian pursued, likely following up further unrecorded discussion, and continued the unusual practice of having his questions noted down: he asked Ursley how she knew the names of Elizabeth Bennett's spirits, something she had not recordedly claimed that she *did* know. At this point, too, she seems to have forgotten about the ferret altogether, further evidence of some disturbance behind the text. Instead of naming that animal, she said that her own lamb spirit Tyffin had told her that Elizabeth's spirits were a black dog called Suckin, and a red lion called Lierd. The idea that an English witch might have a lion as a spirit seems to have created less surprise than one would expect. It might have helped that the Red Lion was a popular inn sign. Possibly the Red Lion inn that now stands in the centre of St Osyth, just opposite the Priory wall on the Colchester road, was there then in an earlier form. It's not clear whether Ursley or Elizabeth originated the idea of the red lion – Elizabeth seems to have been questioned on the 22nd, so it may have been her – but surely the notion of a heraldic sign had some influence. Perhaps Ursley was just echoing what she knew Elizabeth had already confessed in a document that doesn't survive.

Anyway: elaborating, Ursley said that Elizabeth's black dog Suckin had killed William Willingall and also William Willes's wife, and that the lion Lierd had hurt a woman named Fortune and her child, and the wife of William

Bonner. Later, it would be alleged that Elizabeth Bennett had also bewitched the farmer John Butler, whom we've already met in connection with Ales Newman. Finally, Ursley told Darcy that Elizabeth's dog-spirit Suckin had killed Joan, the wife of William Byette, whilst Lierd had killed two of his cows and made a third so sick that William had concluded the animal was dying. He and his farm workers had lit a fire in the straw on which the cow was lying, because a cruel but decisive remedy against witchcraft was to set fire to an animal that was afflicted, or to some of its severed body parts. Later we learn that William was accused of wider animal cruelty. This cow, however, would not submit to being burned, and got up and walked away apparently cured: which strengthened suspicions that she was bewitched. William Byette's wealthy merchant friend John Tendering confirmed the story of William's cow.[12]

When Brian Darcy questioned Elizabeth Bennett on 22 February about her interactions with William and Joan Byette, an unpleasant story of neighbourly dispute emerged. Initially Elizabeth refused to confess anything to Brian. She was a capable woman and the possessor of some modest material resources, which made her appear quite well off in comparison with some of the other accused women. Elizabeth and her husband John owned

---

[12] Phyllis M. Hendy, *The History of St Osyth: Pubs, Pints and Publicans* (St Osyth: Tooseyprint, 2009) 37–40; *ATAJR* B4, table, B3; on 26 February, 2A5v, Cockburn, *Calendar: Essex: Elizabeth* record 1316. See also Phyl Hendy, *The St Osyth Witch Story: 1582 and All That* (St Osyth: n.p., 1993). Mrs Hendy took four years to 'translate' *A True and just Recorde* (2). She died in 2018 and I wish I could have shared this book with her.

cows and pigs, and instead of begging from others she managed her own bread making and dairy processes in some comfort. She stood up to Brian's questions stoutly, until he asked her whether she had a pot or pitcher stood under her stairs in which her spirits slept on wool. Elizabeth denied this. Brian had prepared a trap, however: 'if it be proved to your face, what will you say to al the other matters you have bin charged with, are they true?' 'Yea', said Elizabeth, not defining which part of the statement was to be proven: that she had a pot, or that she had a pot in which her spirits slept on wool. Brian then had the pot brought to her – without, of course, its spirit occupants. The trap snapped shut.

Elizabeth held out as well as she could: she admitted it was her pot, but denied that the wool was hers (had someone planted it, or was she mistaken or lying?). Either way, Brian began to bully her in earnest, and at this moment his text, as it later appears in *A True and just Recorde*, slips into the first person. It seems to me that we can feel his excitement and his personal investment in the witch-hunt growing with his emergence into authorship. In effect, Brian took a selfie with the woman whom he was trapping into a confession of witchcraft:

I calling her unto mee, saide, Elizabeth as thou wilt have favour confesse the truth. For so it is, there is a man of great cunning and knoweledge come over lately unto our Queenes Majestie, which hath advertised her what a companie and number of Witches be within Englande: whereupon I and other of her Justices have received Commission for the apprehending of as many as are within these limites, and they which doe confesse the truth of their doeings, they shall have much favour: but the other they shall bee burnt and hanged.

But as Brian displays himself, so he also exposes himself to criticism. His statement to Elizabeth was largely untrue, some of it a deliberate lie.

Brian probably had in mind a man of great cunning who actually had visited Queen Elizabeth: the French jurist and demonologist Jean Bodin, whose book we know Brian and his friends had read. Jean Bodin had visited England in 1581 in the retinue of Francois, Duke of Anjou and Alençon when the Duke was attempting, unsuccessfully, to win Queen Elizabeth's hand in marriage. Whilst in London, he had visited the English Parliament, presumably in pursuance of his interests in governance, and he had also engaged in some controversy over English treatment of Catholics. There is no record of his having discussed witchcraft with the Queen or her advisers, but it is not unlikely that he did so given his interest in the subject. It certainly suited Brian to claim that this was the purpose of Jean Bodin's visit. However, there is no evidence for the assertion that he, or other magistrates, had been given a special Royal Commission to investigate witchcraft locally at this time. Peter Elmer suggests a Commission of 1580 may be being referred to here, disingenuously.[13] Finally, Brian threatened Elizabeth Bennett with the punishment

---

[13] *ATAJR* B6–B6v; Barbara Rosen, *Witchcraft in England 1558–1618* (1969; Amherst: University of Massachusetts Press, 1991) 121 n.4; Leonard F. Dean, 'Bodin's Methodus in England before 1625' *Studies in Philology* 39:2 (1942) 160–6 summarises the incomplete evidence for Bodin's activities and reception in England (especially 160–1) and see also Summerfield Baldwin, 'Jean Bodin and the League' *Catholic Historical Review* 23:2 (1937–8) 160–84 for details of the sources (especially 165–7); Rosen, *Witchcraft in England* 122 n.25; Peter Elmer Witchcraft, Witch-Hunting and Politics in Early Modern England (Oxford: Oxford University Press, 2016) 30.

for heretics, burning, as well as the hanging that was the actual punishment, and – as he had done with Ursley Kempe – he offered a leniency for confessing witches that he had no intention of granting. All this adds up to a piece of intimidation that, whilst it was not illegal, would become controversial once it was widely known. We'll see that controversy later in the book.

However, Elizabeth Bennett could not know this. She may have been a substantial householder, but with her reputation already tainted by being hauled up to the big house in front of her neighbours, she would have felt fearful and shocked. She was now being told by this well-fed, warmly dressed gentleman, with his books, his quills, his wax candles and his roaring fire, that if she refused to cooperate she would be burned or hanged.[14] Like Ursley, when thus threatened and deceived by Brian, Elizabeth collapsed, 'falling upon her knees distilling teares'. She began her cooperation with the magistrate by explaining her vexed relationship with her neighbour William Byette. She was apparently smarting from the betrayal of accusation by this hostile man, and painted an unflattering picture of him. William had lived next to Elizabeth and her husband for three years, she told Brian, but in the second year the families had quarrelled and he began to call her 'olde trot and olde witche'. One day he cursed her and her cattle, to which she retorted that he should end his curse with his own name because 'it wil light upon your selfe'. Turning his own curse upon him, she implied, may have caused him to lose three of his cattle.

[14] I found Tracey Norman's play *Witch* (Circle of Spears, 2016–present) helpful in thinking about the power dynamics of questioning: www .traceynormanswitch.com

William and his wife Joan already mistreated their own and her animals, Elizabeth went on to state, which explained at least one of the deaths. They had even stabbed one of her swine with a pitchfork. She had had to offer the dead or dying pig to the butcher Henry Durrant, but it had proved to be a sick animal and the butcher gave it back to her without any payment. All this was perfectly safe to admit, but after this preliminary discussion, Elizabeth moved inexorably towards confession. Perhaps she accepted a story Ursley Kempe had already told about her in gaol, or she created her own tale. Either way: 'above two yeeres past' she suddenly said 'there came unto her two spirits, one called Suckin, being blacke like a Dogge, the other called Lierd, being red like a Lion'. Perhaps Elizabeth was confused, tired, experiencing an episode of dementia (she was 'old' according to the insults heaped upon her). Perhaps she tried to invent a story that would please Brian Darcy and save her from burning or hanging. Perhaps, something of all of these. The Red Lion inn sign might have entered her thoughts as a site of temptation, or perhaps she knew that certain kinds of dogs – like mastiffs or bandogs – were supposedly related to lions. In a treatise on dogs in 1576, Abraham Fleming called mastiffs 'vaste, huge, stubborne, ougly, and eager ... terrible, and frightfull to beholde ... fearce and fell', adding 'they are sayd to have their generation of the violent Lyon'. This seems to be the sort of dog that Elizabeth described to Brian, to which she added an actual lion for good measure.

In the story of her dog and lion spirits we might also see some indication that, like Ursley, Elizabeth had some pretensions to magical knowledge. When her neighbour

William Bonner gave evidence against Elizabeth, he told Brian about the strange illness of his wife and said that Elizabeth had come to visit her. Although he presented Elizabeth as his wife's loving friend, noting that during her visit she had kissed and hugged her, he also said that she had used the same phrase that Ursley had used in trying to cure Davy Thurlowe: 'a[h] good woman', Elizabeth had said, 'how thou art loden'. Did Elizabeth, like Ursley, see herself as a healer? Or was this a kindly use of a phrase commonly thought to ease sickness? Elizabeth was clearly close to William Bonner's wife, whose Christian name we don't know, and his testimony conveys her painful eagerness to bring comfort. William said the two women 'did accompanie much together' before his wife fell ill. He even described them as 'lovers', as well as 'familiar friendes' and although this word covered a wide range of friendly early modern relationships it could point to a mutual attraction, a deep love. Perhaps William was jealous of the women's connection, because he implied that by her intervention Elizabeth had made his wife ill: her kissed lip had swelled, he said, and her eyes were now sunken. Overall she was in 'a very strange case' and William by implication, though not directly, blamed Elizabeth and her spirits.

The spirit Suckin, in particular, has a vivid doggy presence in Elizabeth's story. Eastern England is known for its black dog folklore or 'Black Shuck': for example, the story of the 'divel' who 'in moste horrible similitude and likenesse to ... [a] black dog' burst into Bungay church in Suffolk in 1577, unleashing a tempest and killing two people. But as well as sounding like these demonic animals, Suckin exhibits behaviour that sounds like a real, attention-seeking dog.[15] Was he a pet or a needy stray? Elizabeth told Brian Darcy that Suckin had intercepted her as she was going to the tide-mill one day, and held her by the coat repeatedly so that she could not move. She had had to stand in the road until he let her go. However, certainly in her story of him if not in real life, Suckin was more than just a dog: he spoke to Elizabeth as well as holding her coat, asking her to go with him. Elizabeth offered a pious response: 'in the name of God, what art thou? Thou wilt not hurt me'. She 'prayed devoutly to Almightie God to deliver her from it', she told Brian. She made it very clear that she did not welcome Suckin.

Instead, she presented the dog to Brian as an 'evil spirite' attacking her and trying to control her actions. This suggests that Elizabeth was a woman well aware of narratives of temptation by the devil. Satan could come in many guises: friendly, aggressive, seductive. Suckin demonstrates all these characteristics and Elizabeth did the right thing in defying him and turning to prayer for help. Her words echo the paternoster or Lord's Prayer, an orthodox plea that God would 'deliver us from evil'. But Suckin did not go away. He literally dogged Elizabeth's footsteps along the mill road and seized her coat again when she was within a couple of hundred yards of her house. However, when Elizabeth prayed again for deliverance, she gained some respite: the dog 'did depart to the Wel'. Here we start to see something

---

[15] Durrant's forename appears in Ales Hunt's indictment and he gave further evidence on 26 March, Cockburn, *Calendar: Essex: Elizabeth* record 1301, *ATAJR* D4v–5, B5v–B6, B7; Johannes Caius, and Abraham Fleming (translator), *Of Englishe dogges* (London, 1576) 25 and Fleming, *A straunge and terrible wunder wrought very late in the parish church of Bongay* (London, 1577) n.p.

of the landscape around Elizabeth, the lands of the Darcys on which she lived and which were her place as well as theirs. The Darcy's lands appear here not as an economic unit of certain acres but as a magical landscape, one with places where evil spirits might lurk.

Perhaps the well to which the dog spirit departed was the one in Well Yard near St Osyth's market square; if so, Elizabeth was walking home along Pond Street, the modern Spring Road, and Chapel Street. However, given the highly charged religious nature of her encounter with the spirit, it is plausible that the well is Nun's Well, a supposed holy well obscurely associated with St Osyth (Figure 2.1).

As we saw in the Introduction, Osyth was abbess of the early medieval religious foundation at Chich St Osyth, and legend said that she was martyred by beheading at a 'fountain near Chich, where she used to wash herself with her virgins'. Despite being decapitated, Osyth stood up, picked up her head and walked to the church door before finally collapsing on holy ground and being buried there. Antiquarians, while pointing out that we must 'not ... expect much of Chronological truth or exactness in the Lives of Saints', suggested plausibly that this fountain became a holy well and that it was sited at Wellwick, towards which are now the remains of fishponds along the line of a stream at Nun's Well. If she passed the Nun's Well ponds on her way home, Elizabeth was walking north, past the Priory and along the Colchester Road towards Wellwick Farm. Later she mentions walking near 'Heywood's' barn and William Hayward lived at Frowick, which is the next farm settlement north of Wellwick across the bleak, flat fields.

FIGURE 2.1 Near Nun's Well, Wellwick, St Osyth.
(Source: Author's photo.)
Note: A black and white version of this figure will appear in some
formats. For the colour version, please refer to the plate section.

The Wellwick waters were probably channelled early
on in the history of the village and according to later
accounts there may have been remains of piping and of a

conduit house there in the 1580s. Elizabeth might therefore have known the place as an old and Popish religious
site, perhaps a place of derided and forbidden magical
water-cures. The Essex rector William Harrison wrote
in 1570 that supposedly healing springs where sick people might bathe were 'but baits to draw men and women
unto them, either for gain ... or satisfaction of [a] lewd
disposition'. Meanwhile, in Parliament they were condemned in 1581 as sites of 'supersticion', including under
that label both the practices of bathing in holy springs
and of people 'casting' spring waters 'over ther shold-
ers and head'. Despite such godly disapproval, however,
some wells continued as spas or washing places and as late
as the 1890s, the St Osyth well was described as being
in use as a healing spring.[16] Also in later times, stories
of St Osyth's ghost were recorded as being attached to
the well, and these stories, along with a reputation for
magic and dubious goings-on, might plausibly date back
to the early modern period. This 'haunted landscape' in
Tina Paphitis's terms, was exactly the sort of place that
a tempting devil might lurk, disturbingly close to the
Priory that hulked at the heart of the Darcys' lands. As
Nicola Whyte has suggested, such 'visible evidence of
antiquity' could become 'a powerful tool in the media-
tion of authority and control of land and society'. The
well both belonged to the Darcys and did *not* belong to

---

[16] *ATAJR* B7–B7v; Morant, *History* vol. 1 456; thanks to Tim Sargeant
for taking me to explore this site; Alexandra Walsham, *The Reformation
of the Landscape* (Oxford: Oxford University Press, 2011) 397–9, 103,
105; Robert Charles Hope, *Legendary Lore of the Holy Wells of England*
(London: Elliot Stock, 1893) xxi, 73.

them. It was older than their possession of the land. And pre-Reformation it had probably been quite intimately known by local people. Now it was closed off, religiously and literally, and occupied a remembered but inaccessible position near the Park's north gate but inside the boundary wall.[17]

After Suckin retreated to the well, Elizabeth escaped the devil dog for an hour and was able to get home with her freshly milled meal. She had begun to sift it for bread-making when the spirit caught up, and he stayed until she had laid her leaven (added her yeast to the mixture). The day after, as she was kneading her risen dough, he returned with the red lion, Lierd. The two spirits asked her pointedly 'why she was so snappish yesterday'. Elizabeth protested that 'I am in the faith of God, and you shall have no power over mee' – again suggesting a good command of the basic expectations and vocabulary of piety – and the spirits left. But they were not gone for long. As she was making a fire inside her oven to bake the bread, Elizabeth had once again to ask 'God and the holy Ghost' for deliverance. And as she stirred the fire with a fork half an hour later before raking it out of the brick

---

[17] Grid reference TM116166; see also drone footage of the Martin's Farm/Wellwick area by MrJaycoo1, 26 November 2016: https://youtu .be/CxTM_IhOYtw. For Hayward, *ATAJR* C3, Cockburn *Calendar: Essex: Elizabeth* record 1301; for folklore see https://megalithix .wordpress.com/2008/09/12/st-osyths-well-essex/ and for building record see Historic England, 'St Osyth's Priory' (1987): https:// historicengland.org.uk/listing/the-list/list-entry/1000237; Tina Paphitis, 'Haunted Landscapes: Place, Past and Presence' *Time and Mind* 13:4 (2020) 341–9; Nicola Whyte, *Inhabiting the Landscape: Place, Custom and Memory 1500–1800* (Oxford: Windgather Press/Oxbow Books, 2009) 127

oven, things got more frightening: Suckin lost patience and, saying 'seeing thou wilt not be ruled, thou shalt have a cause', he tried to push Elizabeth into the oven. She burned her arm, a burn that she showed Brian as evidence of her struggle against the spirits. Now Elizabeth's own body was marked by the creatures that came out of the well, tying her to their demonic, chthonic world under the Priory park. As she exhibited this demonic mark, Elizabeth was being bound not just to the devil but to the Darcys, the lords of the land on which she lived who would determine her fate.

A month passed before Suckin and Lierd returned to bother Elizabeth again as she went about her business. Then they accosted her walking in a small enclosed field, a croft, near Hayward's barn, likely in the fields near Frowick. Later, they disturbed her milking a red and white cow: the spooked animal suddenly snorted and ran away. In her panic, she broke Elizabeth's wooden pail and spilled all the milk. Elizabeth's husband John was angry about the loss of this valuable resource, particularly as the cow refused to stand still again that night to be milked. On this occasion, Lierd appeared in the less ferocious guise of a hare, and although the two spirits seemed threatening to Elizabeth they did not attack her. They then let her alone for over four months; indeed, she said that she had seen them no more than three times since Midsummer 1581. Perhaps Elizabeth was trying to draw the conversation to a close at this point. She had admitted meeting some spirits, had explained to the magistrate that she had resisted their advances, and that they had stopped pursuing her. Would that be enough? It was not. Brian must have kept pushing.

Whatever he said, it worked and there was a substantial shift in Elizabeth's story.[18]

Returning to the start of her statement, Elizabeth worked up to her final confession by emphasising to Brian that 'Byet had oftentimes misused her ... and her Cattell'. And so, in a crucial and clear-cut admission, she concluded that when at Midsummer she and William had another quarrel, 'shee caused Lyard in ye likenes of a Lion to goe & plague the saide Byets beastes unto death'. Even so, Elizabeth was not yet ready to confess to murder. Instead she suggested inventively that her spirits had begun acting alone. At Whitsuntide 1581, she said, Suckin announced to her that he had met Joan Byette twice, once in the Bennetts' yard and once at a stile between their lands and the Byettes'. And there, Elizabeth explained carefully, Suckin had 'plagued [Joan] to the death'. Elizabeth strove to distance herself: 'it was done by the spirite, but not by the sending of this Examinate'. Brian's scribe recorded her spelling out this difference with as much clarity as she could manage. But Brian must have asked more questions, suspicious, probing: why, he probably wondered sceptically, would Suckin do such a thing? Elizabeth said she thought that by killing Joan, Suckin was trying to 'winne credit' with her, because he knew her neighbours had wronged her. And, in her story at least, he did win credit.

So, at Lammastide – August 1581 – Elizabeth gave in to the spirits' temptation. Echoing Suckin by describing again how 'William Byet had abused her, in calling

---

[18] *ATAJR* B7v–B8v.

her olde trot, old whore, and other lewde speaches', she explained to Brian that she had told the spirit to go and plague William. This time she confessed to being the motive power behind the spirit's actions: Suckin killed William, but he did so at Elizabeth's instigation. This was murder, and Elizabeth had confessed to a crime for which she could be hanged. She said that after the murder she gave her spirit some milk as a reward and, completely submitting to Brian's will, she ended her confession by admitting that she then let both spirits lie in a wool-filled pot – yes, the very one that Brian had used to jolt her into confession. Brian had won, again. How easy it was to get women to confess! All you had to do was lie to them, tell them you would show them favour, threaten them with execution, and they told you everything. Imagine his smugness: they let you do it, you could do anything.

And of course, it was not just Elizabeth Bennett whom Brian was playing like a fiddle in late February of 1582. At the same time as she was telling Brian about Elizabeth on 24 February, Ursley Kempe was also naming other witches. Ursley said that on the 14th or 15th of January she had seen another ferret spirit, a brown one, at Ales and William Hunt's house. William was a mason, as his wife's indictment shows: probably the William Hunt, mason, who appears in Quarter Sessions papers in 1572 as masterless. Times would have been hard for masons after the Darcy mansion was substantially finished in the 1570s. Perhaps Ales was needy and fell out with her richer neighbours, although she later denied it. Whatever the reality, Ursley said that her lamb-spirit Tyffin had told her that Ales Hunt's spirit killed six cattle belonging to William Hayward of Frowick, the same man who was neighbour to Elizabeth Bennett. William Hayward must have agreed that he thought someone had bewitched his cattle, because Ales was accordingly indicted for killing them, supposedly on 1 January 1582.[19] Ursley added that Ales had rewarded her familiar after its costly killing spree by giving it a drop of blood. Brian must have asked 'upon what place of her body it was' that the blood was drawn because Ursley said she had not asked Tyffin that. Ursley had not been interested in her neighbour's bodily relationship with her ferret, but Brian was: as we know, he had his suspects stripped and searched for evidence of suck-marks where familiars had fed. To Elizabeth Bennett's burn mark was added a search for the place where Ales Hunt's ferret nipped her.

Ursley continued with her accusations: a shoemaker, Michell, had met with Ursley – perhaps as part of her practice as a cunning body – and told her that he believed Annis Glascock, wife of the sawyer John Glascock, had bewitched his child to death. Michell is probably Mychell Stevens, who is mentioned later in connection with this crime, the murder of Martha Stevens. According to an indictment, his child Martha was bewitched on 20 December 1581 and had died only recently, on 1 February 1582. Ursley had asked Tyffin whether Annis Glascock was responsible for Martha's death, and he confirmed that she was, adding that Annis had also bewitched an illegitimate child which was being nursed by William Page's wife, Ursley's former client. This child may be

---

[19] *ATAJR* B8–Cv; ERO Q/SR 41/21. There was a twenty acre piece of land called Hunts along East Street, the Clacton road, a century later, ERO D/DCr M1; Cockburn, *Calendar: Essex: Elizabeth* record 1301.

Abraham Hedg, said in Annis's indictment to have been bewitched on 20 February 1582 – after the start of Brian's investigation – and to have died on 1 March, by which time Annis was in custody. William Page may be the gardener at St Osyth Priory who is named in a will of 1587. The accusation that Annis killed a nurse child in the Page family's keeping may also relate back to an earlier tragedy, the death of Charity Page in May 1581. Annis was accused of causing this death in another indictment that went to the Assizes, even though there is no exploration of it in Ursley's statement.[20]

When Annis Glascock herself was questioned on 23 February, she denied all the allegations made against her by the Pages, 'Mychel the shoomaker', a couple named Fortune and a lodger of the Glascocks' named Sparrowe (of whom we hear no more). In fact, like Ursley, Annis told a story presenting herself as the past victim of a witch attack, one that caused aching bones. Like Ursley too, Annis had visited a cunning person for a cure. And like Cock's wife of Weeley, this practitioner – a caulker named Herring who lived at Sudbury in Suffolk – provided a remedy. He gave Annis 'a little lynnen bagge of the breadth of a groate, full of small thinges like seeds' and told her to sew it into her clothes and wear it where the pain was most intense. All this, though, had happened 'long sithence' when Annis was about twenty and lived

---

[20] *ATAJR* B3v–4, C3, Cv, table; will of Nicholas Croydene, 21 April 1587, Emmison, *Essex Wills … Commissary Court 1578–1588* 251; Cockburn, *Calendar: Essex: Elizabeth* record 1304; ERO D/DCr M1 shows a family named Glascock tenanting property on East Street, the Clacton road.

with her brother: she thought the witch who had attacked her had been jealous of her because the witch's husband lodged with Annis's brother and seemed sweet on the young woman.[21]

Now Annis and her sawyer husband lived in another place, and they kept a lodging house of sorts in St Osyth. Perhaps it stood in Mill Street where the boatyards created demand for timber and where mariners needed accommodation. In any case, Annis was desperate to show Brian that she knew nothing about the accusations of her new St Osyth neighbours. She rebutted them individually, adding that not only did she never hurt 'the base Childe, which Pages his wife kept' but also she 'knoweth not, whether the sayde Childe bee a base Childe or not'. Also, she protested, she had not fallen out with the Pages. If they worked at the Priory with Grace Thurlowe, though, perhaps they were hyper-vigilant about suspicions that witches were attacking the children of Priory workers. If there were thought to be evil spirits at Nun's Well, they could easily slip across the park to lurk in the gardens of the old monastic buildings, and prey on the workers there. Someone certainly thought that, like Elizabeth Bennett, Annis Glascock had gained access to the spirits of the locality and sent them to hurt her neighbours at the Priory.

We learn more about the haunted landscape of wider St Osyth when we follow another group of spirits across the fields to the south of the Priory park. These were the familiars of Margerie Sammon or Barnes, whom we

[21] See also Gibson, *Early Modern Witches* 94, 146–50.

FIGURE 2.2 Frowick Farm. (Source: Author's photo.)
Note: A black and white version of this figure will appear in some
formats. For the colour version, please refer to the plate section.

met in Chapter 1, and they draw us across St Osyth's
fields, away from the well and down towards the creek.
Margerie Sammon was the daughter of the 'witch'
Mother Barnes, and after her mother's death earlier in
1582 she allegedly acquired two of her mother's spirits.
They were first described to Brian Darcy by her sister,
Ales Hunt, when Ales was questioned on 24 February –
the same day as her accusation by Ursley Kempe. Ales,
you'll remember, was said to have a brown ferret-spirit
and to have killed six cows belonging to William
Hayward of Frowick (Figure 2.2). Brian began his questioning of Ales by exploring this claim, and his question
is recorded, continuing the unusual practice that he
adopted in late February. He asked Ales Hunt 'whether
there was any falling out beetwene [her] and Haywarde

of Frowycke, or his Wyfe'.[22] Ales answered that there was not, adding that in fact she was 'beeholding unto them' because Hayward's wife had once christened a child for her, something that was done if the baby appeared sickly and likely to die unbaptised. She had been grateful, and hoped this bit of personal history showed that she had no reason to attack the Haywards.

William Hayward's will, written in February 1583 by one of the probable authors of *A True and just Recorde*, William Whetcrofte – of whom more later – tells us a good deal about the Haywards, William and Margaret. William was a substantial farmer with aspirations to better the Haywards in future generations. His will charges his brother Edmund to send William's son – another William – to school for three years and then bind him apprentice to 'some good trade or science'. William the younger was also to have twenty pounds at the age of twenty, and three of his sisters – Joan, Elizabeth and Margaret – were to have the same at twenty one. Another sister, Jane, was to have ten pounds. William Hayward the elder thought that his wife Margaret might well be pregnant at the time that William Whetcrofte wrote his will for him, and this child was also to have ten pounds at twenty one. In recompense for his trouble as executor and guardian, William's brother Edmund was to have four pounds and William's dun nag, a horse called Bucke, with his tack. Margaret was to have twenty marks, with all the household goods. And the animals she was to inherit are particularly revealing of how damaging it would have

---

[22] *ATAJR* Cv–C2v, C3.

been for the Haywards to lose six cows to witchcraft in 1582. In 1583, the family had eighteen milch cows, thirty lambs and ewes, a black bob-tailed mare, a black sow and some poultry. In the shed at Frowick was corn and hay for them, and that completed the inventory of the family's wealth.[23] The six cows who died in 1582 would have been greatly missed.

Ales Hunt, however, strongly denied that she had any hand in the death of the Haywards' cattle. She also denied that she had any kind of spirit. But her assertion of innocence was undermined by information that Brian had gathered from her eight-year-old step-daughter, Febey Hunt. This piece of evidence was subsequently given the date of 25 February, but in order to be used against Ales on the 24th – which it was – it must actually have preceded her statement. This demonstrable inconsistency in the written record returns me to my suspicion that elements of the questioning process went unrecorded or the records were subsequently lost or altered. Alteration might have happened accidentally – in transmission from rough to fair copies and transit to the printing press. But, much more worryingly, it might have been done deliberately. If targetted changes in date, order or content were made, this may have been a process designed to obscure dubious questioning practices. These might include the eliciting of evidence from very young children, and we shall see more of this in Chapter 3. The rules around child evidence were hazy, and Brian Darcy was clearly attempting to push the boundaries, as in other areas, with his use of Jean Bodin's

---

[23] Emmison, *Essex Wills … Commissary Court 1578–1588* 100.

methods: *De la Demonomanie des Sorciers* advises magistrates to 'arrest the witches' young daughters'.

So Febey Hunt was useful to Brian in his attempt to incriminate her stepmother Ales and her aunt Margerie. We don't know what he asked her (an interesting silence) but Febey guilelessly explained that Ales, had 'two litle thinges like horses', one white and one black, which she 'kept in a litle lowe earthen pot with woll' and fed 'with milke out of a blacke trening [wooden] dishe'. So when Ales was summoned to meet Brian Darcy, he asked her about this fantasy, probing, by using Febey's exact words, whether Ales had 'never' fed any spirits out of a 'lyttle trenyng dishe'. Of course, she said no and Brian sprung his trap, just as he had done with Elizabeth Bennett. He sent the constable to Ales' house by the creek, accompanied by Febey, to fetch the identified dish and presented it to Ales. Panicked, she denied that it was her dish or that she had anything similar. Compare Elizabeth Bennett's reaction to Brian's similar trick with the pot. Was the dish Ales's, or was it planted? Or did she lie, unable under pressure to convincingly untangle the physical object from its supposed use, the feeding of familiars? Having easily discomfited her, Brian then used another technique to intimidate her, making her wait while he had the warrant drawn up for her committal to prison.

When Brian read the warrant to her, Ales cracked. Like Ursley and Elizabeth before her, she changed her story. Like them too, Ales tried to take the initiative. This time, she asked to speak privately to Brian – or so he says, in the first person: 'I wente into my Garden, and this Examinate followed mee'. St Clere's Hall garden was moated, its very shape suggesting the security of its owner and the entrapment of any visitor who had come there under duress. The house and grounds exuded wealth. When Brian inherited the Hall from his father, it had been in poor repair. Its last tenant, William Peverell, had – at least according to the aggrieved St Clere family – allowed his employees to store corn in the chief room of the house and damage its windows. Peverell had, they alleged, also illegally killed deer, pigeons, doves and rabbits from the estate and fished some hundred and sixty carp from the moat. There between the glass-windowed house and the carp-filled moat, 'falling uppon her knees with weeping teares', Ales Hunt confessed. She told Brian that she had indeed kept two spirits like little colts until six days before the examination, 18 February, exactly as Febey had said. These spirits were called Jacke and Robbin. But, presumably thinking how to save herself from committal to gaol, she added what she hoped would be a crucial fact: the spirits had left her six days ago, because they had known Ursley Kempe would betray Ales to the magistrate. Callously, as was the way of demonic spirits, they had told her to 'shift for her selfe' and she had not seen them since.

But as well as capitulating on her own behalf, Ales went further. She told Brian that her sister, Margerie Sammon, also had two spirits. They were like toads, one unimaginatively called Robbyn, like Ales's mini-horse, and the other Tom. Returning to the central theme of cunning magic that united her with Margerie and Ursley Kempe, Ales explained that 'her sayde Syster and shee had the sayd spyrites of their Mother, Mother Barnes'.[24] Mother

---

[24] Bodin, 188v; *ATAJR* 2A6–2A6v, C3v; TNA C/139/32, C3/11/50, C3/166/31; *ATAJR* C3, C4.

Barnes was the woman whose death on 12 February perhaps contributed to the crisis of magic currently engulf-
ing St Osyth, and whom Ales readily described as skilled
in witchery. Of course Brian pursued this line of enquiry,
and the next day he had Margerie brought to St Clere's
Hall and questioned her about her mother. Margerie
admitted that Mother Barnes had lived with her recently
for about six months – since September 1581 – and that
Margerie had attended on her when she was very sick and
at the time of her death. But she said that her mother had
not possessed any spirits, much less bequeathed them to
her daughters. Disbelieving, Brian handed her over to the
constable. By now the village lock-up on the Colchester
Road must have been full.

On 26 February, Brian tried a new trick to break
down the resistance of his suspect. He summoned both
the grown-up Barnes girls to St Clere's Hall and confronted Margerie with her sister, Ales. Painfully, he had
Ales repeat to Margerie's face the accusation that she had
two toad spirits. Ales was in effect denouncing her sister to the magistrate who could have her killed. Margerie
responded robustly to this act of apparent betrayal: 'I
defie thee', she said, 'though thou art my sister'. But Ales
contrived to communicate despite the glare of the magistrate's attention. She pulled Margerie's arm and drew
her towards her so that she could whisper in her ear, all
of which was breathlessly recorded by the scribe. Ales,
it seems, was not intending to betray Margerie. Instead,
like the others, she seems to have believed that confession was the only response that would help both of them.
The documents surviving from the examinations do not
tell us that Brian made the same false promise of favour

to the Barnes sisters that he had made to Ursley Kempe (confess and you'll be treated well) or the threats he had made to Elizabeth Bennett (fail to confess and you'll be killed). But Ales' behaviour suggests that this was what she understood.

And her reading of Brian worked in his favour, as did pretty much everything else in his society, on his and his family's lands. Margerie responded exactly as he hoped to Ales' intervention, capitulating with 'great submission'. She cried, as the other confessing suspects had done, and she embarked on a story. Her mother, she said, had indeed given her 'two spirites' on the day she died. She did not explain how Ales came by the other two spirits, but she said that she had 'caryed' her two, Robbyn and Tom, 'awaye with her ... in a wicker basket, more then half full of white and blacke wooll'. Like other witches' spirits, hers were housed in wool baskets, lying snugly on the material that brought income to women like Margerie through spinning and that was exchanged daily with clothiers like John Johnson and dyers like Ursley Kempe. Margerie said that she had asked Mother Barnes 'what shee should doe with them' – implying that she wished to present herself as someone unacquainted with the idea of witchcraft – and her mother had told her to 'keepe and feede them', adding 'if thou doest not give them mylke, they will sucke of thy blood'. Perhaps Margerie understood that suckling spirits with blood would be perceived as an admission of guilt. When questioned more closely by Brian about feeding her animals – when? how? – she stuck rigidly to the line that she had fed them only with milk. In the last two weeks, they had eaten only twice.

Margerie then carefully explained to Brian what had happened to the spirits: she had not only given them away, but had distanced herself from them physically. They would not be found waiting at the end of the long drive to St Clere's Hall, or in Margerie's house. Instead, Margerie explained, Mother Barnes had suggested that if her daughter did not want to keep the spirits herself, she should 'send them to Mother Pechey, for I know she is a Witch, and will bee glad of them'. That was exactly what Margerie did, in her story. On the evening of 19 February, as news spread through the village that Ursley Kempe had been arrested, she walked across 'the grounde of her Master, and so into Reads grounde' taking the spirits with her in their basket and there she set them free. She told them to go to Joan Pechey, and she said a protective farewell prayer: 'all evil goe with you, and the Lorde in heaven blesse mee from yee'. We see the twilight St Osyth landscape through Margerie's eyes as she describes how the spirits 'skypped' most untoadishly ahead of her, dwindling into the early dusk of the February night. They came 'towarde a barred style, goeing over into Howe lane', climbed over and went 'the readye way to mother Pecheyes house'. And there Margerie thought they would still be.

Howe Lane is no longer marked on maps of St Osyth, but it is possible to discover where it was. Its name draws attention to the fact that the area was studded with howes (barrows or tumuli) so-called in the dialect of the sea-borne Norse people who settled in north east Essex in the early Middle Ages. The land that was formerly Hoo or Howe Wick farm, in the tenure of the Cotton family, and is now Howlands Marsh, lies to the west of Lord Darcy's mansion, just south of Nun's Wood. Here howes once marked the rising ground above the creek before they were ploughed out or eroded. A few traces remain and Barrow Hill on Mersea Island west of St Osyth has another tumulus.[25] Most pertinently, the will of John Butler of Lee Wick farm mentions both cattle grazing 'which I have at the howe' and also his 'Messuage or Tenement ... called Reedes' in the Southfleet or Crossfleet area of St Osyth, which he let to his servant Simon Leap. This locates Margerie on John's land south of the fleet on the evening when she released her spirits.[26] John was the victim of attack by both Ales Newman and Elizabeth Bennett, as we have seen, and now he would know that another woman had set demonic spirits free in his fields!

Some of the St Osyth mounds were certainly Bronze Age, since 'Beaker' artefacts were found in similar burials on the heaths around the village; others might have been early 'Anglo-Saxon', like the burials at Sutton Hoo thirty miles to the northeast. And such barrows were often associated with magic, especially with the fairies who were thought to live inside them. Margerie's familiar

---

[25] *ATAJR* C4–C4v, C5; ERO D/DB M160, 161; on prehistoric St Osyth see Mark Germany, *Neolithic and Bronze Age Monuments, Middle Iron Age Settlement at Lodge Farm, St Osyth*, East Anglian Archaeology report 117 (2007) and 'A Causewayed Enclosure at St Osyth, Essex' *Past* 44 (July, 2003); see also *An Archaeological Evaluation of Old School Chase, St Osyth, Essex*, CAT Report 43 (September, 1999).

[26] TNA PROB 11/65/120 (1583); Thornton and Eiden, eds., *The History of the County of Essex* 79–80; ERO D/DCr M1. A single 'Tumulus (site of)' remains on the OS map TM11/21 at TM116162. Barrow Hill is at TM023143. See also will of Henry Read, 1616, TNA PROB 11/127/700. A house 'at the Howe' is also mentioned in a will of 1583, will of Nicholas Huer, Emmison, *Essex Wills ... Commissary Court 1578–1588* 98.

spirits were being imagined in a landscape filled with the fey associates of the prehistoric and pagan dead. As they skipped towards Howe Lane, away from Reads, across the mill dam and towards the Priory, they were travelling into haunted lands. Some of the howes were close to the holy well where Elizabeth Bennett imagined that her dog spirit had its hideout, and they may have been associated with it as a site of old, fearful religion. Off the spirits went into the marsh and Margerie was rid of them. Her description of this parting as having happened only days before in the cold dark not half a mile from St Clere's Hall must have sparked a shiver even in the most warmly wrapped magistrate and his sharp-quilled clerk.

When we see the Darcys' lands in this haunted twilight, suddenly they come alive. Most of St Osyth's records may be lost, and an economic and social reading of the witchcraft accusations there may be hard to attempt. I have done my best in these first two chapters to research and infer what I can from wills and deeds, inquisitions post mortem and records of lawsuits. But a reading based on the reconstructed landscape of feeling and imagination is surprisingly effective in adding to that more traditional historical reconstruction. Think about it: the Darcys' heartlands, the very homes of Lord Darcy and Brian Darcy, were ringed by pagan burial mounds and Catholic ruins. Many of their lands were reft from the church at the time of the Dissolution, still a comparatively recent memory in the 1580s. Like so many others across the country, St Osyth's was a landscape haunted and choked with memories of past spiritual lives, pagan and Christian. If the witches' creatures were thought to be holed up in landscape features associated with these old beliefs, with all their unresolved fears and tensions and their rich imaginative power, why would anyone be surprised? Fairies, the magic of cunning people and the malice of witches meet in this story at a specific landscape location, the well wick and the howelands around the Priory.[27]

And so Margerie Sammon's spirits went off down Howe Lane into the February night. If Joan Pechey lived among or beyond the howes, she likely lived in the medieval strip of St Osyth along the banks of the fleet. There was a line of buildings north of the water near the Priory Farm, and more buildings along the south side at Southfleet. This creekside part of the village was called Nether Hoo and contained a sizable group of cottages. One of the properties had a saltcote, a salt store: this one was known as 'le hoo cum le Salt Coate'. It was next to How Pightle and the marsh. There was also a property named Little How, one nearby in Mill Street called How's and a 'hoofeild', all in the same holding, and there were houses called Maynard's and Piper's – Maynards seems to have been in both Mill Street and Nether Hoo, presumably on a corner.[28] This mapping of a lost part of St Osyth locates

---

[27] M. R. Hull, 'Five Bronze Age Beakers from North East Essex', *Antiquaries Journal* 26 (Jan–April, 1946) 67–9; see also Whyte, *Inhabiting the Landscape*, chapter 5; a useful context (fairies/familiars) is *The Wonderful Discovery of the Witchcrafts of Margaret and Phillip Flower* E2v–E4; see also Victoria Carr, 'Witches and the Dead' and Emma Wilby, Cunning Folk and Familiar Spirits.

[28] Harding, Gibson and Cooke, *St. Osyth, Essex* iii; for Howe Wick Farm ERO D/Db M161; for Nether Hoo ERO D/DCr M1 – in the mid-seventeenth century the holdings were those of James Greene, of the Grene shipwrighting family, and one of the tenants in the 1670s was the oyster-dredger Thomas Pilgrim, both suggesting Nether Hoo's location by the water; Thornton and Eiden, eds., *The History of the County of Essex* 79.

Howe Lane in Nether Hoo, which can be placed north east of Mill Street and north of the fleet. Margery thus let the spirits go up Howe Lane, in the direction of the tumuli and also of Joan Pechey's house. As well as her howeland location, Joan's reputation made her a good suspect for Margerie to accuse: Joan was the woman that Ales Hunt had named already as a witch on 24 February, saying that Joan was as skilled in witchery as Mother Barnes was. She was also the next door neighbour of Ales's family: Ales and her mason husband William lived with his mother 'Widow' Hunt in the next house to Joan, also therefore in Nether Hoo.[29]

Joan Pechey was in her sixties and had lived in St Osyth for over forty years, so it's likely she first came to the village as a young working woman or a bride in the 1540s. You have probably already guessed that we learn these personal details about her because she gave the information to Brian Darcy when he questioned her. That was shortly after he had heard the testimony of Margerie Sammon on 25 February following that of Ales Hunt on the 24th. The emphasis on Joan's age might suggest the other suspects were younger than that, and that her age was seen to be remarkable. She must have been a determined woman with her wits about her, since, like Ales Newman, she put up a stout defence. Joan also used her long residence in St Osyth to make a point about how long she had known Mother Barnes, and to add that she had never heard her

---

[29] It is interesting that Margerie does not mention the fleet or creek and perhaps my mapping is slightly faulty, for all its detail. Was crossing water thought by St Osyth villagers to be significant in distancing oneself from spirits, or not?

called a witch or to have any witchcraft skill attributed to her. This does not mean that Mother Barnes was not a magical figure: in addition to being regarded as such by her daughters Margerie and Ales, she was named as a witch by Henry Durrant, a St Osyth butcher. Henry was quoting Ursley Kempe's diagnosis of the cause of his daughter Rebecca's death, which Ursley attributed to the Barnes-Hunt family. To her friend Joan, Mother Barnes was at worst a practitioner of good magic, if that, but others thought differently and wanted to know more.

Mother Barnes was dead, and could not be asked, but Henry Durrant was inventive and quite well-connected. He was friendly with some of the upper servants at the Priory – one of whom, Robert Spencer, had only recently in February 1582 willed to him a grey horse, saddle and bridle along with several pieces of pewter and brassware. Henry was flush, mobile and resourceful. So he decided that when he was next on business in Colchester he would talk, and probably pay, his way into the Castle, where Ursley Kempe had by then been imprisoned for several weeks. He wanted to ask Ursley, as a fellow-practitioner of Mother Barnes, for help. So as well as telling us more about the magical atmosphere surrounding Mother Barnes, her daughters and Joan Pechey, Henry's statement to Brian adds a new detail about the prison-visiting that we have already seen happening at the St Osyth lock up. This time it happened over a much longer distance. And Henry took some of his neighbours with him to Colchester, he explained to Brian Darcy on 26 March. They must have been persistent to get in: the Castle is a moated and walled fortress. And once inside the dungeons – which still exist – Henry and his neighbours were told by Ursley that Ales Hunt and her mother 'widow Barnes' had killed his child.

But long before Henry Durrant's finger-pointing, Joan Pechey's refusal to accept that Mother Barnes was a witch buttressed her resistance to the label of criminality for any of her own activities.[30] So Joan also denied other stories told about her: that like Ales Newman she had fallen out with the Collector for the Poor (in her case because her dole of bread was not good enough) and bewitched him, and that she had committed incest with her son. This shocking accusation comes from nowhere in the textual record of the trials, and it might be being used to soften up the suspect, in the unpleasant way that Brian Darcy had mastered with others. The likely source is Ales Hunt, because in her statement on 24 February she had admitted listening through the thin wall between Widow Hunt's house and Joan Pechey's house, as Ales Newman's neighbours also did. Like them, Ales Hunt said that she had heard Joan talking strangely: to someone or something, although she knew there was no-one else in the house at the time. She had concluded that Joan 'used those speeches unto her Imps' or familiars rather than to the non-demonic kitten and dog whom Joan later said shared her home. Likewise Ales might also have heard Joan asking her twenty-three year old son Phillip Barrenger to 'lye uppon the bedde at her backe', which was what Joan said she sometimes did.

---

[30] Will of Robert Spencer, 24 January 1582, Emmison, *Essex Wills ... Commissary Court 1578–1588* 187–188; *ATAJR* D5; Cockburn, *Calendar: Essex: Elizabeth* record 1301. Rebecca was said to have been bewitched on 4 November 1581, and she died on 24 November. Durrant discusses Spencer interestingly (18) noting that he knew Robert Rosse.

Phillip is likely the agricultural worker Phillip Barrenger alias Cowper who at the Midsummer 1578 Quarter Sessions was bound to serve Roger Steven of Frating, six miles north of St Osyth, in return for food and clothing. These powers of binding workers, effectively indenturing them in barely paid labour to masters in need of 'hands', were given to magistrates to help them deal with the otherwise unemployed and 'masterless' – like William Hunt – and stop them becoming a burden on the parish poor relief.[31] So while Joan described her dependence on charitable relief when she was asked about her relationship with the Collector for the Poor, her son Phillip was denied similar charity and required to work for his keep, a status little better than penury. Brian, being Brian, had the young man brought in for questioning and persuaded him to admit that he had lain naked in bed with Joan, after which this sordid distraction disappears from the narrative of witchcraft. Joan and Ales were committed for trial, and joined Ursley Kempe and Ales Newman in the prison at Colchester Castle. We'll hear later what happened to Margerie.

The relationships between the Barnes-Hunt family and Joan Pechey, neighbours in poverty, the recurrent theme of masterlessness and the return to stories about the Collector for the Poor illuminate the economic and social landscape of the Darcy estates. But this chapter has shown how there is more to the story than that: the

---

[31] *ATAJR* 2A4v, C6; ERO Q/SR 67/63. On the Statute of Artificers see Tim Wales, 'Living at Their Own Hands: Policing Poor Households and the Young in Early Modern Rural England' *The Agricultural History Review* 61:1 (2013) 19–39.

statements of Elizabeth Bennett and Margerie Sammon in particular also show us the spiritual landscape of St Osyth, the haunted lands of the Darcys across which witchcraft accusations had now begun to spread. It's harder to reconstruct the landscapes of the other villages of the witch hunt, because we have less information in the informations and examinations about specific locations. We are lucky that in St Osyth, where so many other records are missing, we do have these details as well as some estate records. The story that we can tell of each village is thus decisively shaped by record loss and survivals. In the remaining chapters of the book, the story of the witches will focus on what we can learn from the classes of record that survive for each one. In Little Clacton, the parish register is a particularly helpful source of information, especially set alongside the register for Great Clacton which also survives. These show us new facts about the witches questioned by Brian Darcy at Little Clacton, and they are the subject of Chapter 3.

3

Little Clacton

Cisley and Henry

∿

Brian Darcy must have been extremely satisfied with the result of his February 1582 investigations in St Osyth. And either this fact, or a drip of further accusations coming into his office in response to gossip about witches, or both, stimulated him to widen his search for them across the Darcy estates in March. Along the coast to the east lay the Clactons, Great and Little. St Osyth Priory had had ecclesiastical interests there for centuries and in the days of the abbey a fine house had been built to lodge their officials. This was Cann Hall, now a sub-manor of the wider unit of Clacton manor, and it passed to the Darcys in the aftermath of the Reformation. Lord Darcy re-acquired Cann Hall for the Priory estate and was also granted Clacton Manor itself in 1553, although previously the bigger manor had been held by the Bishop of London. Clacton carried ancient privileges, like the right to hold an ecclesiastical court outside the jurisdiction of the local archdiocese, and its peculiarities reflected the long history of power struggle between church and secular authorities in the area. Victorious in this battle after the Reformation, the Darcys also gained another sub-manor at Clacton, the scattered parcels of land that comprised Skirman's or Skyrman's Fee. Brian Darcy was thus well-acquainted with his lordship's tenants at Clacton, people like the manorial bailiff Philip Cawston of Weeley, who held Great Clacton Hall, the Hubberds at Bovells and the Thurstons at Colbaynes. It was not surprising that he should be asked to go to Clacton to investigate an accusation of witchcraft there about six weeks after he started his investigations in St Osyth.

Clacton is as low-lying as St Osyth, with clayey, fragile cliffs facing onto the North Sea. The coast turns north east as it sweeps round from St Osyth and whilst St Osyth Creek is sheltered behind Beacon Hill and the marshes, the Clacton coast is bare and wild. It was also extremely vulnerable to erosion in the past, as it is now. Tens of acres were lost in big storms, and the coastal farms shrank over the centuries until some if them were little more than a few fields. The land was also often water-logged, and transport was difficult and costly, over miry roads. This challenging environment meant that the farmers at Clacton were often poorer than their St Osyth neighbours. There were also fewer opportunities for merchants at Clacton than there were to the west. The villages had no south-facing creeks or bays that could form a naturally safe landing place, so their inhabitants conducted most of their trade through St Osyth. Even the fish weirs that had dotted the coast in the Middle Ages were almost all gone by Tudor times, swept away in gales, and at Little Holland a few miles further east the flooding was so bad and the population so keen to leave that the church was demolished in the mid-seventeenth century.[1]

In the 1570s an epidemic swept through the Clactons, further reducing the already scattered population. The

---

[1] Thornton and Eiden, eds., The History of the County of Essex 241–2, 244, 246, 251, 257–8 and see Chapter 2, this volume; ERO D/DB M160, 161, D/DHt M47.

Great Clacton Parish Register is especially helpful in showing us the sudden increase in mortality in September 1570, and also in allowing us to conjecture that it was due to a single disease. In a normal month in Great Clacton, one person would be buried at the church of St John. But in September 1570, this death rate abruptly quadrupled. At the end of August, husbandman John Cole died and his widow Dionese was buried on 6th September. Two children and a labourer also died that month. The next month five more people died, two labourers and three children. Another five people died in November. One of them was a servant of the Parby family, one of whose members had died in October, and another was a servant in the house of the Myllsopp family, one of whom had died in October. In December eight people died, including Thomas Thurston of Colbaynes Hall and Johane Cawston, wife of Philip Cawston of Great Clacton Hall. Two of the victims were a couple: Symon Lavender, carpenter, and Alice his wife, buried nine days apart. Eleven people died in January 1571. Two were father-in-law and daughter-in-law in the Boreflete family, two were mother and son and two were children of William Rogers. In February another member of the Boreflete family and the widow of one of the January victims died. By March the epidemic seems to have ended, although it probably affected adjacent communities too.[2]

---

[2] ERO D/P 179/1/2 Great Clacton parish register, volume 2, 1560–1710, ERO D/P179/1/2. There is a gap in December, perhaps because William Simpson would have been in St Osyth for the Darcys' seasonal festivities? There are a number of deaths in Moze in the same families over the period (ERO D/ACA 5, D/AZ 1/8).

In Little Clacton, mortality rates also rose in 1570 and 1571. In a normal year in the 1560s up to twelve people were buried at the Church of St James per month. But in 1570 and 1571 this rose to eighteen. There are recurrent names and some close relationships are recorded although not as fully as at Great Clacton. A member of the Cole family was buried on 10 September 1570, perhaps a relation of John and Dionese. Two members of the Dale family died in January 1571. Raphe Purle lost his wife Ann and daughter Judith in February and March. Two members of the Orris family died. Georg Jerman died in February and Alice and Robert, children of Widow Jerman, died in May. And in 1580–1581 came another apparent epidemic. Only five people were buried in 1579 but in 1580 this rose to seventeen including three members of the Crow family, two Peppers, Susan daughter of Thomas and Dorothy Short, Barbara Martin, Joane the wife of Edmund Hudson, Gyles Badghott gentleman, and two members of the Wheeler family, Nycholas and Hellen, who are connected with the witchcraft accusations in Thorpe (see Chapter 4). In 1581–1582 twenty were buried, including two sisters from the Hunt family, three Shorts including two more of Thomas and Dorothy's children, two Clarkes, another Wheeler, another Crow, another Martin, Edmund Hudson husband of Joane, Raphe Purle and his second wife Elizabeth, and two people important to the story of witch accusation at Little Clacton: Avis Smith and Margaret Redwoort. By October the death rate has slowed, but there were four deaths in February and March that may have looked like another wave starting. These losses must have marked the community of the Clactons in ways that we understand better in mid-pandemic 2022 than we could when I began this book in 2018.

As Jonathan Durrant suggests, 'it is possible to hypothesise a correlation between the sudden increases in burials in the villages nearest St Osyth and the witchcraft accusations made there' in 1582, driven perhaps by 'increased anxiety and fear'. So it is not surprising that four days after Raphe Purle's funeral, Brian Darcy travelled to Little Clacton to continue his investigations, presumably at the invitation of local people. This was on 1 March 1582. No doubt he was accompanied by his clerk and perhaps other observers. A woman travelled with the magistrate too, Margaret Simpson was probably a relative of the former Little Clacton vicar and St Osyth curate William Simpson, and we first met her in Chapter 1. She was expert in searching for witch marks and had already searched Ursley Kempe and others in St Osyth. So Margaret probably rode over to Little Clacton with Brian: she had a similar job to do that day. There must have been an air of expectation as the party trotted onto Little Clacton green. Spring was coming, and they would have heard wrens and robins singing, passed banks of primroses and the odd early celandine. Little Clacton was further inland than Great Clacton, so the riders would have jogged along the Clacton Road to Bocking's Elm and then turned north between Giddy Hall and Bovells Hall, two medieval sub-manors that faced each other across the lane. Once they crossed the Picker's Ditch stream they were in Little Clacton parish. There Brian found the witch accuser Richard Rosse or Rose waiting.[3]

---

[3] ERO D/P 80/1/1 Little Clacton parish register 1570–1571, 1580–1582 and see also Durrant, 'A Witch-hunting Magistrate?' 26–7, which also discusses Great Oakley and the other parishes where records survive.

Richard wanted to meet to Brian in order to accuse his neighbours Henry and Cisley Selles of witchcraft. He told Brian that about six years ago he and Henry had been working together in the fields. Henry, a labourer, was using Richard's plough on Richard's land (Figure 3.1), forcing the heavy blade round the field with Richard's team of horses. They had completed two or three circuits of the strip of land when two of the horses fell down 'in a moste straunge wise' and died.

Shocked by this upsetting and expensive loss, Richard began to think about what might have caused the deaths. He recalled that 'a little before' a negotiation over the price of malt had gone wrong. He had refused to sell Cisley Selles two bushels at the rate she wanted to pay for them, three shillings. Richard held out for ten groats instead, and Cisley would not give him his price. Cleverly, she then went to Richard's wife Alice, hoping to strike a better bargain. She brought a poke or sack with her, asking to buy a bushel or a bushel and a half – presumably as much as she could realistically afford – or as much as the bag would hold. But once again Cisley tried to haggle, and Alice Rosse would not compromise. Cisley lost her temper and, 'using many harde speaches' left without buying any malt.

Unfortunately there were also other sources of tension between the Rosse and Selles families. The Selles's cattle one day trespassed onto Rosse's land, and Alice

The same pattern is less obvious in Great Clacton in 1580–1582 perhaps because the population was by then so small; *ATAJR* C8; Little Clacton parish register, burial of Alice, 'wife of Richard Rose' 22 December 1592.

FIGURE 3.1 Ploughing. (Source: GRANGER / Alamy Stock Photo.)

drove them out. But Cisley was angry about it, and once again attacked Alice verbally, with 'lewd speeches'. Soon afterwards many of Rosse's cattle were 'in a most straung taking' and, with suspicion building up in his mind, Richard then concluded that this was as a result of witchcraft done by Henry or Cisley Selles. He also thought that they might have been responsible for a more direct form of attack on his assets. About twelve months ago, he told Brian Darcy, one of his barns had suddenly caught fire. It stood 'a good way from his dwelling house', so he had seen nothing, and was full of corn which was all burned. This too was a significant economic blow to Richard: when the matter came to trial the barn and corn was valued at one hundred marks. However, he was reluctant to blame Henry or Cisley Selles outright for this crime. He said that he did not have any evidence other than that he had heard their youngest son John say one day, speaking of Rosse's stores, 'heere is a goodly deale of corne'. This innocent comment was answered by a male voice which said nastily that it 'was the divels store'. Richard, or whoever was overhearing this conversation, could not identify this speaker.[4]

In the context of their previous dealings, however, this exchange evidently felt to Richard like a continuation of the Selles family's carping about his wealth. It is possible that he was a professional dealer in corn and malted grain, or that he was simply a richer farmer than those around him, with surplus to sell. He might even have been an engrosser, a merchant who bought up large stocks of corn when it was cheap, hoarding it until prices rose again so as to make a large profit. Engrossing was illegal from 1552 onward, and was perceived as an important modern

---

[4] Cockburn, *Calendar: Essex: Elizabeth* record 1302; *ATAJR* C8–C8v.

problem. From 1562, stricter regulation of markets was policed by magistrates at the Quarter Sessions. Whether Richard was an engrosser or not, his barns were full of grain but many of his neighbours could not afford to buy it. The Selles family were among these poorer people and had previously said they couldn't pay him what he asked. And they or someone else had now gone further to suggest that the inequitable level of his wealth was sinful: greedy, uncharitable, corrupt, devilish. Richard was upset by this anti-capitalist slander.

Interestingly, he does not seem to have mentioned in his evidence something that later came to be significant in the case against Henry and Cisley Selles. In addition to the Selles's supposed attacks on his goods, Richard's maid Ales Baxter had been taken strangely ill one night. It took until 19 March for this story to come out, although the next witness who met Brian on 1 March, Henry and Cisley's son Henry junior, would refer obliquely to it. The Selles's children had been mentioned in Richard's evidence and, given the success that he had enjoyed previously with Febey Hunt in St Osyth, Brian Darcy had probably already made up his mind to repeat his trick of questioning the children of suspected witches in the hope that they would incriminate their parents. And that is what he did, sending for the eldest son of Henry and Cisley, who was nine years old. Brian began to question young Henry and was rewarded by being told about a recent nightmarish experience. Sometime since Candlemas (2 February), Henry said, one night about midnight his brother John woke up screaming.

John Selles's nightmare is vividly recreated by his brother. 'Father, Father come helpe mee, there is a blacke thing yt hath me by ye legge, as big as my sister', the little boy shrieked. Henry said this thing was 'a spirite', and was 'like his sister, but that it was was al blacke'. The boys' parents comforted them, but Henry said that they also fell out with each other. His father said a shocking thing to his mother 'why thou whore cannot you keepe your impes from my children?' Cisley did not shout back, or rebut this insult. Instead, she responded mutedly, by telling the 'blacke thing' to 'come away, come away'. The next day, young Henry told his mother that he was terrified of the black spirit that came out of the dark: he 'swett for feare, and ... could scarse get his shirt from his backe'. But instead of giving him the expected sympathy and reassurance, he said that Cisley was angry with him. Indeed, she called him a name that recalled his father's attack on her in the night 'thou lyest' she spat at her son, 'thou lyest whoresonne'.

Brian Darcy listened attentively, and chose his moment perfectly to ask a key question. The boy was evidently upset and he sounded angry with his mother. So the magistrate led his nine year old witness by apparently making an assumption that his mother did keep some 'impes' and asked: 'wherewith hee had seene his mother to feede her Imps, and wherein'? Young Henry fell into the trap, and said that 'she fed them out of a blacke dish'. The familiar spirits were given milk every alternate day, near 'a heape of wood and brome standing under a crab tree by the house'. They lived there under the broom faggots. Brian asked the spirits' names. The black one had two, said Henry, 'Herculus' or 'Jack', and it was male. The other one was called 'Mercurie' and was a white female spirit. Elaborating, he added that 'their eyes bee like unto goose eyes'. Presumably these geese were the creatures that actually lived in the Selles's family's yard. The night that Richard Rosse's maid Ales Baxter was taken ill, Henry concluded, his mother had confessed to his father that she had sent the spirit Herculus to attack her. Presumably this attack was intended as revenge for Richard's refusal to trade with the Selles family: there's no indication that Ales Baxter herself had angered them. Henry said that his father had then called his mother a 'trim foole'. Cisley had some further words for little Henry about this exchange later on. Walking through Richard Rosse's broomfield, where the Selles's broom faggots probably came from, on the way to see Brian Darcy, Cisley told Henry junior that he should 'take heed ye say nothing'.

Sadly, by the time he walked back across the broomfield Henry had already said enough to get his parents into deep trouble, and Brian would move on to question them after he had finished with the boy. The incriminating words were then published to prove the criminality of Henry and Cisley. As with the evidence of eight year old Febey Hunt, the questioning of Henry Selles junior reveals that Brian and his assorted advisors and clerks rearranged the dates of his witnesses' testimony for publication in *A True and just Recorde*, making it appear that the evidence given by young children was merely a supplement to adult confessions. Even the testimony of nine year old Henry is confusingly dated to 'the saide day and yeere' rather than being clearly labelled. But we know from the statements of Henry Selles senior that his evidence, dated 'the first day of Marche' – and which we'll discuss in a moment – was given after that of his son Henry, which we've just read. And, despite the dating of the evidence of his youngest son John to 'the third of March', it likely comes after this as well because Henry quotes words used only by John. So Brian Darcy spoke to John, who told the magistrate himself that he was just six and three quarters, before he spoke to his father. We'll look at John's evidence first, therefore.[5]

John was the boy to whom the black spirit supposedly came during February 1582, and he was the Selles's youngest son. He expanded upon the story told by his brother Henry of that frightening night. Perhaps the boys were even questioned side by side, for company. John added to the insult to his mother that his brother had reported: he said that his father had called her 'stinking whore' not just 'whore', and had asked her 'what meane yee? Can yee not keepe your imps from my children?' He confirmed that one imp was black and the other white, and – like Henry junior – commented on their eyes. He said his father 'bad[e] his mother put them away or els kill them', and he detailed what had happened to the familiars which meant that they were not now available to be seen. His mother, he said, had 'delivered them to one of Colchester', ten miles away, and 'he thinketh his name is Wedon or Glascock'. Wedon's wife, he added 'had a cap to dresse of his mothers', and he thought that the spirits were taken away in a basket at that time. The man who carried the spirits away 'gave his mother a pennie', saying 'that when she should goe to him she should have another pennie'. He must have been asked why his brother Henry had not reported this,

5 *ATAJR* D–Dv.

and told Brian that Henry was away 'from home at one Gardeners house' when the courier came. This may be the house of Thomas and Alice Gardener, who appear in Little Clacton's parish records.

John also talked about the relationship between him and the shadow that had attacked him in the night. He said that his father had 'mocked him because his name was so' – one name by which the black spirit was called was Jack, commonly short for John, and that was the boy's name too. Fatally, he added that his father as well as his mother fed the spirits, 'out of a blacke dish with a woodden spone'. The spirits were fed on 'thinne milke' without the cream. Brian must have asked him, as he had asked Febey Hunt, if he could identify the feeding dish and he answered confidently that 'he knoweth the same dishe'. Brian also sought further physical evidence of witchcraft and John showed him his leg, the place where he and Henry said that the black spirit had attacked him. Pleased, Brian had this detail recorded. As we know, he was interested in physical marks made by spirits, and this was excellent evidence of that. 'Note also', Brian or the scribe wrote, 'it is to be considered, that there is a scarre to be seene of this examinats legge where it was taken, and also the naile of his little Toe is yet unperfect'. This injury seemed to confirm that a corporeally present demonic creature had indeed held onto John's leg.[6] The child must have been terrified by this confirmation, and its actual origin – an injury? a congenital disability? – remains obscure.

---

[6] Little Clacton parish register, marriage of Thomas Gardener and Alice Cooke, 16 May 1574; *ATAJR* D2–D2v.

With his examination of the two Selles boys complete, Brian summoned their parents. Henry was first. Yes, he confirmed, he had ploughed with Richard Rosse in the past. Yes, one time two of Richard's horses had 'upon a sodaine fell downe and were in a most strange taking'. But 'what the occasion should be thereof (he saith) he knew not'. Henry was asked about other fallings out with Richard but – perfectly fairly, because they had happened to Cisley rather than himself – said he did not remember any. But he also denied the more intimate matters alleged against him: 'yt his childe cried out unto him, saying, father, come helpe me, or that he called his wife stinking whore' (the phrase which is the exact quotation from his son John, and was not used by Henry junior). Clamming up under this highly personal assault, he then denied 'all the residue of the matters in general enformed against him, &c'. Cisley was then questioned, and took the route of denying absolutely everything: 'yt Rosse his wife did at any tyme hunt her catell being in her ground, or yt shee used any hard speeches … or yt shee fel out for yt she could not have any mault at her price … that her childe cryed out in the night' and so on. Together, Henry and Cisley must have appeared unconvincing, set against the detailed and immersive stories told by their adult accusers and their own children, with physical evidence backing them up.

Cisley did say that she remembered Alice Rosse making some sort of derogatory remark to her, saying that 'I shall see at your ende what you are', which suggests ongoing tensions between the two women and that Alice regarded Cisley as a ne'er-do-well. She was also asked a question that has no link to any other evidence recorded against her, which implies that some accusations went unrecorded or were lost. Perhaps there were other accusers, or multiple statements by some accusers. Whatever the case, Cisley was asked if she knew 'mother Tredsall'. She said she did. But she was then asked whether she had once informed someone that 'if she were a witche, she learned the same of the saide mother Tredsall'. She replied that she had never said this, and then denied 'all the residue of ye matters in general enformed against her', like Henry. However, Brian had a nasty surprise for her. He called in Ales Gilney, Joan Smith and Margaret Simpson, 'women of credite', to strip and examine her for evidence of suckling familiars. They did so, and said that she had 'many spots very suspitious'. Margaret said of her marks that 'they bee much like the sucked spots, that shee hath seene upon the body of Ursley Kempe and severall other'.[7] Ales and Joan were likely Little Clacton villagers, and Joan may even be Cisley's accuser of the same name, who gave evidence later.

Joan was the wife of Robert Smith, who – like Henry Selles – worked with Richard Rosse on his farm. She told a sad story. One Sunday afternoon sometime since Michaelmas, 'shee had made her selfe readie to goe to Church' and, neat and well wrapped against the September chill, picked up her young child to leave her house. 'Opening her dore, her mother (grandmother to the child) one Redworths wife and Selles his wife were at the said dore readie to draw the latch'. The women had

---

[7] *AJATR* D3v–D4. Maybe Mother Tredsall is Edithe Tredsolle, widow, of Great Oakley, who had died in 1570? It depends whether 'knew' is past or present tense; Great Oakley parish register 24 January 1570.

come visiting together, and perhaps planned to walk to church as a group. Joan's mother took the little child's hand and shook it, saying playfully to the baby 'a[h] mother pugs art thou coming to Church?' Redworth's wife said cheerfully 'here is a jolie & likely childe God blesse it.' But Cisley Selles struck a sour note. Looking at Joan, she said 'shee hath never the more children for that, but a little babe to play w[i]t[h]all for a time'. Joan felt that her fertility and the healthiness of her baby were both being questioned. And sure enough 'within a short time after her saide childe sickned and died'. Joan was a fair-minded Christian woman, though. She scrupulously told Brian Darcy that 'her conscience wil not serve her to charge the said Cysley or her husband to be the causers of any such matter, but prayeth God to forgive them if they have dealt in any such sort'. Nevertheless, the damage had been done.

Robert, Joan's husband, was also questioned, but not until three weeks later and then he was either not asked about the death of his child, or declined to accuse anyone of causing it. Instead, he confirmed the evidence of Richard Rosse's maidservant, Ales Baxter, who – as we have already heard – was believed to have been attacked by Herculus, Cisley Selles's spirit. Ales came to see Brian Darcy on 19 March when he was travelling back from investigations in Little Oakley (see Chapter 5) and was passing through Little Clacton on the way to resume questioning at Thorpe le Soken (see Chapter 4). She said that around the time of Hallamass (All Saints' Day) in November 1581, at about four o'clock in the afternoon as it was getting dark, she was milking in one of Richard's enclosures two fields' distance away from his house. She had eight or nine cows to milk, and had nearly completed her task. But as she was milking the last cow, the animal was startled and kicked over the milk-pail. Ales saw that the other cows were staring around them too. She carried on milking, but suddenly 'shee felt a thing to pricke her under the right side, as if she had been striken with ones hand'. This sensation of having been touched upset her, but she picked up her bucket and set out for home. As she neared the stile into the next field, however, 'there came a thinge all white like a Cat, and stroke her at the hart, in such sort as shee could not stand, goe, nor speake'. She sank down against the stile, remaining there until she was missed.

When Ales did not come home with the milk, Richard Rosse came out from the farmhouse to see what had happened to her. Ales said that she had not recognised 'her master' when he arrived, so strange was her state of mind. There was general alarm. Richard was used to giving orders, however. He organised two of his workers – Robert Smith and another man – to fetch a chair, put Ales onto it, lift her over the stile and carry her back to the house. Three weeks later and she was fully recovered, able to explain that the white creature she had seen had vanished into the bushes after assaulting her. Robert Smith confirmed the he had helped Richard Rosse to fetch her home at about five o'clock that night, and that she really had been seriously ill.[8] Her description certainly suggests this, although it was not unheard of for contemporaries to be suspicious of young servants who made up stories of strange illnesses to explain failure to complete their tasks.

---

[8] *ATAJR* D3, D4–D4v.

The spilling of Ales' employer's milk would fall into that category and being 'strangely taken' would account for this unfortunate accident. Perhaps, though, Ales had suffered a minor stroke, severe migraine or fit, something that would cause strange nerve sensations and possibly visual disturbance or hallucinations.

A True and just Recorde will take us this far in telling the story of the witch accusations in Little Clacton, and allow us to speculate to a certain extent on the motives and lives of those involved. But there are other sources that can be drawn upon too. Little Clacton's and Great Clacton's parish registers survive from 1538 onwards and we can learn a good deal about the community there by reading them. The manorial records of Little and Great Clacton are lost, which frustratingly means that we don't know exactly which lands were held by Henry and Cisley Selles, or by Richard and Alice Rosse, or about other aspects of their businesses. This limits economic and social understandings of the relationships between the participants in the Little Clacton witch hunt. The account of Little Clacton's landscape is also less specific than the account of St Osyth, with less clarity about the location of particular incidents, so that it's not possible to reconstruct where Ales Baxter was attacked by the spirit, or find the location of Richard Rosse's broomfield.

However, a will of 1583 names Richard Rosse as a tenant of the manor of Cann Hall in Great Clacton. You'll remember that Cann Hall was a small Darcy submanor. Its lands were grouped around an early Henrician timber-framed and jettied house. The Stubbes family lived there and farmed the Clacton lands of Cresswick or Crayswick, Bishopswick and Clactonwick, and Richard

Rosse would have been a close neighbour of theirs, one of the sub-manor's wealthier tenants. In a recognisance of 1599 he is described as a 'yeoman'. It seems fair to infer that the people whom we have seen contributing evidence against the Selles family were connected to him by ties of employment and obligation, like Robert Smith and Ales Baxter. Like some of the other male accusers that we have seen, and will see, Richard was also involved in local administration and justice: for example, in 1574 he sat on a coroner's jury with other local landowners like William Hubberd of Bovells Hall, and Robert Hulwood of Great Holland and Kirby, finding that their neighbour Robert Hill had strangled Margaret, his wife. Robert's case went to the Assizes and he was hanged.[9]

The murder of Margaret Hill reminds us of the vulnerability of women not just to the sort of suspicions that engulfed Cisley Selles but to outright physical violence. No-one's life was easy in early modern Little Clacton, but sustaining a good reputation, marrying wisely and keeping safe as a woman was especially hard, then as now. For some women this proved too much to bear, as we can see from a particularly shocking incident in 1592. In late June of that year, Nicholas Lambert died at Clacton Lodge in the Great Park, leaving a young widow, Prudence. Two months later, on Tuesday the 15th of August, Prudence married another gentleman, Clement Fenn, and he moved into the Lodge. But, as the Parish Register records, on

---

[9] Will of Robert Clerk, 1 May 1583, names Richard as both 'Rose' and 'Roose', Emmison, *Essex Wills … Commissary Court 1578–1588* 48–9; Cockburn, *Calendar: Essex: Elizabeth* record 741; TNA PROB11/88/189, 11/121/787, 11/98/147; ERO Q/SR 146/19.

Wednesday morning Prudence got out of bed, hid herself from her husband's sight and 'desperatelie hanged her selfe, to the intolerable grieffe of her new maryed husband, & the dreadfull horror & astonishment of all the Countrye'. Why Prudence killed herself is a mystery, but instead of mourning her wretched state of mind at the time of her death, the vicar Richard Schofield described her in his register as a 'most accursed creature' and had her buried 'out of the compass of Christian burial; in ye furthest syde of the Churchyard Northward'. Northward was the devil's direction – he was thought to enter churches through their north doors, like the one at St James', Little Clacton – and beyond the churchyard wall to the north Prudence joined Cisley Selles in the parish's roll of devil-led female shame.[10]

In the twin contexts of unequal status of gender and class, day-to-day economic conflicts seem to have driven some aspects of the accusations made at Little Clacton: Cisley Selles in particular is portrayed as being easily angered by business transactions, and as an unreasonable woman to deal with. She is not begging from her supposed victim Richard Rosse, which many suspected witches were portrayed as doing, but instead she is trading with him and his wife. Cisley is shown trying to buy their goods affordably and becoming angry when she fails to strike a deal. There is also conflict over land with Cisley, when cattle stray across into adjacent plots and she is seen shouting at female neighbours. Henry Selles,

---

[10] Little Clacton parish register 16 August, 17 August – see also Clement's remarriage, children and burial; 'St James Parish Church, Little Clacton' at www.littleclactonparishchurch.co.uk/Church-History/; Walker, The Story of Little Clacton n.p.

meanwhile, seems to be imagined as envious of Richard Rosse's success: an unreliable male co-worker who harms his employer's horses and burns his barn full of corn, plotting with his whorish, turbulent wife. In *A True and just Recorde*, Henry and Cisley are also set against Robert and Joan Smith by their similar position in relation to the Rosses. Unlike the Selles family, the Smiths are ideal neighbours and employees: a diligent, obedient fieldworker and a demure housewife who dresses up for church and speaks readily of her Christian duty.

But beyond the observations that can be made from *A True and just Recorde*, the parish records give us further context which helps us to understand the emotional and psychological world of Richard Rosse's evidence about the Selleses. In particular, there is reason to imagine tension between the Smiths and the Selleses over fertility and mortality, especially of very young children. The Redworth family were important in this as well. To begin with, the Smiths were a large family in a small parish. The Parish Register at times gives the impression that everyone in Little Clacton whose surname was not Outlaw was called Smith instead. In Little Clacton between 1544 and 1561 William and Elizabeth Smith had at least twelve children, of whom at least eight sadly died young. Robert and Joane Smith, meanwhile, had two children in 1554 and 1556, both of whom died within a year of their birth.[11]

11 William and Elizabeth's children who died were two Joans born 1544, 1557, Barbara 1546, twins William and Austen 1553, Agnes (died 1553), two Johns 1554, 1556; those who apparently survived were Dorcas born 1548, Helen 1549, Thomas 1555, and Avis 1561. Robart and Joane's were Joane born 1554, Emma born 1556. Little Clacton parish register.

Perhaps they then relocated to another parish, since they disappear from the surviving record, although they may perhaps have been the parents of the Robert Smith who worked for the same or a later Richard Rosse thirty years on in the early seventeenth century.

Parish records confirm, then, that Robert and Joane Smith did indeed have only one child and 'never the more' when they encountered Cisley Selles in autumn 1581. Their daughter Avis Smith was baptised on 9 April that year. And, as *A True and just Recorde* reliably reports, the little girl was buried on 24 September and her name recorded in the Parish Register – actually just before Michaelmas. To Durrant's suggestion that we can hypothesise a general correlation between the apparent epidemic and witchcraft accusation, we can helpfully add a specific link in the mid-epidemic death of Avis, daughter of one of the accusers. Robert and Joane went on to have another daughter, Plesance, in 1583 but she also died as a baby.[12] Meanwhile, Redworth's wife, who with Cisley Selles met Joane at her door in September 1581, is also significant in this story. She was Margaret Redworth or Redwoort, who was married to Josias Redwoort in 1579. Her comment that Avis Smith was a 'likely childe' is given depth of feeling when we know that her own firstborn child Robert had died just two months

---

[12] A Richard Rose of Wix died in 1587 (ERO D/ACA 14 16 June) but our Richard was alive in 1592 when his wife died and I have found no further record of him (yet); there was a Rosse family in Great Clacton in the 1540s (parents John and Margaret, son William), Great Clacton parish register 8 August 1545; Avis 'daughter of Robart Smyth & Joane his wyfe'; Plesance, baptised 20 October 1583, buried 3 November, Little Clacton parish register.

before, in July 1581. And she probably did not come forward to support her friend Joan Smith in giving evidence on either the 1st or 3rd of March 1582 because she was ill, perhaps with whatever the epidemic disease was that swept Little Clacton in 1581–1582: Margaret was buried on 12 March. When Robert Smith gave his evidence in support of Ales Baxter on 19 March, Margaret had been dead for a week.

The Smiths' fragility and recent bereavements contrast with the relatively rude health of the Selles family, although as we shall see this had not always been a given. Henry Selles senior and Cisley were older than the Smiths and Redworths. Henry was baptised at Little Clacton on 28 January 1543, the son of Christopher and Katheren Sylles (the surname is spelt variously including Cilles, Sellys, Sells, Cylles and so on). His parents had another two children, Isabell who died in 1542 and John who died on the day of his birth, 21 January 1551. By then Henry's father Christopher had also died, in September 1550, and his mother Katheren had remarried Henry's first stepfather Robert Kirkman. Robert and Katheren had a daughter, Agnes, who then died in 1551, and Robert died in 1553. Katheren married a third time, to Stephen Mason in 1554, and she died in February 1565. In winter 1566 comes an entry that explains a lot of things about the Selles family and the events of 1582. One thing at a time. First, the Little Clacton Parish Register for 14 November 1566 records the birth of 'the base sonn of Cicilie Sills' who 'was baptised, the xxiiiith daye of November'.

The wording of this part of the entry – 'base sonn' – is notable. 'Henrye Sylls', had in fact married 'Sysley March Singlewoman' in *Great* Clacton church on 24 June 1566

FIGURE 3.2   Great Clacton parish register, marriage of Henrye Sylls
and Sysley March. (Source: Author's photo; reproduced by courtesy
of the Essex Record Office. D/P 80/1/1.)
Note: A black and white version of this figure will appear in some
formats. For the colour version, please refer to the plate section.

(Figure 3.2).[13] They were married by the Vicar there,
John Marckant, also known to history as a composer of
metrical psalms.

Whilst it was obvious that Cisley's baby had been conceived before their marriage, and this was a fault punisha-
ble in a church court, he was not born 'base'. The choice
to label him in this way seems aggressive and it was likely
made by the vicar of Little Clacton, William Simpson,
also curate of St Osyth among other ecclesiastical roles.
William was also quite likely to have been the husband of Margaret Simpson, the woman who would one
day search Cisley for witch marks. This parish register
entry certainly contextualises, although it does not fully
explain, the references to whoredom made so woundingly

[13]   Little Clacton parish register, *passim*; Great Clacton parish register,
book 2, 24 June 1566.

by Cisley's children in 1582. Their mother did indeed have a bad sexual reputation recorded officially, at least in the mid-1560s. It apparently clung to her, although she and Henry went on to have a large legitimately born family together, christened by William Simpson and his successor at Little Clacton William Chaplen: John baptised 2 May 1568, Robert baptised 15 April 1570, Henry baptised 21 December 1572, John baptised 17 July 1575 and Joyce baptised 26 October 1578.[14]

These baptismal entries do help us to understand the Selles' boys' statements to Brian Darcy very well. Joyce is the 'sister' referred to in John and Henry's description of the black spirit, which they say is about as big as and 'like' their sister. The Selles' first son named John must have died, before the birth of the second John in 1575. It is interesting that in his account of the familiar Jack, this second John makes reference to another being who shares his name: he says that his father 'mocked him because his name was so'. The boy John must have had the nickname Jack, and there really was another John or Jack in the Selles family once. And the name of Cisley Selles's 'base sonn' – the one born in November 1566 and who must also have died before 1582 – shows clearly that this is the way the minds of the two living Selles children

---

[14] Little Clacton parish register; Chaplen was buried 12 August 1589. In correspondence, Chris Thornton suggested – rightly I think – that Simpson was also Vicar of Kirby le Soken and Rector of Great Oakley, perhaps sequentially, changing roles in 1579 (see the forthcoming *Victoria County History* XII volume 2, which will include reference to him in these roles and as a simoniac non-preacher, perhaps with Catholic leanings). Subsequent research at LMA found him as Rector of Little Oakley in 1577 as well as curate of St Osyth: LMA DL/B/A/002/MS09537/004.

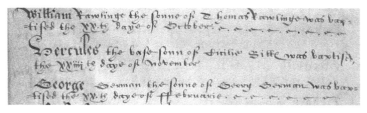

FIGURE 3.3 Little Clacton parish register, baptism of Hercules Sills.
(Source: Author's photo; reproduced by courtesy of the Essex Record
Office. D/P 80/1/1.)
Note: A black and white version of this figure will appear in some
formats. For the colour version, please refer to the plate section.

is working: when asked to name their mother's familiars,
Henry and John choose the names of two of their dead
siblings, Jack and the 'base sonn'. That 'blacke thing' that
came in the night, the one that was 'like' their sister, is in
fact the ghost of their dead brother and he is mixed up in
their minds with the idea of witches' familiars. We know
this with certainty, because the illegitimate baby's name
was Hercules.

The parish register entry for 14 November 1566 that
records the baby's baptism reads in full 'Hercules the
base sonn of Cicilie Sills was baptised, the xxiiiith daye of
November' (Figure 3.3). Thus the familiar spirit named
'Herculus' or 'Jack' represents not one but two dead
Selles boys, returning to terrify their living brothers. The
name Hercules is caught up in their minds, too, with the
sense that their mother is untrustworthy, and had once
nurtured other children – like the milk-fed familiars in
the woodpile – in some way that was wrong. The Selles
children knew their mother was called a 'whore' by some
people and the two boys were then persuaded during
their examination to consider that she may be a witch too.

They blend whores and witches, and they name Cisley's spirit Herculus when Brian Darcy questions them about something secret that their mother has done, something from the past that they don't fully understand. It all makes very neat sense and the discovery of the baby's name and status satisfyingly ends speculation about why the boys chose Herculus as the name for a familiar. There are 'ghost familiars' recorded in other witchcraft cases from the period, and Hercules is newly identified here as one of these.[15]

Maybe Henry and Cisley didn't tell Brian about Hercules and Jack, and didn't try to explain the nightmare their children had described. Whether they did or not, Brian apparently felt no stir of compassion. He committed Cisley for trial at the Assizes and possibly Henry too (although he does not appear to have been indicted immediately, he was asked to post bail). But maybe we shouldn't be quite so quick to feel superior to Brian, who failed to ask the right questions of Henry and Cisley in 1582. The record of Hercules should make us wonder: why haven't historians thought to look for it before? If I'd looked at the parish register when I first researched this case in 1996 or so, we would have known for twenty-five years the fact that the familiar's name was also the boy's name. Digitisation makes the information possible to find

---

[15] See Millar, Witchcraft, the Devil, Sharpe, 'The Witch's Familiar' and Wilby, Cunning Folk, and Victoria Carr, 'Witches and the Dead: The Case for the English Ghost Familiar' *Folklore* 130:3. (2019) 282–99 and Malcolm Gaskill, 'Witchcraft and Power in Early Modern England: The Case of Margaret Moore' in Jenny Kermode and Garthine Walker, eds., *Women, Crime and the Courts in Early Modern England* (London: UCL Press, 1994) 125–45.

anywhere in the world now, but why did no-one research the history of the Selles family in the physical archive before? Perhaps because parish registers are documents that professional historians do not tend to read? Perhaps because these records are associated with family history and local history? As Tanya Evans has summed up:

academics, sometimes even feminist historians, have been quick to distance themselves from genealogists in the desire to set themselves apart from and better than, those 'amateur' family historians; from those who supposedly 'wallow in self-indulgent nostalgia'.[16]

Additionally, of course, some academic traditions have traditionally cared less about 'ordinary' labourers and women than others, and those who do care about them have often assumed that their stories must be totally irrecoverable.

In this way, we share some attitudes with Brian Darcy and with the creators of the parish registers. Often, these men looked at life through a magisterial lens – they looked for data on sin and crime, in particular – and they recorded only the information that was necessary for their clerical purposes. Sometimes they did so in a coldly bureaucratic manner. Pastors, for instance, recorded the paternal parentage of infants, the names of spouses, and sometimes the marital status of the deceased but usually nothing else. A few went further, recording the names of the mothers as well as the fathers of babies, and occasionally godparents, or a detail of life or employment – age

[16] Tanya Evans, The Emotions of Family History and the Development of Historical Knowledge *Rethinking History* 24:3–4 (2020) 311.

at death, relationship with an employer. Choices also record attitudes to individual parishioners and sometimes a bad choice made by a recorder at the time can be a good choice for the historian. When he uncharitably described baby Hercules as the 'base sonn' of Cisley Selles, William Simpson gave us exactly the information that we need to understand his dim view of her reputation and to guess at why she was later suspected of witchcraft. He helped us, although we may disapprove of his choice of descriptor.

Conversely, John Marckant, who married the pregnant Cisley March to Henry Selles in 1566 did not do what we needed him to do: record the pregnancy of the bride. It was not common to do so, to be fair, and perhaps Cisley's baby bump was not clearly visible – although with the pregnancy at about eighteen weeks it is more likely that a blind eye was turned. If so, John Marckant appears to the historical record as a better human being than William Simpson, but paradoxically on this occasion less helpful. Interestingly, his other detailed recordings of his parishioners' lives suggest that he did not treat them exclusively as clerical data. Occasionally, like William Simpson, he would note down a 'bastard', like Thomas the son of Johane Farrow, buried in 1562. But with more frequency than most vicars and rectors he took the trouble to record his flock as individuals in ways that served no religious purpose. He tells us, for example, that Dionese Cole was only recently bereaved, a 'late widdow', that Thomas Welsom and Roger Wade were husbandmen, Moyses Wickes was the servant of William Rogers, Johane Sayer a single woman and servant to Umphrye Parbye, and so on.

Perhaps this tendency to see the names he wrote as rounded individuals was reflected in John's treatment of

Cisley March and Henry Selles in 1566. Certainly in his religious writings, he stressed the importance of mercy. The clearest example of this is his 'Lamentation of a Sinner' from 1562:

> O Lord turn not away thy face
> From him that lies prostrate:
> Lamenting sore his sinfull life,
> Before thy mercy gate:
> Which gate thou openest wide to those,
> That do lament their sin:
> Shut not that gate against me Lord,
> But let me enter in.
> And call me not to mine account,
> How I have lived here:
> For then I know right well O Lord,
> How vile I shall appear.
> I need to confesse my life,
> I am sure thou canst tell,
> What I have been and what I am,
> I know thou know'st it well.

Cisley and Henry might even have gone to Great Clacton church to be married because they feared the righteous wrath of William Simpson and knew John Marckant would be kinder: their choice of parish might have had a practical explanation but it might not. Whatever the case, the record of their marriage, of the baptism of Hercules and all the other records of Henry and Cisley's children and their own parentage have been overlooked by historians. Yet together this is a mass of information, all of it relevant to their accusation as witches and to the precise details of the evidence given against them by their children. We should have looked more thoroughly.

Maybe we should imagine more thoroughly too. Squeezing the information further, we can perhaps learn more about the personalities of Henry and Cisley Selles. Their first baby's name, Hercules, is an interesting one, telling us about their choices as parents. They didn't hide their child behind an ordinary name, but wanted him to be noticed despite the sneers about his conception. Classical names were occasionally used in early modern England, but they were not common. My survey of all the parishes of north east Essex from 1550–1650, depending in each case on the survival of registers, threw up only a handful of examples. Dionese or Dionysia was popular. In addition to Dionese Cole in Great Clacton, Dionysia Style lived in Little Oakley in the 1520s, and Dionysia and Cassandra Galloway in the 1530s. Cassandra married Robert Sylls of Little Oakley, who may have been related to Henry and Cisley. They named their eldest surviving son Robert – he was twelve in 1582 – and that may have been a family name.[17] Perhaps the family also had a fancy for classical names like Cassandra. There's a boldness and aspiration here that marks out the Selles family from their neighbours. Whatever the story of his unusual naming, the death of unique little Hercules must have brought Cisley and Henry great pain. The rest of their children all have more common names and would have blended into their society with much greater ease.

Cisley Selles not only reared her own surviving children with Henry but she also acted as a wet-nurse to the children of others. Wet-nursing was a common way for child-bearing women to earn a good income over several

---

[17] ERO D/DEl M76, and also see 1552.

years, as their milk fed not only their own children but also those of wealthy neighbours. It is interesting that the accusations made against Cisley by her sons Henry and John are about giving milk to other nurslings than themselves. Not only were they conscious of the ghosts of dead brothers, they also perhaps felt jealousy over the time and resources that Cisley devoted to her professional nursing.[18] This activity also fed into the swirl of neighbourhood suspicion about her which, as we have seen, focused on fertility, infant mortality and care for growing children. As a wet-nurse, Cisley was feeding the children of her neighbours and this was a risky relationship where tensions were very likely to arise. The parents of nursed children would have worried not just about the watchfulness and health of wet-nurses, but also about their morality, which was thought to influence the development of the young. And when concerns did surface about Cisley, they were not only in relation to the nursed children, but also revealed there had been conflict over the lucrative activity of wet-nursing. Nobody wanted their wet-nurse to be quarrelling in the street with her professional rivals.

Cisley had done exactly that, and as a result she was accused of harming two children in the Death family of Great Clacton. On 15 March, when Brian Darcy was on his way back from Thorpe and about to go north to interview accusers in Little Oakley, the mariner Thomas Death and his daughter Marie spoke to him about their concerns. Thomas said that his wife (her name, given in

---

[18] As Deborah Willis first suggested, *Malevolent Nurture: Witch Hunting and Maternal Power in Early Modern England* (Ithaca, NY: Cornell University Press, 1995) 56–8.

Great Clacton's parish records, was Agnes) had fallen out with Cisley around two years ago. This was when a neighbour, George Battell, had taken away from Cisley a child that he had given her to wet-nurse and instead placed it with Agnes Death. Great Clacton's parish register shows that George's wife Rachell had died in February 1578, so his child must have been in need of a nurse from then onwards.[19] But presumably in 1579–80 George began to have doubts about Cisley and asked Agnes Death to take the baby instead. Agnes had had many children – Thomas, William, Marie, Martha, Susan or Susannah, Amy, Ann, Elizabeth, another William, John and Robert – and since wet-nursing was well-paid work she was probably glad to have it. However, Cisley railed at Agnes about the baby the next time they met, saying 'thou shalt loose more by the having of it then thou shalt have for the keeping of it'. Within a month afterwards, the Death's four-year-old son John, born 1576, horrifyingly fell down in their yard and died. Shortly afterwards several of their swine and a calf died too.[20]

However, more worryingly, their eldest child Marie had also by then fallen ill. Marie was eighteen, baptised on 17 December 1564 as 'Marye', and while her father

[19] Great Clacton parish register 15 March 1573 (birth of Elizabeth Death); 10 February 1578.

[20] *ATAJR* D8v; the children are named in the will of John Death, Thomas' brother, written 23 June 1581 and proved 6 July 1581 (Emmison, *Essex Wills … Commissary Court 1578–1588* 57) and Great Clacton parish register (17 December 1564, 8 February 1566, 28 March 1568, 1 March 1570, 23 December 1571, 15 March 1573, 2 February 1574, 1 April 1576, 15 December 1577. Elizabeth died in 1573 and Martha in 1588). Cockburn, *Calendar: Essex: Elizabeth* record 1302.

was away at sea two years before she had experienced a numbness in her neck and back which was so severe that she could not turn over in bed. Resourcefully, her mother Agnes sent a messenger bearing her daughter's urine to a physician in Ipswich. The man met Thomas by chance as he returned to port, and together they went to the physician to ask if Marie was bewitched. Evidently they had already decided that the deaths of John and of their animals were not natural. The doctor was more cautious, according to Thomas: 'hee saide that hee woulde not deale so farre to tell him'. Thomas was not satisfied with this, however, and shortly afterwards he met a friend who advised him to visit a cunning man – a magical practitioner like Mother Ratcliffe or Ursley Kempe. Thomas wisely told Brian Darcy that he could not remember the name of this sage – otherwise Brian might have wanted to talk to the cunning man as well – but he did say that on being shown Marie's urine the cunning man said that 'if hee had not commen with some great haste to seeke helpe, hee had come too late'. He gave Thomas some 'thinges' to be 'ministred' to Marie, and told Thomas that 'within two nyghtes after the parties that had hurte his daughter shoulde appeare unto her, and remedie her'. Thomas went back to sea reassured.

When he at last came home Agnes confirmed to him that what the cunning man had promised had indeed happened. The night after the messenger had arrived home with the 'thinges', she had heard 'a noyse like a groning' in the night, got up and went to Marie to ask how she was. The girl replied: 'ah mother that you had commen a little sooner, you shoulde have seene Celles wife and Barkers wife here standing before mee'. Brian Darcy asked Marie for her account and she explained that she had heard a voice saying 'looke up' and had then seen 'Celles wife and Barkers wife standing before her in the same apparell that they did usually weare ... shee thought they saide unto her bee not afraide, and that they vanished away'. This was a fairly standard version of the 'spectral evidence' that victims of witchcraft were sometimes thought to be able to produce, identifying those who were afflicting them. Judging by Marie's description of the women, Brian probably even asked the classic question 'what were they wearing?' which was intended to aid identification of suspects and trip up anyone who had not thought this far ahead in describing their vision, fantasy or dream. After the spectral women faded away Marie was soon better, and could get up.[21]

All this was very bad news for Cisley and Henry Selles. Cisley looked particularly guilty because of the volume of accusations made against her, but Henry too had been forcefully accused and the couple's children had implicated both their parents. Most likely both man and wife were committed for trial at the Assizes, although possibly Henry was allowed to return home in the interim, posting bail to ensure his attendance at the trial. Either way, the children almost certainly went home without their mother, perhaps in the care of their shaken father or eldest brother Robert, who at twelve years old would have been expected to help provide for his family. What was said as the little group trailed home across the broomfield? Did Henry and John come to the sudden, corrosive understanding that they had betrayed their parents? How

[21] *ATAJR* E–E2.

would the younger children manage now that Cisley was gone? This chapter leaves a bitter taste in the mouth – certainly mine, perhaps yours too. Henry and Cisley Selles were horribly unlucky in that once they were suspected the troubled internal dynamics of their family propelled their children into fabulating stories of witchcraft that could easily be used against their parents.

Cisley's poor sexual reputation seems to be the origin of many of the couple's troubles, and this is newly laid bare by my reading of the two surviving parish registers of the Clactons. The story of the Little Clacton witches is thus rich in emotional atmosphere. We are also lucky that the record keepers of both of the parishes added additional detail, of different kinds, about their congregations. However, the economic picture is less clear and depends primarily on inference from *A True and just Recorde*. The Selles family appear poorer than Richard Rosse and a group of people associated with him (the Smiths, Ales Baxter) added to his evidence to create a damning series of accusations against both Cisley and Henry. Meanwhile, Cisley stood in problematic relation to the young Smith couple and their friends and possibly an epidemic intervened to add to Joan Smith's suspicions that she had killed their little daughter. Cisley had also fallen out with the Deaths over wet-nursing, taking us back to the central theme of her life: suspicions about her fertility, maternity and nurture. In uncovering this complex of tensions among neighbours, which seemed to provide very clear evidence of witchcraft, Brian Darcy was no doubt pleased. He already had plans to move on to other villages on the Darcy estates to ask similar questions and his next target was Thorpe le Soken.

4

The Sokens

Ales, Margaret, Elizabeth and Joan

~

The Sokens are a group of three villages – Thorpe le Soken, Kirby le Soken and Walton le Soken – which lie between Hamford Water to the north and the North Sea to the south and east. The land forms a long marshy hook, curled around Hamford Water like a cat's claw, with Thorpe furthest west and Walton furthest east. The Sokens are connected by a series of ecclesiastical and judicial oddities, because their area is a large former manor with unusual ancient rights. The Soken manor was held by the Dean and Chapter of St Paul's Cathedral in London until the 1540s. Its ecclesiastical 'peculiar' rights included a distinct ecclesiastical court, separate from the jurisdiction of the Archdeacon of Colchester. There was also a legal liberty: immunity for its inhabitants from arrest by external agents such as bailiffs. This immunity reflected a long history of shifting power balances in the area, of which the Clactons are another example. The Soken villages split into sub-manors in the Middle Ages and then into independent units, but many of their business and legal affairs were still handled together – for example, the manors held a common manorial court, and many families leased land and homes in several of the Sokens. Lord Darcy gained the manors and their big houses – Thorpe Hall, Kirby Hall and Walton Hall – after the Reformation in 1551 but although all were now part of the Darcy lands,

FIGURE 4.1 Hamford Water. (Source: Ricky Leaver / Alamy Stock Photo.)

they were also part of the 'Soke' – or 'Sooke' as local people spelt it. The word 'Soke' referred to the area's peculiar jurisdictional rights to hold its own courts.

Also part of the Soke was the manor of Birch Hall and the sub-manor of Landermere Hall or Landmer, whose name reflected its origin in a landing place on the marshy south shore of Hamford Water (Figure 4.1), just north of Thorpe. There was another sheltered quay on the Water north of Kirby and tide mills at Kirby and Landermere. But as in the Clactons to the west, the long southern coast leading around to Walton was prone to violent storms and erosion. Entire estates and settlements had disappeared into the sea here and the landscape was also marked by old fortifications against human invaders. Just like St Osyth, there were howes in the Soke, with How Streate Lane in Kirby marking that fact. The naming of the howes again recalled the language of seafaring Norse invaders, who had also named the Soken promontory the 'ness' or Naze. Walton on the Naze, as it is now called, was a little embattled world unto itself – almost an island, particularly when roads and bridges were ill-maintained as they were all across eastern Essex. Every strong wind and heavy rain was a challenge and descriptive place names such as Waterfields reflected this.[1]

Also like St Osyth, Walton made use of the power of the sea: it had a tide-mill, which in the late sixteenth century was held by the Sadler family, and was occupied by the Malls as the village's millers. There was also a windmill on the heath at Thorpe, with an adjoining cottage held by the millers, the Havill family.[2] The heaths were a little above sea level, but not far below them the yellow and grey sandy cliffs slipped and slid onto the beaches. Behind the ness were vast mudbanks that disappeared under each high tide and were prone to tidal surges. Seals lounged fatly on the shores of marshy islets and the immense skies belonged to curlews and marsh harriers. Even at Thorpe, the furthest inland of the three Soken villages, there was a feeling of wild wet flatness that matched that at St Osyth and the Clactons, despite the green fields and rising ground to the north. With their Norse names and misty mudflats, the Sokens belonged

---

[1] Christopher Thornton, 'St Osyth to the Naze: The Soken: Kirby-le-Soken, Thorpe-le-Soken and Walton-le-Soken', work in progress, https://boydellandbrewer.com/9781904356554/ a-history-of-the-county-of-essex/ and 'Before the Resorts', www .tendringcoastalheritage.org.uk/wp-content/uploads/2019/06/ Tendring-Before-the-Resorts-.pdf, 17, 20; ERO D/DBm M89.
[2] TNA PROB11/56/325; ERO D/DBm M89.

together on the edge of England and their few inhabitants usually stuck together too.

On 13 March, three people from the neighbouring villages of Thorpe le Soken and Walton le Soken came forward to give information about a suspected witch, Ales Manfield, who lived at Thorpe. The unusual interconnections of the Sokens might have brought the accusers together: at the manor courts, juries often sat for two or all three of the villages together, and manor and parish officials were often in contact with each other – indeed, sometimes they were the same people filling different roles. Although their settlements were scattered, villagers with this sort of status would have known each other well. This interconnection is evident in the witch-hunting approach of John Sayer, one of the constables of Thorpe, Joan Cheston, a farmer from Walton, and an unidentified woman called 'Lyndes wife' to Brian Darcy of 13 March. It is possible that Lynde and his wife came originally from Great or Little Oakley, where there was a family of that name. A John Lynde died in Little Oakley in 1584 and his will was proved by the bailiff John Wade, whom he described as 'my master'. We'll meet John Wade as a witch accuser later in this book.[3] Meantime, the three accusers John Sayer, Joan Cheston and Lynde's wife had all had suspicions about their neighbour Ales

---

[3] Will of John Lynde, probate 6 March 1584, F. G. Emmison, ed., *Essex Wills: The Archdeaconry Courts 1583–1592* (Chelmsford: Essex Record Office with Friends of Historic Essex, 1989) 170; See also in Great Oakley John Lynde, died 1562 leaving land to his wife Anne, Richard Lynde, died 1581, and Jone Lynde, married 1581 – Emmison, *Essex Wills … Commissary Court 1578–1588* 127, 162; Great Oakley parish register.

Manfield for a long time and perhaps, as constable, John Sayer organised them to come forward and speak to Brian Darcy when he arrived in the Sokens on 13 March.

John said that more than a year ago he had employed a thatcher to re-roof a barn of his near Ales Manfield's house. Ales had asked the thatcher if he could also re-thatch an oven of hers. Like Elizabeth Bennett, she had her own oven, in a separate structure away from her house. Her expectation suggests that John Sayer might have been her landlord, although sub-tenants were usually expected to make thatch repairs themselves. The thatcher explained that he could do the work if John told him to do so, but otherwise he could not. Unfortunately, as he later reported to John, Ales had angrily replied 'hee had beene as good as to have willed you to doe it. For I will bee even with him'. Soon afterwards, one of John's carts broke down immovably outside Ales's house and he blamed her for this. Problems with haulage were the kind of difficulty that might be interpreted as natural: mud, deep ruts, skittish horses, a wheel binding on the body of the cart, that sort of thing. But occasionally witches were blamed for the stopping of carts or the running away of horse teams, as with a group of Bedfordshire carters who in 1613 blamed the repeated loss of their cart's wheels and spillage of their cartload of corn on a witch's familiar.

Meanwhile, John's co-accuser Joan Cheston said that in the summer of 1581 she had refused to give Ales Manfield curds, for the excellent reason there were at that time none to give. Shortly after, though, some of her cattle went lame so that they were unable to range about grazing in the fields. Joan instructed her servants to mow grass and bring it to the cattle, a time-consuming and costly nuisance. After this had gone on for over a week, Ales returned to ask again for curds. This time Joan spoke forthrightly to her, saying to Brian that:

shee then telled the saide mother Manfielde, that shee had bewitched her Cattell, and that shee then sayde unto her, that if her cattell did not amend and become well, shee would burne her.

After this violent, and judicially inaccurate, threat Joan's cattle recovered which confirmed her belief that Ales had been responsible for their lameness. Perhaps she saw Ales's attack on her cattle as a kind of blackmail: give me curds, or you'll see your cattle go hungry – or worse. Lynde's wife had a similar, though less developed, story: Ales had asked her for milk, and when she was refused the Lyndes' twenty day old calf died.[4]

These three stories were all fairly slight, but they were enough for Brian Darcy to call Ales Manfield to him for questioning on the same day and perhaps this was organised by John Sayer in advance. Ales's examination preamble states that her meeting with Brian took place in Thorpe, confirming that he was now on a tour of the Darcy lands, coming from St Osyth through Little Clacton to Thorpe, and then beyond the Sokens too, as we shall see in Chapter 5. In Ales's confession, he found in profusion the kind of evidence that he needed, showing that he was right to widen his investigation and take time out from his other activities to pursue witches.

---

[4] ERO D/DGh M45/16 describes the customs in Moze and related manors, which excepted only tile repairs; *ATAJR* C6v; for the Bedfordshire carters see *Witches Apprehended* (London, 1613) B–B2; *ATAJR* E2–E2v.

Unfortunately for him, however, it also looks as if he was not the only traveller between Darcy villages: others had likely preceded him and they had come telling stories. Ales Manfield seems to have paid attention to gossip about Ursley Kempe and Ales Newman in St Osyth, because her confession was closely modelled on Ursley's. Accordingly, she immediately blamed another woman for bringing familiars to her to be looked after, and then borrowing them back to do harm to the neighbours, just as Ales Newman was said to have done. She had also heard about the accusations against Henry and Cisley Selles at Little Clacton and mentioned these. Perhaps Brian was the only vector of transmission of these stories, but as we shall see he became suspicious of Ales's loquacious willingness quickly, and that suggests that Ales got her ideas from someone else.

In this case of shared familiars the other woman in partnership with Ales Manfield was Margaret Grevell, another resident of Thorpe. Ales said that about twelve years ago, Margaret had been going to move house within Thorpe. She had been worried that during the relocation her neighbours would notice that she was a witch. In particular her spirits might 'be espied or seene'. So Margaret brought to her friend Ales Manfield her four black cats for spirit-sitting, with the proviso that 'shee should have them upon condition that shee the sayde Margaret might have them at her pleasure, otherwise shee should not have them'. Ales was to feed the spirits, and Margaret told her 'with what, and howe'. The spirits were called Robin, Jack, William and Puppet or Mamet – a name meaning 'doll' but also sometimes used to refer to the images witches supposedly made of their victims, which they then mutilated to cause sickness. Two of the spirits were male and two female and Ales said that when they were in her house they lived 'in a boxe with woll therein: And yt they did stande upon a shelfe by her bed where she lay'. Margaret would borrow these companionable, wool-snuggled spirits whenever she liked, and the spirits would often tell Ales where they had been and whom they had harmed.

According to Ales's story, this meant that she knew as long as seven years ago that Margaret had sent her spirits to hurt Joan Cheston. Joan had only mentioned a recent dispute with Ales in her statement to the magistrate, but Ales referred to a longer history. She stated that Margaret and Joan had 'fallen out, & had chidden very much', seven years ago. As we have seen, Joan's chiding of her neighbours was vigorous, and Margaret told Ales that Joan 'gave her evill speeches' which had offended her greatly. According to Ales, she therefore requested to borrow the spirit Robin to retaliate against Joan, and turned Robin onto the Cheston family's cattle. A seemingly healthy bullock died. However, this was not the end of the matter. Two years later, Margaret also sent her spirit Jack to 'plague' Joan's husband Robert, as he came home from ploughing. The spirit had attacked Robert 'upon the great Toe' and Robert had later died. It was not clear why this second, deadly, attack had been made – Ales did not specify. But a version of this story went into Margaret's Assizes indictment, which states that she attacked Robert Cheston on 20 April 1577, causing his death on 20 November. At about the same time, Margaret had killed her own husband by witchcraft, Ales added casually. He had died of unspecified sores. Ales went on to make some more mundane accusations too: Margaret had damaged bread-baking and brewing at 'Reades', 'Carters' and 'Brewses'.[5]

As well as accusing Margaret Grevell, Ales also confessed floridly to her own supposed crimes. She confirmed the story of being refused curds herself at the now-widowed Joan Cheston's house and bewitching her cattle. Ales said that she had sent the spirit Puppet or Mamet to Joan's cattle so that four of them became lame; the spirit had then sucked her blood as a reward. She also admitted afflicting John Sayer's cart, adding the detail that its cargo was dung, being transported from an orchard near her house. John's team, she explained, had inadvertently scraped and made muddy 'a greene place before her doore' so that in annoyance she sent Puppet to stop the cart. She said that in trying to move his load, John had snapped both a hawser and the harness on his horses, turning an apparently simple problem into an expensive breakdown. Ales thus accepted some guilt herself for recent witchcraft events in Thorpe and Walton, but she also accused another woman of far more serious offences including two murders, and she went on to spread further blame. At about Michaelmas last year, she told Brian, the four spirits had petitioned her to be set free: 'I pray you Dame' they chorused 'give us leave to goe unto little Clapton to Celles, saying, they would burne Barnes, and also kill Cattell'. On their return, they reported burning Richard Rosse's barn 'and also tolde her that Celles his wife knewe of it, and that all they foure were fedde at Cels house by her'.

5 *ATAJR* D5v–D6v; Cockburn, *Calendar: Essex: Elizabeth* record 1303.

Incriminating Margaret Grevell and Cisley Selles was not the end of Ales's evidence, however. After their trip to Little Clacton, she said, the spirits had left her and she thought they had gone 'unto saint Osees unto mother Gray [Ursley Kempe], mother Torner [perhaps Elizabeth Turner of St Osyth], or mother Barnes two daughters [Ales Hunt and Margery Sammon]'.[6] Evidently Ales had heard their stories as well, and was prepared to corroborate them. She went on to accuse another woman in Thorpe, Elizabeth Ewstace. About three months ago, she said, she had gone to 'mother Ewstace' to speak with her, at which time she had seen three cat shaped spirits in an earthen pot near Elizabeth's hearth. Like her stories about an accomplice, this story of seeing spirits in other women's homes echoed accusations made by Ursley Kempe. Ales Manfield even used the same phrase as Ursley in explaining how her spirits gave her information about other people: contradicting her earlier description of them as black, she said that 'her white spirit told her' that Elizabeth Ewstace had hurt an unnamed child.

This kind of inconsistency and apparent plagiarism appears to have been suspicious even to Brian. Although he forcefully pursued accusations, he was evidently concerned that they should be believable. He therefore recorded at the end of Ales's examination that:

---

[6] *ATAJR* D5v–D7v, D8. This may be Elizabeth Turner of the Turner mercer family, widow of Thomas who died in 1573. The family had properties in Great Bentley, St Osyth's East Street (Clacton Road) and next to the almshouses in St Osyth in the mid-seventeenth century: ERO D/DCr M1, Emmison, *Elizabethan Life: Wills of Essex Gentry* 157.

I the same Brian in the presence of they [*sic*] cunstables & other the Townesmen of Thorpe, sayde as I had severall tymes before unto the sayde Ales, what a danger it was, and how highly shee should offende God if shee shoulde charge any person with any thing untrue, and also telled her that her saide confession should bee read agayne unto her, willing her that if shee hearde any thinge read that she knew was not true, that she should speake, and it shoulde be amended.

He also called the two Thorpe women Margaret Grevell and Elizabeth Ewstace to him so that Ales could accuse them 'to their faces', which she did. Why did Ales confess and incriminate others? Was she bullied or lied to? Knowing Brian's previous methods, it seems fair to suppose that she might have been, but he does not record any such trick, as was his normal practice. Perhaps Ales confessed glibly, surprising Brian and causing him momentarily to doubt his case. Was Ales a fantasist, confabulating her stories from gossip and imagination, perhaps suffering from dementia? Maybe: all we know about her is that she was about sixty three.[7] As with so much of the story of the St Osyth witches, it is impossible to know the complicated truth. Creditably, we might suppose that either Brian or, more likely, the Assize authorities worried more about the plausibility of later accusations in Thorpe, Walton and Little Oakley than they did about the earlier ones in St Osyth. It is noticeable that only lesser charges were proven against those accused later, and we'll return to this question in Chapter 6.

---

[7] *ATAJR* D8, D5v.

Ales's stories had terrifying consequences for her and for those she had accused, however. We don't know what happened to 'mother Turner' and I'll come back to Margerie Sammon later, but Cisley Selles, Ursley Kempe and Ales Hunt were already in gaol, and the three suspected Thorpe women – Ales herself, Margaret and Elizabeth – were now also held overnight. On 14 March, Brian questioned Elizabeth Ewstace, who said that she was about fifty three years old. She seems to have known that Ales had named several suspects and was dismayed to find herself on the list: 'out upon her', she exclaimed, 'hath shee tolde anye thing of mee?' This phrase was noted down as if it was suspicious, but in fact there was nothing else to write since Elizabeth denied not only the practicing of witchcraft and the keeping of spirits, but also other alleged contacts with Ales Manfield. However, she did say that she remembered a meeting when she had taken Ales some 'ointment to annoynt her lamenesse that shee was troubled with'. Perhaps, as had also happened in St Osyth, Elizabeth had fallen under suspicion partly because she did claim herbal, magical and other healing abilities.

The presence of healers in Thorpe is also illuminated by another witness who came to Brian on 14 March to give testimony against Elizabeth and also against her daughter Margaret Ewstace. This witness, Robert Sannever (also referred to as Stannivette), said that about fifteen years ago Margaret had been his servant, and that he had discovered some 'lewde dealynges and behaviour by her doone'. Robert had responded with 'threatning speeches unto her, being his servaunt': presumably he felt that her supposed moral lapse reflected badly upon his household.

Margaret was a live-in servant, but when she went home to visit her mother she reported Robert's behaviour, as he conjectured. The next day he was strangely afflicted with a facial disfigurement as he sat by his fire. His 'mouth was drawne awrye, well neere uppe to the upper parte of his cheeke'. He sent for 'one of skill' to come to him, a term which might refer to a chirugion of some sort or a magical healer. If Robert believed Elizabeth or Margaret to have bewitched him, he probably hoped that the healer could turn their witchcraft back against them. But the man of skill adopted a primarily physical remedy: blind-folding Robert with a linen cloth he 'stroake him on the same side with a stronge blowe'. Whatever was dislocated or spasming was cured, 'his mouth came into the right course' and Robert sacked Margaret immediately on the advice of the healer.

Robert had further accusations of more recent date too. In 1578 or 1579, he said, his brother-in-law Thomas Crosse had been taken ill and 'at tymes was without any remembrance'. This memory loss and 'weak state' could not be explained, and Thomas told Robert that he believed Margaret Ewstace had bewitched him. Robert was passionately angry and said that if so 'hee then wished a spyt red hotte and in her buttocks'. This graphic sugges-tion of a fiery torture relates back to Joan Cheston's belief that witches could be burned. Of course the outburst was reported to the Ewstaces and rumour then related Elizabeth's response. She intercepted a neighbour going to Robert's house to say to them 'naye goe not thyther, for he saith I am a witch'. Continuing the conversation, she incautiously made reference to Robert's wife's preg-nancy, either diagnosing or threatening that while his wife was presently in 'lustie' health, 'it will bee otherwise with her then hee looketh for'. And indeed, Robert's wife fell strangely ill. Her baby was born prematurely and died soon afterwards. Elizabeth's prediction of this tragic outcome again suggests that she claimed some medical and cunning knowledge, perhaps as a midwife and keeper.[8]

Accusations continued to be brought forward. One of the 'other … Townesmen' present on 13 March was probably John Carter, who was listed with Joan Cheston as being present to give an information against Ales Manfield that day. However, no accusation was recorded, and he apparently returned again on 20 March to give his testimony, which was in fact against Margaret Grevell. Ales had intimated as much when she said that Margaret had attacked brewings at Carter's. John Carter confirmed this. He said that Margaret had come to his house asking for yeast ('Godesgood' as it was called), and was refused. A few days later 'his folkes' began brewing, using at least a cartload (a seam) of barley, split into two mashes. If the Carters followed the practice of their Essex neighbour Marion Harrison – who left an account of her recipe – they or their servants would first have ground the malted barley in a quern or hand-mill, or paid the miller to do it for them. They might have added in small quantities of wheat and oats. Then they boiled water and transferred it slowly into the malt mixture, leaving it to stand without stirring so that the water could be absorbed, infused, into the grain (Figure 4.2). This process was called 'letting the mash run' and it produced two substances. The first was a mush of damp grain, 'about the consistency of a pudding'

---

[8] *ATAJR* E6, C7–C7v.

Der Bierbreuwer.

Auß Gersten sied ich gutes Bier /
Feißt vnd Süß / auch bitter monier /
In ein Breuwkessel weit vnd groß /
Darein ich denn den Hopffen stoß /
Laß den in Brennten kůlen baß /
Damit füll ich darnach die Faß
Wol gebunden vnd wol gebicht /
Denn giert er vnd ist zugericht.

as F. W. Steer describes it, which was called the 'mash'. The second was a liquid remnant that was strained off, called the 'wort'.

Whilst waiting about an hour and half for the infusion to work, the Carters would have boiled up a second quantity of water and had hops, spices or flavoursome flowers ready to add to the wort that had been strained off – depending on the kind of drink they were making. After infusion and fermentation, the result would be beer or ale, of varying strength and taste. But both the Carters' mashes failed to produce alcohol on this occasion. The mixture stank and neither mash was working its processes properly. The mashes both had to be put 'into the swill Tobbe' for the pigs and the toiling brewers began to suspect witchcraft. Therefore they sought a magical remedy. John called his son, 'a tall and lustie man of the age of xxxvi' and told him 'to take his Bowe and an arrowe, and to shoote to make his shaft or arrowe to sticke in the Brewing Fatte'. The arrow was supposed to lodge its point in the wood. As with the knife in Ursley Kempe's unwitching spell, when a sharp metal object defied gravity and stuck then the charm had been effective. John's son tried this three times. As with the brewing, the first two attempts were a failure, which surprised his father: he emphasised in his statement that his son was in the prime of his archery skills. At last, with the third shot the arrow lodged in the vat, and after that the brewing yielded good beer.[9]

Other Thorpe townspeople joined John Carter on 20 March to give evidence. The butcher Nicholas Strickland

---

[9] Francis W. Steer, *Farm and Cottage Inventories of Mid-Essex 1635–1749* (1950; Chichester: Phillimore, 1969) 33; *ATAJR* E2v–E3.

recounted how he had denied Margaret Grevell's son a rack of mutton. Nicholas had given the reasonable excuse that the sheep was too newly killed for the meat to be cut out – it was too 'whot' or hot, and not ready for butchery. The meat should be chilled as fast as possible in a cold larder and ideally also aged for a couple of days before it was ready to cook. Nicholas was willing to skip the aging but not the chilling, and he told Margaret's son that he should return in the afternoon. Then he would give him the meat. Whether he did or not is unclear. The next Monday, however, Nicholas's wife was boiling milk to make 'the breakfaste of his woorkfolkes' when it began to stink and taste bitter. A few days later, his wife 'went to chearne her Creame that shee had gathered' into butter. But she spent the whole day 'from the morning until tenne of the clocke in the night' at the churn, and no butter would come. This was a common problem. If the cream was insufficiently fatty or too warm it might not coagulate and no butter would form. But although it was a common problem, it was also often attributed to witches. Sometimes it was thought that the witch had her hand in the churn by supernatural means, and was literally holding back the butter.[10]

Watching his wife sweat over her churn long into the night, Nicholas intervened with suggestions. He 'caused his wife to power the saide Creame into a Kettle, and to set it upon the fire'. The tired couple built 'a great fire' under the vessel, but it would not heat enough to boil

[10] H. R. McIlwaine, *Minutes of the Council and General Court of Colonial Virginia* (Richmond, VA: Virginia State Library, 1924) 136, a case from circa 1600–1610.

the milk, never mind achieve the Stricklands' aim, which was to make the milk 'seeth over'. They wanted it to be piping hot and some of it to touch the fire, because as we have seen fire was believed to be a remedy against witchcraft. But the milk would not boil and Nicholas became impatient. Frustrated, he ill-advisedly poured 'one halfe' of the milk into the blaze. Of course the fire smoked and steamed and the room filled with the stench of burnt milk. In fact, it 'stancke in suche exceeding sorte, as they coulde not abyde in the house'. So as the church clock ticked on towards eleven the Stricklands fled into the dark night, choking, and had to wait until the fumes had cleared. Further churning failed to bring any butter, and the rest of the milk was fed to the pigs. After that, the head cow of Nicholas's herd of five miscarried her calf and began to limp so that he thought it best to kill her rather than waiting for her to die. All this had happened, Nicholas thought, because of a small inconvenience caused to Margaret Grevell's family.

The final witness on 20 March spoke against Elizabeth Ewstace rather than Margaret Grevell. Felice Okey was Robert Sannever's sister and the widow of Thomas Crosse, whom Robert had described as losing his memory several years ago. Felice said that when she was married to Thomas, she had one day found Elizabeth's geese in her grounds and driven them out. 'By mischance', one of the geese was hurt. Elizabeth had been furious, threatening Felice that 'thy husbande shall not have his health, nor that whiche hee hath shall not prosper so well as it hath done' and also that 'thou haste not so good lucke with thy gooslings, but thou shalt have as badde'. Felice's geese did indeed stop breeding, and her cattle's milk became bloody for eight days after the quarrel – a phenomenon usually caused by mastitis but often linked with witches. Meanwhile, as Robert Sannever had described a week before, Felice's husband Thomas fell ill. One day he became insensible and 'was cast amongst Bushes' which distressingly marked his face so that it was 'all to beescratched'. Thomas 'coulde neyther see, heare, nor speake' after this fit. Later he wandered in his mind as Robert had described. But when conscious 'hee woulde always crye out upon the sayd Elizabeth even unto his dying day' saying 'that sithence shee the sayd Elizabeth had threatned him he was consumed, and that shee had bewitched him'.

A deathbed statement of this kind was regarded as powerful evidence, but there was an element of confusion in the allegations made against Elizabeth and Margaret Ewstace that would be unhelpful if anyone were to ask the right questions about it. Some of the questions would be legalistic ones about motive, date of attack and the precise means of its operation. Between them, Robert Sannever and Felice Okey had not explained how or why Elizabeth had threatened Thomas Crosse, nor why he had also blamed Margaret Ewstace for his illness. Their statements lacked the neat stories of offence taken and revenge meted out that characterised some of the accusations made at St Osyth and Little Clacton. Thomas was dead, and so there was no opportunity to hear his version of events. And whilst his death had been painful for Felice and Robert, such symptoms were known to have other causes than witchcraft. Medical questions might be asked, therefore: why was it not the 'falling sickness' (epilepsy) or a stroke? Nevertheless, the evidence would go to court, since Brian Darcy committed Elizabeth Ewstace for trial. Did someone at the Assizes ask these questions? Margaret Ewstace was not interrogated by Brian, it seems, and perhaps she had left Thorpe since we hear no more of her pre-trial or in the Assize court.

Margaret Grevell, however, remained at home to be arrested and four days after hearing the evidence against her Brian Darcy questioned her about it. Like Elizabeth, Margaret told him her age, suggesting that both had been asked this because they appeared aged, like Joan Pechey back in St Osyth, who also gave an estimate of her age. Margaret was about fifty five years old. Like Elizabeth, she denied all the accusations against her, pointing out acutely that her own domestic processes were sometimes unsuccessful and her animals died: 'shee her selfe hath lost severall bruings, and bakings of bread, and also swine, but she never did complaine thereof'. But Margaret's initial resistance was followed by despair: she lamented her falsely accused state, saying that 'shee wished her gere [trouble] were at a stay' and that 'shee cared not whether shee were hanged or burnt, or what did become of her'. Before falling silent, she did comment on Joan Cheston's long-running suspicion of her, however. Joan had once denied her a pennyworth of rye meal on the grounds that 'it was pitie to doe her any good'. This was, Joan had said, because Margaret had 'told master Barnish yt shrifes dogge did kill a Doe of his by the parke pale'.[11] After this, there is no record of further accusations, or indeed examinations of suspects, and Brian committed Margaret Grevell for trial.

---

[11] *ATAJR* E3–E4v, E5–E5v.

Here then is the outline of the evidence given against Elizabeth and Margaret Ewstace and Margaret Grevell and printed in *A True and just Recorde*. But once again we can learn more from the few surviving records of the Sokens, particularly their manor courts and the wills of key figures. Contemporary records of the localised ecclesiastical court and parish registers are all lost, but some wills went to the Prerogative Court of Canterbury, and there are also some manorial court and estate records from the last few years of the sixteenth century. They illuminate some, though not all, of the accusers of the Soken witches. The first of these is John Sayer, the Thorpe constable, who was the son-in-law of the local magnate Henry Moyce or Moyse and brother-in-law to the Wheeler family, at least two of whom you might recall had died in the Little Clacton epidemic. Both these wealthy families held land in Thorpe, the Clactons and St Osyth (the Wheelers at 'the ffen' and the Moyses in Mill Street). When Henry Moyse died in May 1576, he left his daughter Jane Sayer, John's wife, houses and land in Thorpe and Kirby, the neighbouring Soken village. The Moyse lands lay across the sub-manors of Birch Hall and Landermere Hall too. Henry also left John Sayer all his unbequeathed goods and debts, making him executor of the will and also entrusting him with the will of Richard Gye of Thorpe which Henry had been unable to execute in full. John Sayer's sister-in-law Hellen Wheeler also chose him as her executor.[12] John was thus a rich,

---

[12] TNA PROB11/58/130, PROB11/63/9, PROB11/39/318; ERO D/DBm M160, 161; Little Clacton parish register 28 October 1569, 22 February 1572, 1 February 1575, 16 March 1577, 22 August 1580.

well-connected man, experienced in matters of justice and administration within the parish and manor systems. Joan Cheston, one of the women who accompanied John on 13 March to give evidence, was also a formidable person. Her interactions with Ales Manfield and Margaret Grevell – threatening to burn one and denouncing the other – suggest her character. Joan was in no hurry to remarry after Robert Cheston's death either: she appears in manorial court records as late as 1598 still a widow and in control of her own property, being reported for failing to clear ditches. Robert had farmed at least seventeen acres, at Cheston's Corner, Tovell's Fleet and Tovell's Marsh, but almost certainly more: Joan had 'servants' to tend her animals and continued to hold other land of Thomas Richmond's until the late 1590s.[13] She knew about the intersecting rights and responsibilities of farming and she respected the power of the Darcy family: hence her awareness of the problematic consequence of reporting a hunting violation of the park boundaries to John Barnishe. This was what she had accused Margaret Grevell of doing. As we saw in Chapter 2, John was an experienced park manager for the Darcys.[14] The word 'shrifes' seems to be a misprint in *A True and just Recorde* for the name of the dog owner who had been reported to him for killing a deer. It might have been 'Berifes' in the original pre-trial manuscript: Berife was a fairly common Essex surname. The Berife gentry family held land in the Sokens, although a London compositor puzzling over handwriting as he set his type might not have known that.

---

13 ERO D/DBm M89, D/DB M160.

14 ERO D/DB M160, 161; Emmison, *Elizabethan Life: Wills*: the will of John, Lord Darcy, 3 February 1581.

There was a park at Thorpe and an adjoining one at Little Clacton, respectively owned by the Dean and Chapter of St Paul's and the Bishop of London. This conjoined parkland area may have been the one Joan Cheston was referring to. John Barnishe may have been its Keeper: he also kept Great Oakley Park, and previously also the Great Park at St Osyth until 1581.[15] If a dog had killed a protected animal in one of his parks – perhaps at Thorpe or in Great Oakley by what is now Parkpail Farm, where the Park paling stood – then it was his duty to take action. If Margaret had reported it to him this might have prompted a prosecution with, at the least, serious monetary consequences. Joan Cheston apparently blamed Margaret for this kind of outcome, although for reasons that are now lost. Perhaps she was related to the Berife family and one of them had been prosecuted for poaching. Certainly other connections of the Chestons were woven into the case against Margaret Grevell and Alice Manfield. Nicholas Carter was the guardian of the child John Cheston, who may have been Robert and Joan's son, in the 1590s. He farmed land in Thorpe and Kirby, including five acres and a cottage called Dorys and a wood. John Carter also tenanted at least twenty acres in both parishes and houses and land with an annual rent of eighteen pounds. He also held a tenement and three acres and one rod of land from the manor of Moze, called Kings. The Carters were regular jurors in the Soken manor courts which Joan also attended. They were connected to the Sayers, too: John and Nicholas Carter witnessed the

---

[15] ERO D/DGh M45/2 – this is its 1617 acreage. Thanks to Chris Thornton for advice on the parks and their owners.

will of John Moyse in 1557, and John and Robert Carter witnessed that of Henry Moyse in 1576, as well as accepting the surrender of his lands into the hands of the lord of the manor. As Henry's executor, John Sayer would have worked with them on the practicalities of administering his father-in-law's estate.[16]

Robert Sannever was a man of similar standing. A regular manor court juror, referred to in the manor court record with the spelling of Standevet, he also appears in the table at the end of *A True and just Recorde* as Robert Stannivette. His wife, whom he describes suffering a miscarriage, died between 1578 and 1597, perhaps even before Robert gave his evidence against the Ewstaces in 1582. We do not know her name, but Robert then married the widow Mary Ryvett, whose former husband John was Bailiff of Little Oakley and Skighawe manors, and held Little Oakley Hall, Skighawe Hall and Moze Park as well as land in Great Oakley, Thorrington and Tendring. John Ryvett was wealthy enough to lend forty pounds to Edmund Pirton and engage in other banking transactions: his illegitimate son Edmund fought a court case after his death over land in Walton, arguing that John Gent, John Brasyer, William Pope and William Gardiner had mortgaged it to his father and defaulted. We'll meet some of these men again. John Ryvett died in 1580, and Mary Sannever inherited his land in Tendring. When she died in 1597, the Sannevers held at least five houses and land called Jordons in Thorpe

---

[16] On the Colchester Berifes (Beriffs) see Laquita M. Higgs, *Godliness and Governance in Tudor Colchester* (Ann Arbor, MI: University of Michigan Press, 1998) especially 166, 192–3; TNA PROB 11/39/318, PROB 11/58/130; ERO D/DBm M89, D/DGh M45/1.

and twenty acres called Hethes, formerly belonging to the Guild of St Margaret which had its hall opposite Thorpe church. They likely also held other lands outside the Soken manors. Felice Okey, Robert Sannever's sister, also had land and Thomas Crosse's heirs John and Thomas inherited from their father a cottage and seven acres called Brache at Thorpe. They were young when he died, and in 1597, aged sixteen, John chose Robert Sadler, the miller, as his legal representative to help him with his landholding.[17]

Other accusers are less well-documented, although Nicholas Strickland was also a regular manorial juror and accepted the surrender of lands. In 1597 and 1605 he acted as surety for two Quarter Sessions recognizances. A John Read was also a Soken tenant, holding land called Mones – perhaps it was his brewing that was disrupted. Nothing further is known about the Manfield, Lynde or Brews families. Perhaps they lived within the Birch Hall or Landermere manor lands, between Thorpe and Kirby but separate from the Soken manors. Most of their records are lost. John Sayer had holdings in these areas, and if Ales Manfielde lived on his land – as seems likely from her story about the oven – then she may have lived there. Some of the Grevell family certainly did: Mighell Grevell accepted the surrender of lands to Birch Hall manor in 1547 and witnessed the will of William Sadler.[18] The Okeys, Crosses and Ewstaces

[17] TNA PROB11/63/54, PROB 11/69/652; ERO D/DB M160, D/DB M161; Emmison and Fitch, *Feet* vol 5 90; ERO D/DBm M89.
[18] ERO Q/SR 137/3–35, Q/SR 173/124; ERO D/DBm M89; TNA PROB11/33/6.

likely held lands of Skighawe and Moze manors, north of Thorpe, in addition to the Crosses' cottage in the village: there were families of all these names on Skighawe and Moze manor land ninety years later, with records of their tenure dating back to at least 1617. There was land called Okeyland and seventeenth century Okeys farmed Threshers, Netherland, Broomes Close, Batemans, Robyns, Sylers and Stubbs, and held a tenement called Smiths. There was also a tenement and nine acres called Howes or Hores described in the 1670s as formerly in the tenure of John Crosse: it abutted on the glebe land of Moze parsonage.

This land of John Crosse's was also right next to land in the tenure of John Eustas in the 1670s. The Crosse and Eustas holdings shared a corner in common. Some of this land had been called Eustac or Eustace and Hopkin Eustac since at least 1582, a date specified on the rental list. Some, to the south and separated from the Crosse family's land by land called Millers, was called Willes or Mershe. The Eustac grounds of Hopkin Eustac and Willes or Mershe had a tenement and twenty-three acres and three rods of land, seven acres and one rod of land and marsh, eight acres and one rod of salt marsh (Hopkin Eustac) and twelve acres and one rod of land and three acres of marsh (Mershe). Mershe – whose name, of course, means 'marsh' – went right down to the shore of Hamford Water on its south side. Some of this Eustac land was in the tenure of John Brock in the later 1580s, but John Eustas was there almost a century after Elizabeth and Margaret Ewstace had been accused of killing Thomas Crosse

FIGURE 4.3 Map of the Manor of Moze showing Eustac and Crosse lands. (Source: Author's photo; reproduced by courtesy of the Essex Record Office. D/DBm P5.)
Note: A black and white version of this figure will appear in some formats. For the colour version, please refer to the plate section.

in the 1580s.[19] It looks as if their lands, and possibly their houses – each parcel of land had a tenement on it – were literally next door (Figure 4.3). A map shows houses clustered tightly together in that area of the manor, and these may be the very homes inhabited by the Ewstace and Crosse families. If so, no wonder

[19] ERO D/DGH M45/14, M45/1, M45/7, M45/15, M45/11, M45/13, M45/12.

Elizabeth Ewstace's geese strayed into Felice Crosse's ground.[20]

Moving onto the second group of accusations in the Sokens in 1582 adds further to our understanding of the interconnections between accusers and suspects, across Walton as well as Thorpe and Kirby. It also provides a further connection to the St Osyth suspects too. On 25 March, returning from his journey to Little Oakley (as we shall see in Chapter 5), Brian Darcy heard evidence from a group of Walton townspeople against their neighbour Joan Robinson. The farmer Edward Upcher said that he and his wife had had occasion to go to Colchester in the previous week and there they had visited the Castle 'to speake wt Ursley Kemp' – just as Henry Durrant had done. Edward asked Ursley 'if she could tell what sicknes or diseases his wife had' and Ursley told him that she was 'forspoken or bewitched'. The couple excitedly enquired about their enemy and received a classic cunning person's reply, narrowing the field but evading a too-certain identification: it was 'a woman yt dwelt in their town ... that ye party hath one of her eares lesse than ye other, & hath also a moole under one of her armes, and hath also in her yard a great woodstacke'. Edward did not name a suspect to Darcy, but other accusers immediately identified the Upchers' target as Joan Robinson.

Joining Edward, Ales Miles said that when she had visited Joan Robinson to buy a pound of soap, she had

---

[20] ERO D/DBm P5. The houses look like Monopoly-style generic buildings with pitched roofs and central chimneys but, given the detail of the map and the care with which it was drawn, they may represent individual dwellings.

gossiped with Joan's maidservant Joan Hewet. The maid told a strange story: 'her Dame made her nose bleed, and then called her Catte to eate ye same'. Thomas Rice added that Joan Robinson had tried to borrow a hayer from him a fortnight ago, a fine strainer made of hair, used in brewing. Rice's wife had refused because she was using the hayer. As Joan left, a squall struck the Rices' house, and next day one of their cows lost her calf. The Rices' goose abandoned her nest and would not be caught. Joan also tried to borrow a hayer from Margery Carter, and three days after she was refused one of Margery's cows drowned. Margery had long suspected Joan. Ten years before, her husband William Carter had refused to rent Joan Robinson's husband pasture for a cow, because he needed it himself. Immediately, two of 'his best and likliest beasts in a strange sort brake their neckes' and the pasture was freed up. Tactlessly, Joan Robinson's husband went to the Carters' house and said breathlessly 'God restore you your losse, nowe you may pastor me a cowe'. The flimsy comma separating these clauses seemed to indicate the events were related. In about 1580 the Robinsons had wanted to buy a house and an acre of land from the Carters, but they refused to sell because Margery's husband said 'he would not have [the Robinsons as] his neighbour'. The next day William's mare, worth at least five pounds, died in a strange manner. A dog had eaten meat from her carcass and also died.[21]

The Robinsons had also fallen out with other farmers over their pig-keeping. Ales Walter said that four years

[21] *ATAJR* F5v–F6v.

ago, Joan had wanted to buy a pig from her. Ales had refused and soon her sow, who had farrowed a week ago, started attacking her piglets. She had begun to 'bite and flye at them, as though shee had bin madde' and had prevented them from suckling. Alarmed, Ales sold Joan the piglet that she wanted for threepence. She told Joan about the behaviour of the sow, and Joan said 'her sowe did the like' and advised her to give the remaining piglets cows' milk if the sow would not suckle them. Ales did so and her piglets thrived. She must have felt more warmly towards Joan, since she then described a friendly visit two years ago to the Robinsons' house. The Walters had 'found her and her husband sitting by the fire' and again the two couples had discussed piglets. Joan asked if she might buy two of Ales's latest farrow when they were born. That night, Ales's sow gave birth to ten piglets, all of which died escaping from their stall. Ales said that she had blocked a gap in the door with a broom faggot, but the piglets had still got out and in death they 'stoode one before an other … lieke horses in a teem'. Nine had died in this strange formation, while the tenth had drowned in the Walters' pond.

Allen Ducke told a similar story: Joan had asked to buy two of his piglets and had twice been refused, after which the Duckes' pigs died. He also said that Joan had tried to buy a cheese from them, and had flown into 'a great anger' when she was denied this. The next day, Allen had 'went with his Cart and foure horses therein to fetch a lode of corne' and he took his wife and two of their children along in the cart for the ride. But his four carthorses misbehaved. He stopped by the river and 'watered his horses at a ware [weir] called the Vicarage ware' but 'when they had drunke, he could not gette them out of the water'. He, his wife and children were held up whilst he waded 'to the forhorse head' to lead him out. The water was a yard deep, Allen said, and it had been no small thing to drag the big horse away. Finally, John Brasyer said briefly but pointedly that Joan had asked to buy from him a particular sow piglet to wean, but he had refused because he wanted to wean it himself. The next day the piglet died. And earlier in the year 'sithence Christmas last past', John's wife had gone to Joan Robinson to pay her 'for wares which shee had beeing due upon scores'. The two women had disagreed about the amount owing: 'his wife would not pay [Joan] her owne reckoning' and they fell out. Soon after one of John's cows drowned.

Joan Robinson was questioned about these accusations on the same day as they were made, 25 March. This was Lady Day, the Feast of the Blessed Virgin Mary and her immaculate conception, and it counted as New Year's Day in the old style of calendar in use in much of Elizabethan England. Brian Darcy would also have known that it was only four days until the Spring Assizes at Chelmsford, which were due to be held on the 29. He would have been notified of this date by messenger, and he was expected to attend with all those who were to be tried. He thus had very limited time to investigate the charges against Joan, commit her for trial and transport her to the Assize town if he wanted to do so. The Walton informations and Joan's examination are brief, perhaps because of resultant haste. Joan confirmed that some of the stories her neighbours had told were true: she had attempted to borrow from and trade with them. But she firmly denied any witchcraft. Everything had happened as Thomas Rice, Margery Carter and Ales Walter had described, she said – she did not comment on the accusations made by Edward Upcher, Ales Miles, Allen Ducke or John Brasyer – but she 'denieth that shee sent any Impes or Spirites ... and all the other matters against her enformed shee denieth in general'.[22] Perhaps Brian committed her for trial, but there is no further record of her. Perhaps he ran out of time and was overtaken by events, which – as we shall see – did not favour further commitals immediately after 25 March.

Meantime, using the same sources as those that cast light on the accusers at Thorpe le Soken, we can learn more about Joan Robinson's enemies at Walton. Some were probably connected to the Thorpe accusers. The relationship between the two families of Carters, for example, is unclear but they are likely to be part of an extended kin network. Men with the right names – William and John Carter – are mentioned together in records, and we can identify the more distinctively named Margery Carter well into the 1590s in the manorial court records. Margery's husband William Carter died before 24 March 1583, when the will of John Shurlock – which was witnessed by John Carter – mentions William's recent death, his widow and the lands that she now held from the Shurlocks. Margery then appears as a widow in the Walton court records in the 1590s, along with William Carter (her son?), one of the homage and jury. This grouping suggests a family connection between William, Margery and John Carter of Thorpe, but there is also a

---

[22] *ATAJR* F7–F8.

further detail connecting this second William Carter to other Walton accusers from 1582. William Carter the second held land called Rosedowne and land at Mones, which abutted land farmed by John Brasyer and where John Read of Thorpe also had land.[23]

Ales Walter's family are also traceable, although there are two Ales Walters among them. One was the wife of John Walter who died in 1596, the other the wife of Robert Walter who died in 1597. John and Ales had three sons (Robert, William and Thomas) and held at least two acres of land and marsh near Walton tide mill, called Holmeground, seven and a half acres of land and marsh and an additional acre and a half called Myddlepightell, an acre and a half called Harmanspightell and five and a half acres in Strodefield (also known as Broadfield). Robert and Ales had one son, Thomas, and held more land: Church Pightle (one and a half acres), three and a half acres in the Newfield, strips totalling five acres in Strodefield, a rod of land with a cottage let to Richard Browne, land called Marshefeild or Berifes, two acres at Oldhowse let to Mathew Master, a house and two acres called Marsheland Pightells with some additional marsh, four and a half acres let to Robert Ryldon, three acres at Smallpightells, and a fish weir which Robert would inherit after the death of his mother Elizabeth Harnes. The Walters and Carters were further interconnected in land dealings the manorial courts throughout the 1590s.[24]

The Brasyers were also a large extended family in Walton. The testimony of John Brasyer in *A True and*

---

[23] TNA PROB11/77/96; ERO D/DBm M89.   [24] ERO D/DBm M89.

FIGURE 1.1 The Mill, St Osyth. (Source: Chronicle / Alamy Stock Photo.)

FIGURE 1.2 Old houses in Stone Alley, St Osyth. (Source: Rodger Tamblyn / Alamy Stock Photo.)

FIGURE 1.1 The Church of St Peter and St Paul in
St Osyth. (Source: Author's photo.)

FIGURE 1.2 St Osyth Priory gatehouse.
(Source: ColsTravel / Alamy Stock Photo.)

FIGURE 2.1 Near Nun's Well, Wellwick, St Osyth.
(Source: Author's photo.)

FIGURE 2.2 Frowick Farm. (Source: Author's photo.)

FIGURE 3.2 Great Clacton parish register, marriage of Henrye Sylls and Sysley March. (Source: Author's photo; reproduced by courtesy of the Essex Record Office. D/P 80/1/1.)

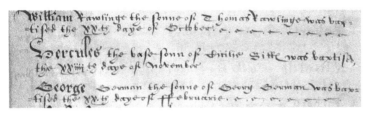

FIGURE 3.3 Little Clacton parish register, baptism of Hercules Sills. (Source: Author's photo; reproduced by courtesy of the Essex Record Office. D/P 80/1/1.)

FIGURE 4.3 Map of the Manor of Moze showing Eustac and Crosse lands. (Source: Author's photo; reproduced by courtesy of the Essex Record Office. D/DBm P5.)

FIGURE 5.1 Annis Herd and William Dowsing Archdeaconry Court presentment. (Source: Author's photo; reproduced by courtesy of the Essex Record Office. D/ACA 5)

FIGURE 5.2 Little Oakley parish register, baptism of Goodlie Weld. (Source: Author's photo; reproduced by courtesy of the Essex Record Office. D/P 388/1/1)

FIGURE 6.1 Horses by a dead tree at St Osyth. (Source: Adrian Muttitt / Alamy Stock Photo.)

FIGURE 6.2 Junction of Rainsford Lane and Rainsford Road, Chelmsford. (Source: Author's photo.)

FIGURE C.1 Field path to Frowick. (Source: Author's photo.)

just Recorde does not suggest he was among the wealthiest members of the family: he reports the loss of a single cow, and his wife visits Joan Robinson in person to pay debts accumulated on credit. The wealthiest Brasyers had held Walton Hall for generations. They were quarrelsome folk. John and Edward Brasyer fell out over land in Walton and pursued each other through the courts in disputes that festered into the reign of James VI and I.[25] In the 1570s Edward and Bartholomew Brasyer were alleged to have assembled unlawfully with others, broken into a barn at Walton Hall and stolen cheese worth seventeen pounds from John Tendering, whom we have already met at St Osyth, giving evidence to support accusations made against Elizabeth Bennett.[26] We have already met John Brasyer, head of this branch of the family, too – this time as a defendant in another court case. In the mid-1580s Edmund Ryvett alleged that John Brasyer, with John Gent and others had defaulted on a mortgage lent them by John Ryvett, whose widow later married Robert Sannever. This John Brasyer and his wife Alice were related to John Gent, and had sizable land-holdings across Walton, Kirby and beyond in the 1590s, when records begin. John Brasyer died in 1597, leaving over eighty acres in the Sokens; John Berife, gentleman of Walton and a major landholder in Brightlingsea, was his executor. Perhaps it was his dog that killed the doe by the park pale.

[25] TNA PROB11/31/627, C2/Eliz/B26/29, 31, and 51; also C2/JasI/P22/46 and C3/301/34, and D/DBm M89, dispute over Stockslands.

[26] ERO Q/SR 38/6, 7 and 8; for the cheese see also F. G. Emmison, *Elizabethan Life: Disorder* (Chelmsford: Essex County Council, 1970) 127.

This John Brasyer could be the man who gave evidence against Joan Robinson. If so, his word was a powerful one, and his enmity was something to be concerned about. There was, however, also at least one other John Brasyer in Walton. In the 1590s, this John and his wife Dorothy held a house and ten acres of land and marsh from Thomas Hurlock, three acres of wood near Longland, a house and six acres and a moiety of a house and nineteen acres previously belonging to Thomas Christmas. A John, perhaps this one, appears in the manorial court records in land dealings with Robert Walter and William Carter, members of the other families who also gave evidence against Joan Robinson. Of these, this second John is the more likely to be the informant against Joan, because of his more modest status. But, importantly, it is not possible to be sure: the records describing these men are mostly from at least thirteen years after the witch trial, because earlier records are lost. They are also only references from one class of document, the manorial court, so cross-referencing is mostly impossible. Finally, the proliferation of people of the same name further complicates matters.[27] Because Walton records and wider records of the Soke are limited in their survival, there is also no trace of the Miles, Rice and Ducke families, and little detail on the Upchers, but the Hewet family seem to have come from the manor of Skighawe, where there was land called Hewetts Pightells and where a John Hewett farmed land at Skinners, Joyces, Hayles and Locks Pightell in the 1620s.[28]

---

[27] ERO D/DBm M89.
[28] ERO D/DGh M45/1, M45/8, M45/11, M45/3, M45/12.

The Robinsons may also have lived on one of the sub-manors' lands, since they too are frustratingly invisible in the surviving records. They were not among the poorest inhabitants of Walton, because they employed at least one servant, Joan Hewet, kept a number of animals and made large quantities of certain goods like soap. Soap making was a skilled business, requiring hardwood ashes (potash) to be soaked in water, which was concentrated to make lye. Then fat – lard for fine soap, tallow for coarse – was refined and added, a lengthy process of draining, boiling and drying. Since Joan Robinson kept pigs, she probably used pork fat in her soap. A barrel of ashes and ten pounds of fat made about forty pounds of soft soap. Joan probably produced it as a home industry as well as for her own use: Ales Miles thought she would readily be able to buy a pound of soap from her, and the Brasyers had bought 'wares' from Joan too, running up credit as if she were a regular supplier. Joan's skills would have brought her income from her soap but also from its by-product: after the soap was made, the remaining ashes were sold and used on unproductive land. A seventeenth-century rental describes how a tenant of the manor of Moze – just up the coast towards Little Oakley – is to land a load of thirty pounds of soap ashes at Beaumont dock in Hamford Water, to be used for farm improvement.[29]

From what we can reconstruct of the witchcraft accusations in the Soken villages, then, it is possible to suggest that the accusers of Ales Manfield, Elizabeth and Margaret Ewstace and Margaret Grevell were often

---

[29] ERO D/DGh M45/16; William and Robert Chambers, *Information for the People* (Edinburgh and London, 1849) vol. 2 779.

from well-off farming families. They were the landholders of middlingly sized acreages, and many of them were interconnected by family and friendship ties. Some, particularly in Thorpe where the accusations began, were active in local justice and were regarded as pillars of their remote and tightly knit community. From Thorpe, accusations spread to the even more isolated Walton, where they were gathered in haste just days before the Assize trial of the group of witchcraft suspects thus assembled. While Ales Manfield is described asking for charity from her community, the other three witchcraft suspects are not notably destitute. Joan Robinson, in particular, was a capable trader and farmer who came to her neighbours' doors to buy, lease, or borrow, not to beg, and they went to her to buy a range of commodities. Elizabeth Ewstace and Margaret Grevell were both older women and perhaps more economically and socially vulnerable, but Margaret is described as carrying out her own baking and brewing and sending her son to buy an expensive cut of meat.

The landscape of Thorpe and Walton is not described in anything like the detail that accompanied the witchcraft accusations at St Osyth, and it is difficult to map out the various localities in such a way as to understand the emotional, magical geography of the Sokens. Walton has been extensively developed, like Great Clacton, as a seaside resort: its street plan has changed, and many streams and lanes have disappeared under tarmac and post-war housing. Thorpe is less developed, but like Little Clacton it is not as well-documented in *A True and just Recorde* as is St Osyth. With the communities of Chapters 3 and 4, we have a better insight into their economic and social patterns than we do into the physical features of their landscape. In the Clactons we have parish registers but no manorial records, whilst in the Sokens this position is reversed. In each case this affects the story this book is able to tell: Chapter 4 is drier, less personal, more dependent on *A True and just Recorde* for its narrative elements. It is still possible to reconstruct some of the story of the witches of the Sokens, especially when we have a rare survival like the map of landholdings in the manor of Moze, but this does remain only a partial reconstruction. However, in the next and final chapter on the villages of the Darcy lands, we are lucky: we have an almost complete survival of records across manorial and parish classes of document, as well as archidiaconal records, wills and deeds. Let's travel north to Little Oakley and Beaumont cum Moze to see what a difference this makes to the story.

5

Little Oakley and Beaumont cum Moze

Annis

~

The village of Little Oakley lies about sixteen miles to the north-east of St Osyth and fourteen miles from the nearest of the Sokens, towards Harwich and the River Stour, facing the North Sea. It is part of a chain of villages that circle the five thousand acre inlet of Hamford Water. Great Oakley and Beaumont cum Moze lie to the south of Little Oakley, and further south and east across the Water are the Soken villages of Thorpe, Kirby and Walton. Little Oakley is a shoreline community, strung out along the Water, which has receded from the village over the centuries due to land reclamation. Its farms included large areas of saltmarsh and mud in the sixteenth and seventeenth centuries. They often had large acreages in theory but much of that was unusable as agricultural land. It was not falling into the sea in landslips, like the farmland at Clacton and Walton, but nothing would grow on it. One seventeenth century surveyor wrote that the estate he was assessing had '758 acres at low water, but all sea at high tides not worth one shilling'.[1]

The threat of flooding was ever-present at Little Oakley, just as it was on the flat land in all the other low-lying villages of eastern Essex. Beaumont Hall, for

---

[1] ERO D/DGh M45/1.

example, had a sea wall about three miles long, and other properties were similar. Lease agreements specified that the 'Wall against the Sea' must be maintained. A seventeenth-century estate survey at Beaumont recommends regular inspection of the sea wall, with a day's labour per year expected from each tenant and more hefty maintenance undertaken by a team of two men, with five horses and a cart. A later account describes the costs of sluice repair and how in the thirty six years to 1727 the sea 'have broke in & overflow'd its banks' three times. On the upside, the farms had 'landings' or 'docks' for boats to bring in goods, especially chalk and ash for the fields, and to transport people across the Water. Like the jetties at Landermere to the south, these little docks were ancient landing places and a lifeline to the isolated villagers. Like other people in the area, the villagers west of Hamford Water were ill-connected to the outside world, in some ways more so even than their neighbours to the south and east.

Although transport on the Water was useful, it was wholly dependent on tide state. The Water is also a giant sink, pulling in streams all along its westward edge, so that although villages like Little Oakley were on high ground, they were connected by many linking bridges over low lying tidal streams. There were long bridges and causeways at Great Oakley and further north at Ramsey and Wrabness, which were often unreliable. In 1573, the people of Ramsey, a mile north of Little Oakley, presented a petition to the Quarter Sessions arguing that Ramsey bridge, a walkway three hundred feet long and with twenty nine piers, was an essential link for them to Colchester and Ipswich yet part of it was 'caryed awaye wythe everye ragyng tyde'. There was, they said, a tidal range of about twelve feet, and they feared loss of life if something wasn't done. Once, they pointed out, the bridge had been maintained by the moneys of the 'brethren and systren' of the religious houses in the area, but now that was 'done awaye'. Hard times, they thought and, as with the people of St Osyth, their perception was that things had once been better. It is easy to overstate this nostalgia – even in the 1530s wills frequently mentioned the roads and the bridge at Ramsey as crying out for repair and left legacies to effect it – but perceptions are important and Hamford Water's people clearly felt that the new masters of their lands could do more for their communities.[2]

As news of Brian Darcy's enquiries spread through the county, several pressured farmers in Little Oakley complained to him about Annis Herd or Heard, whom they suspected of witchcraft. Brian, his scribe and perhaps his female searcher visited Little Oakley from the 16th to the 18th of March to hear their evidence and investigate the suspect. They came up from Thorpe and then returned to the Sokens, going out east to Walton to collect evidence against Joan Robinson: a long trip over difficult ground in a cold spring. The Little Oakley group's accusations look to have been recorded together in a single document, which was then transcribed into *A True and just Recorde* as 'the enformation of John Wadde, Thomas Cartwrite, Richard Harrison with several others'. The accusers' complaints focused primarily on the economic hardship that they believed Annis had caused them although, as

---

[2] ERO D/DEl M76 and D/DGh M45/16 and 18; Q/SR 43/17; TNA PROB11/25/95, PROB11/27/116.

we shall see, there were other factors at work too and these may have been more important. The first to speak seems to have been John Wadde or Wade, who explained to Brian that about two months ago Annis Herd had come to him to talk about her recent presentment to the Archdeaconry Court on a charge of witchcraft. This was not, however, a neighbourly visit to someone who might help her with her legal troubles. In fact, it was John and his fellow accusers who had presented Annis.

Archidiaconal visitation records and archdeaconry court Act Books tell us that John was a churchwarden at Moze and also an important presence in Little Oakley's religious community. Both parishes were in a group of Hamford Water churches linked by ancient ties and serving church personnel. The Act Books don't show Annis's presentment but that is probably because the pages of Volume Ten are especially badly damaged by water and the record has been torn away. When Annis spoke to John around December 1581 or early January 1582, she was asking about her projected court hearing. She requested that it be postponed until 'the dayes were longer', presumably so that she could get to the court at Colchester and back in daylight. John Wade replied with the assurance of a man who knew the forms of law. The Register (Registrar) of the court lived in Colchester, he told Annis, and 'it must be hee that therein may pleasure thee'. Brushed off, Annis said that she would speak to John Aldust or Aldus instead to see if he could help her. John Aldus was a churchwarden in Ramsey, and a man with wide connections across the archdeaconry: Annis hoped that she might be able to persuade him to 'speak to the officers for her' on his travels.

And so she went away to make her request. John Wade, however, was uneasy. Soon afterwards he drove forty sheep and thirty lambs to his eighty acre pasture in the adjacent parish of Tendring, a field of grazing that he said he had been keeping especially for them: he had 'spared [it] by some long time, and knew the same to be a good sheepes pasture'. John appointed a shepherd to keep an eye on them. Despite all these precautions – sufficient grass and careful watching, he emphasised – when he visited these animals eight or nine days later he found one dead, one lame, and a further sheep and a lamb sick. All these died, and another two continued sick, one weak and one with its neck curiously awry. Across his wider flock, he said, more than twenty sheep and lambs had fallen lame or died since he and his neighbours reported Annis to the church court, and he had lost cows and other cattle too. In her Assizes indictment, the attack on John's animals is described as taking place on 1 January 1582, and it is stated that one cow died, as well as ten sheep and ten lambs, together worth about four pounds.[3]

John Wade's neighbour Thomas Cartwrite or Cartwright echoed his concerns. In winter 1579 there was a big snowfall and during the storm one of his trees had lost a bough. Annis Herd had taken the branch to use as a footbridge over a 'wet or durtie place' but Thomas innocently removed it. Later he heard Annis was angry with him. Reportedly she had said 'that the churle (meaning this examinat) … had carried away the peece of the bough that she laied to go over, saying, that shee woulde

3 ERO D/ACA 10, D/ACV 1; *ATAJR* E6v–E7v; Cockburn, *Calendar: Essex: Elizabeth* record 1312.

bee even with him for it'. Manor tenants were usually allowed to gather wood under their rights of ploughboot, cartboot and fireboot, to repair wooden items, cook and heat their homes. Some properties had hedgeboot, for fencing. Thomas probably took the branch because it was his right. But because it was being used as a bridge, Annis was displeased. Not three days later, Thomas continued, there was more snowfall and two of Thomas's cows got lost. He could see where they had lain in the snow and could not understand how they had wandered from the herd. When he found the lost cows, one had died calving and the other – the head cow, a sensible animal – had fallen into a ditch and broken her neck. She had survived, but was in pain and would not eat, so that after two weeks' Thomas had to kill her. These distressing, costly losses he blamed on 'some witchery of the saide Annis Herd'.[4]

Annis's third accuser was Bennet Lane, the wife of William Lane. Again, her accusation was a historic one although she dates it only to 'when she was a widdow' before her remarriage. In contrast to the accusations of John Wade and Thomas Cartwrite, Bennet's is an oddly reluctant, lengthy statement. The picture she paints of her relationship with Annis Herd is a surprisingly friendly one. Annis came to Bennet's house often to borrow items, but unlike many witch-accusers, Bennet did not turn her away empty-handed. Instead, on several occasions she gave her a pint of milk, once with butter, and another

---

[4] TNA PROB11/74/256: John refers to himself as Aldus; ERO D/ACA 8 – no location is visible; for instance, ERO D/DGh M45/7 lists the boot rights of the manors of Beaumont, Moze and Skighawe; *ATAJR* E6v–E7v.

time she lent her tuppence or allowed her to run up a tuppence debt. However, Bennet began to be troubled by fears. With one pint of milk she lent Annis a dish, but after Annis had kept it for a fortnight or three weeks she felt constrained to ask for it back. So when Annis's daughter, probably her illegitimate child Annis Dowsing (of whom more later), visited with a message Bennet spoke firmly to her. 'I gave thy mother milk to make her a posset', she said, but 'I gave her not my dish'. Little Annis went home and brought the dish back.

Shortly afterwards, however, Bennet's spinning went wrong. Like other needy women – Ursley Kempe and Ales Newman, for example, and Annis Herd herself – Bennet was a spinster, taking in wool from clothiers like John Johnson to make into yarn. So when Annis Dowsing left and Bennet's thread broke, she was alarmed. The quality of her thread likely impacted on her wages. She took her spindle to the grindstone and smoothed it: it might be catching on the thread. But this did not help. Then, she says, she 'remembred her self'. What she remembered was that bewitched items could be purified by heat, as with Nicholas Strickland's frantic attempts to unwitch his milk at Thorpe. Bennet heated her spindle red hot, after which she was able to spin again. This must have confirmed her suspicions. Another time, Bennet continued, Annis Herd owed her tuppence. When Bennet had to pay her rent she, 'beeing a poore woman', was obliged to call in her debt and to borrow more money herself. Apologetically, she asked Annis for the sum. But Annis said she had laid out eight or nine shillings that week and could not pay. Bennet had to insist: 'you must needes helpe me with it now, for this day I must paye the Lordes rent', she said, referring to the rent she owed to Lord Darcy as Lord of the Manor.⁵ Annis borrowed the money and paid Bennet, who told her 'now I owe you a pint of milke, come for it when you will and you shall have it'. Annis claimed the milk and Bennet threw in some butter. But then her own milk and cream gave her trouble.

Just like last time, Bennet did not initially put her problem down to witchcraft. When she tried to skim her milk she just could not get the cream to lift off cleanly. She tried boiling the milk, but it burned onto the pan. She worried that the cows had been eating the wrong food, or that there was some taint of sour, turned milk in her pots. So she scalded them out with hot water and scoured the pots with salt, but nothing helped. She 'was full of care, that shee shoulde loose both milke and cream'. But at last 'it came into her minde to approove another way', or to try another approach. It was Nicholas Strickland's way, again. Bennet took a horseshoe, heated it to red heat and put it into her milk. After that, she could skim and boil her milk and make butter as normal. The hot iron, and perhaps also its lucky horseshoe form, seemed to have scared away the witchcraft – if there had been any. But interestingly Bennet made no explicit accusation that there had been: her stories have an open end like Joan Smith's at Little Clacton or William Bonner's at St Osyth. Did Bennet really want to accuse Annis or was she under pressure from someone else?

---

⁵ The phrase 'Lordes rent' has troubled editors including myself (Gibson, *Early Modern Witches* 114 n.133), but it means the rent owed to the Lord of the Manor rather than a tithe. It is used in this way in, for example, the will of John Hulwoode TNA PROB11/98/147.

Others at Little Oakley also came forward to accuse
Annis Herd in a way that suggested both suspicion and
reluctance to express it fully. Andrew West and his wife
Anne had a similar relationship with Annis to that of
Bennet: friendly, but concerned. Another long conversation about small details ensued, as if the accusers were
trying out aspects of their stories. Andrew West told
Brian Darcy that one day he had met Annis coming back
from the mill, presumably the one by Millpond Farm,
where she had been asking for meal or bread but getting
neither. 'Knowing her neede', he told his wife to give her
some bread but he also questioned her about her reputation: 'Annis, thou art ill thought of for witchcraft' he
probed. This suggests that others, not the Wests, thought
ill of Annis and we know that these included the churchwarden John Wade. Annis denied that she was a witch,
however, and the Wests accepted her assurance. Indeed,
they began to talk about their pigs, offering to sell one
to Annis. She agreed to buy one, although she was concerned that as a 'poore body' she would struggle to find
the cash and if the pig died she would have nothing. She
also needed to ask her landlord if she might keep one, and
she went to do this. So far, so good.

However, the Wests had heard nothing from Annis.
Instead, they sold the pigs to Edmund Penly, a neighbour
who was probably also a family member. He had married
Ales Weast or West, a widow, in 1575 and they had a large
family from 1576 onwards.[6] Predictably, after Edmund

---

[6] Great Oakley parish register 17 July 1575, 11 April 1576 and 10 March
1581; Little Oakley parish register 17 November 1577, 19 November
1579, 1 January 1580, 12 November 1581, 20 September 1584, 21
January and 12 December 1585, 23 September 1586, 25 May 1588.

had taken his pig, Annis turned up to collect it and had to be told she had missed her chance. The day after, Anne West sent her nephew over with a pound of wool for Annis to spin. Annis appeared resentful of her subordinate status as an out-worker. She carped at the boy: couldn't the weeders who worked on the Wests' farm do the spinning? His aunt might as well have given her one of their pigs as give it to Edmund Penly. Immediately one of the Wests' remaining pigs began to behave strangely. Panicked, Andrew West called the weeders and asked their advice. 'Some of them said, burne it' Andrew told Brian Darcy, 'other said, cut of[f] the eares and burn them'. He favoured the latter option and so the poor pig was mutilated. Surprisingly, it recovered well. The Wests began to think Annis might actually be guilty of witchcraft. Two days later, Anne West recited to Annis the words she had spoken to the Wests' nephew, and told her about the sick pig. 'Thou saidest the other day thou hast no skill in witcherie' she remarked, but 'I will say thou hast an unhappie tongue'. This approach insinuated but didn't confirm an accusation. However, Anne's brewing then went wrong until like Bennet Lane she remembered to drop a hot iron into her vat.

And others in their community echoed the Wests' new concern. Just like Anne West, Godlife Osborne found her brewing affected after a brush with Annis. She had sold Annis a peck of apples – thirty to forty depending on fruit size – for threepence and allowed her to have them on credit. Just before Christmas 1581 she sent her boy to Annis to ask for payment. The boy reported that Annis said curtly she could not pay until the wool man had visited: likely he was going to pay for her spun yarn.

Back at home, Godlife was brewing with top-quality Manningtree malt that her husband Edmund had bought. The sprouted and kiln-dried Manningtree grains were known for being especially sweet and hard, a fresh yellow outside and chalky inside, the finest available. As she gave her statement to Brian, Godlife remembered Edmund bringing home his malt and saying jovially 'good wife, let us have good drinke made of it'. Well-off women brewed in large quantities about once a month, and this special brew would have been for the Christmas and New Year festivities. But Godlife began to have difficulties fulfilling Edmund's expectation. When her boy came back from Annis's house to report her annoyance with the Osbornes, Godlife was adding her second quantity of boiling water to her mash. But it began to froth and stink. It bubbled up a hand's breadth above the rim of the vat, she said, and even when poked with a stick it kept rising.[7]

Eventually, Godlife put a hot iron into the vat hoping that this would unwitch it and this worked: the mash calmed down. But Godlife was now suspicious: surely Annis had ill-wished her drink and it would not now brew as it should. And so it proved. When the second infusion was finished, an hour and a half later, Godlife strained out a second quantity of wort. She boiled this up with the flavouring and prepared for a third and final infusion. But there was now something wrong with the second batch of wort. Wort had to be boiled and then cooled quickly, killing its enzymes and sterilising it. Then it was added

---

[7] For brewing see William Harrison, *Elizabethan England: From The Description of England* ed. Lothrop Withington (London: Walter Scott, 1876) 99; Steer, *Farm and Cottage Inventories of Mid-Essex* 33.

to active yeast to ferment. But Godlife's wort 'stancke in suche sorte, as that they were compelled to put ye same in the swill tubbe' – just like the Carters' mash. Having invested four or five hot and tiring hours in her brewing, far from having the finest drink for the Christmas season Godlife had to discard at least part of her brew, feeding it to her pigs. Did she lose all the mash? Certainly the second batch of wort was a duff one, and either it or possibly even the third and final mashing might have had to be abandoned. As well as the disruption to the current brew, alewives and beer-makers also kept a kind of stockpot of wort from previous brewings to add to new ones: this contained the active yeast.[8] This wort may have been spoiled. Godlife blamed this disappointment on Annis Herd, although like some of the other accusers she did not say this in so many words.

This, then, is the story that *A True and just Recorde* tells. But other sources reveal more about the Little Oakley families. There are at least two John Wades and they are connected with the Herds. John Wade I was a substantial farmer and Quarter Sessions juror with lands of his own and also lands worth eighty pounds held in trust for his young brother-in-law John Marven. John Wade's wife was Barbara Marven and John's other brother-in-law, married to Barbara's sister Christian, was Thomas Herd. This John Wade died in 1574 leaving his wealth to his brother Robert's children, and it is very likely that the John Wade of *A True and just Recorde* was one of these. In the pamphlet, John's statement describes extensive lands

---

[8] Harrison, Elizabethan England 100–2; see also Ruth Goodman, *How to be a Tudor* (London: Penguin, 2016) 246–53.

in Tendring, and a John Wade had some of his children baptised there: Margaret (1565), Jonas (1566) and John (1575). A John Wade also held at least forty acres and a tenement (Chapmans and Cookes) from the manor of Moze. In 1574 – the year John Wade I died – this John also took over from Alice Wade, widow, over fifty acres: four tenements and lands (Brownings, Youngs, Goodiers and Skinners) three houses, and Fulhold pightle. He also took Kings from John Carter before 1602 (see Chapter 4). Skinners abutted land belonging to Beaumont rectory and also Gobyns or Gubbins Pightell, of which more soon.[9] This John Wade II was probably the heir of John Wade I, and the son of Robert Wade. He tenanted Little Oakley Hall, inherited by Barbara Wade from her father, John Marven the elder, and had at least two servants Katherine Hils and John Cock, buried in 1583 and 1584 as 'servant wt John Wade'. John Wade proved John Lynde's will in 1584 (see Chapter 4) and is described there as Bailiff of Little Oakley manor.

So Annis's accuser John Wade was a wealthy and well-connected man across Little Oakley, Beaumont and Moze. But as well as being related to the Herds he had an ongoing business relationship with some of them. Young John Marven's 1584 will reveals a debt of six shillings and eightpence rent to John Wade and John Herd, 'for grounde I hyred of them'. These interconnections of

---

[9] Tendring Parish Register: Margaret 15 April 1565; Jonas 27 April 1566 (buried 18 August); John 3 March 1575. His daughter Joane was buried 14 January 1573, and an earlier John buried 27 January 1574. ERO Q/SR 26/29, 36/49, 40/37, 53/5; which he left to Robert Wade, who also served often on the panel (Q/SR 32/32, 40/37, 55/18, 77/28); D/DGh M45/1, M45/7.

Wades and Herds raise questions about how far Annis's own relatives believed her to be a witch. Her immediate family was small, in size and in wealth, and we'll meet them later. But they were part of a group of Herd families in Little Oakley and beyond. The wealthiest branch was that of John Herd, son of Robert and Ellen and the likely relation and business partner of John Wade. When he died in 1601, John Herd held about forty acres in Little Oakley: Glovers, Overshoggs, Whitewayfield, Syersland and Little Stroggs next to Clubber's Pond, Church Acre, Brookhouseland, Wyllmaryes, Mereland or King's abutting on Clubber's and two acres called simply Lands. His death prompted digging in the records and he was found to be holding without a proper grant a further twelve acres: a meadow and pightle near the mill, Thurstons or Barkehouselands, Hurlocks, Longpightle, Brookmeades, and other lands. These had moved in and out of Herd holdings: after Robert Herd's death Ellen had married John Leighton and then Thomas Borham, while her daughter Elizabeth Herd, later Hickman, had also taken some lands into her marriage.[10] They were part of a web of kinship going back centuries and only partly penetrable – as the inability of the manor court and its clerks to keep track of John Herd's holdings over the decades nicely demonstrates.

Part of the clerks' trouble, and now the historian's trouble, is that there were also other Herds in Little Oakley

[10] TNA PROB 11/63/54; Little Oakley parish register 13 December 1583, 16 April 1584; ERO D/DEl M76; Marvin, *The English Ancestry* 117–18; Emmison, *Essex Wills ... Archdeaconry Courts 1583–1592* 170; ERO D/DEl M76, 1556; Little Oakley parish register 6 October 1567, 7 August 1568.

and adjoining villages, and there were lots of them. For example, there was Christian, daughter of Stephen. Stephen was the son of Edward and Agnes, he married a woman named Isabella and died in 1546. We know from land descent from Edward that Stephen's daughter Christian (born 1546, died 1600) married George Cowbridge, after which the couple bought the holding of Bennet Lane's house and land in 1591. Here we can pause for a moment in this genealogical tangle to note that we can again see a Herd interacting with someone who gave evidence against Annis Herd in 1582 – Thomas Herd and John Wade were connected, and now Bennet Lane is connected to Christian Herd Cowbridge. This may or may not be significant, however: business relationships are not a proxy for friendship just as blood relationship does not equate with shared views. A land transaction between a Herd and a Lane does not imply endorsement of Bennet's actions nine years before by Christian or the rest of her family. But the Lane–Herd connection is worth noting: the court record makes it clear that Bennet trusted George Cowbridge and Christian Herd Cowbridge to let her continue as a sitting tenant for the rest of her life.

Equally, Annis had defenders among the Herd-Wade-Cowbridge family group as her plea to John Aldus for assistance with her church court presentment shows, since John was another wealthy member of the family. In his will, witnessed by Edward Herd, he mentions his 'coosen' Elizabeth Herd, sister of John. Other less direct connections between the Herds and John Aldus went back into the 1570s when Thomas Herd, widower of Christian Marven, married Barbara the widow of Thomas Marven (formerly his sister-in-law). The couple entered a 'plaint' in the manorial court against John Aldus, claiming a third part of the tenement of Barons as her dower. Herd–Aldus dealings continued after Annis's trial. In 1587 John Herd, son of Edward Herd, sold to John Aldus the Little Oakley tenement Longmans or Mayes, which had been in his family for generations. John Aldus added this to his property portfolio: Read's Pightle, land in Eastfield, Aylwyns and Trumpers, Warehouse, Mockings and Cross House in Little Oakley (over fifty acres), with other lands at Ramsey and Dovercourt. Although his will shows he could not write his name, John Aldus was, like Annis's accusers, a regular Quarter Sessions juror. Yet she trusted him to make her case to the ecclesiastical court at Colchester. As a churchwarden at Ramsey, John was well-placed to do this and Annis seems to have wanted to play off John Aldus, Wade–Herd family member and Ramsey churchwarden, against John Wade, Wade–Herd family member and Moze churchwarden, to get her way. Although the evidence is deeply confusing, a broad conclusion might be that she had friends as well as enemies in high places and in her wider kinship network.[11]

One of Annis's other accusers, Thomas Cartwrite, was a churchwarden like John Wade and John Aldus – this time for Little Oakley itself, Annis's home parish. He was a lively controversialist, presented in January 1579 for not receiving communion and for 'brawling speaches' in the

---

[11] The notion of kinship has been much debated in Essex, especially because of Keith Wrightson's study of Terling in *Poverty and Piety*. Here kinship networks were famously interpreted as being relatively loose and insignificant, but further discussion has questioned this thesis and Wrightson sums up the nuances in 'Terling Revisited' in the 1995 edition, 192–7.

church and churchyard. Inevitably, Thomas Cartwrite was linked to the Wade–Herd clan too, indirectly through the Marvens. Thomas witnessed John Marven's will with John Herd and before her marriage to Thomas Cartwrite, his wife Cecily had been married to John Blosse, whose mother (also called Cecily) was a Marven.[12] Thomas shared in the wealth of that family group and had his own resources too. His father William Cartwrite or Cartwright's will shows that in 1571 and thereafter Thomas was able to draw on substantial sums of money. After his father's death he was told to pay his brothers and sisters over forty pounds between them, and after his mother's death he would inherit the family home and land in Great Oakley. In 1572, he married Cecily Blosse, formerly Thurlethorpe, who brought him more land and properties. John Blosse had built a new house in Little Oakley, Winters, and there were lands at Merelandes, Gladwyns and Paynes in the village that came to Cecily, as well as lands in Great Oakley and Ramsey – although some would go to her sons John and Robert Blosse and daughter Bridget Sack too. But Cecily and her new husband Thomas Cartwrite were well-off. They had at least one servant, as we know from the burial of Alice 'ye servant of Thomas Cartwright' in 1584 and held land across the Oakleys.[13] Like John Wade, Thomas was a regular

[12] ERO D/DEl M76 1546, 1556, 1573, 1579, 1590, 1591, 1600, 1601; Emmison *Essex Wills: Archdeaconry Courts 1583–1592* 193; Emmison and Fitch, *Feet* vol. 5 232 with Thomas Godfrey; Marvin, *The English Ancestry* 39, 44–8, 84, 117–18; TNA PROB11/74/256; ERO Q/SR 61/17, 54/40, 58/18, 81/7; D/ACA 8, D/ACV 1.

[13] Great Oakley parish register 7 January 1572 (burial of William); Little Oakley parish register: marriage 6 October 1572, Cecily's burial 3 May 1602; ERO D/DEl M76 1542, 1546, 1588, 1598; Little Oakley

juror, including at the Midsummer Quarter Sessions of 1582.

If Annis Herd was connected in some way to the wealthy Herds and though them to men like John Aldus, what happened to cause her to become a suspicious burden to her neighbours? Annis is the best documented 'witch' of the St Osyth group, well represented in manor and church records, and we can now tell her life story for the first time. First, there are land transactions. Annis appears in the manorial records as Anne Herd or the Latinised version of Anne, Anna. It's important to note that the names Anne, Agnes, Anna and Annis were used interchangeably. For example, William Lane's first wife is called both Anne and Agnes, 'Agnes' and 'Annas' are used interchangeably in a will of 1578 and the rector's wife Anne Harrison – whom we'll meet later – is also called Agnes. In a church court presentment of 1588, our Annis is referred to as 'Anna' which is then crossed out and 'Agnetam' substituted. To make identification even surer, there is only one Anna Herd in the manor records. Annis's father was Robert Herd, holder of a cottage and three acres called Boroughs or Brymleys. He had inherited a two-thirds share of it from his father John, who died in 1537, leaving the other third to his widow Anne. Anne died in 1538, so her son Robert held the whole property. After Robert's death in 1568, he left the land to his widow Charity, who had married Roger Blanchflower. Charity was still living in this cottage in 1582. If Annis and her

parish register 1558–1571 Blosse children, 20 September 1584 (burial of Alice, no surname); will of John Sacke, Emmison, *Essex Wills ... Commissary Court 1578–1588* 186.

mother or stepmother (Charity could be either) were on good terms she might have shared in the little house and garden. But Annis may have been estranged from her family: she had a reputation for sexual and other immorality which appears in the records of the archdeaconry court.[14]

Like Ursley Kempe and Cisley Selles, Annis Herd had 'base' children. As part of his investigation, Brian Darcy questioned one of them, the little girl named Annis Dowsing. When she was questioned, young Annis told Brian that 'shee is of the age of vii yeeres the Saturday before our Lady day next' and since she was speaking to him on 18 March that was just a few days away. Brian asked her 'whether her mother had any little things, or any little imps' and unfortunately she replied that 'she hath in one boxe sixe Avices or Blackbirds', which were 'white speckled, and all blacke'. In another box, little Annis continued, were 'vi spirits like Cowes ... as big as Rattes ... and they lie in the boxes upon white and blacke wooll'. Annis also said her mother had given her one of the spirits, a black and white cow named Crowe. Another, called Donne, had been given to her brother, Annis Herd's second child. The spirits fed on wheat, barley and oats, straw and hay, bread and cheese, water or beer, but sometimes they would suck on the children's hands and legs. Little Annis showed a burn on her hand as evidence of this. Sweetly, she added that her brother would sometimes comment on the birds as they flew around him:

[14] ERO D/DGH M5, Emmison, *Essex Wills ... Commissary Court 1578–1588* 12; D/ACA 14 19 April 1588, another presentment for non-attendance at church (see later); ERO D/DEl M76 1537, 1568, 1586.

FIGURE 5.1 Annis Herd and William Dowsing Archdeaconry Court
presentment. (Source: Author's photo; reproduced by courtesy of
the Essex Record Office. D/ACA 5)
Note: A black and white version of this figure will appear in some
formats. For the colour version, please refer to the plate section.

'they keepe a tuitling and tetling'. Following Brian's usual
practice, this guileless accusatory evidence was re-dated
to after that of the adult who was accused: supposedly
on 17 March, Annis Herd denied that she had any spirits
called Crowe or Donne. She was, of course, quoting her
daughter Annis Dowsing directly.

Annis Dowsing had been born in late March 1575
and she was the daughter of Annis Herd and William
Dowsing. We know this both because *A True and just
Recorde* claims that Annis Herd had bewitched to death
'two wives of William Dowsing, as it is supposed' but also
because Annis was presented to the archdeaconry court
for carrying on an affair with William (Figure 5.1).

She was fairly young – from other evidence which
we'll look at later, I would suggest she was in her twen-
ties or early thirties in the 1570s. In May 1573 she was
first accused of fornication with William Dowsing.
Initially the court misrecorded his name as 'John' but
this was erased and corrected. At the June court of 1573

Annis admitted she had indeed slept with William and was required to do penance, confessing her error both at Colchester and Little Oakley. Evidently, their relationship was ongoing in 1574 too. Although she does not seem to have been presented nine months later for giving birth to a 'bastard', Annis Dowsing, Annis Herd was called back to court in March 1577. Perhaps this was because of this or the conception of her son? It is not clear – and she did not respond to this second summons. This led to excommunication, which she did nothing to reverse. Excommunication sanctions included exclusion, even when requested, from the church community: for example in receiving parish alms or participating in church ceremonies. Thus Annis Herd and her children are absent from the parish register and we don't know her son's name or who his father was.

However, since Annis was accused of killing two of William Dowsing's wives, we can assume that she either continued to have sex with him or was thought to be doing so throughout the 1570s. The parish registers of Little Oakley and Great Oakley show that William's two wives were Susan Orris and Anne Smyth. William married Susan at Little Oakley on 15 December 1575, nine months after Annis Dowsing's birth, and when Susan died in childbirth at Great Oakley in March 1579 he married Anne Smyth at Great Oakley on 12 July 1579. Anne had died before March 1582, if *A True and just Record* is correct and Annis was thought to have murdered her. Little Oakley's churchwardens brought relatively few cases to the church court, unlike those of some parishes (Coggeshall, Dedham) but Annis was regularly reported, far more often than any other resident. This may well have estranged her from her birth family.[15] Certainly Annis had limited means compared to other Herds. This was probably true even at the start of her life and by 1575 she had fallen decisively from grace. We'll return to Annis's life story later but her sexual history is a key part of her reputation and likely influenced her accusation as a witch by the churchwardens John Wade and Thomas Cartwrite. Her reportedly fatal attraction to William Dowsing, and her two illegitimate children, meant that scandal hung around her.

Alongside the group of churchwardens who repeatedly presented Annis – Thomas Cartwright for Little Oakley and John Wade for Moze – other pious-seeming local people across the connected parishes disapproved of her. One group was the West–Osborne family. Like the others the family's men were active in local justice. Andrew West was an occasional Quarter Sessions juror and Edmund Osborne served very frequently, most recently at the Epiphany Quarter Sessions on the 11–13 January 1582. Edmund was a comparatively wealthy man and influential in Little Oakley, but he was not at the Wade– Herd level and neither was Andrew West, who was his brother in law.[16] Andrew was, however, connected to the

---

[15] *ATAJR* F4–F5v; ERO D/ACA 5 and 6 (May–September 1573), D/ACA 7. The records of the court are very thin for parts of 1574–5; Little Oakley parish register 15 December 1575, 27 October 1576 (son Edward baptised); Great Oakley parish register 20 March 1579, 12 July 1579; there has been detailed investigation of such presentments as possible evidence of the growth of godly religion in Dedham: e.g. A. R. Pennie, 'The Evolution of Puritan Mentality in an Essex Cloth Town: Dedham and the Stour Valley 1560–1640' unpublished thesis (University of Sheffield, 1989).

[16] ERO Q/SR 41/21, 64/4, 67/12, 79/51, 82/11; F. G. Emmison, ed., *Essex Wills: The Archdeaconry Courts 1577–1584* (Chelmsford: Essex Record Office and Friends of Historic Essex, 1987) 175.

Wades and Thomas Wade of Beaumont Hall was his cousin. In addition to these good connections, Edmund and Andrew's wives had brought them a moderate amount of property. Edmund and Godlife Weld were married on 20 May 1575, when she was seventeen, at which time she was the youngest survivor of four siblings whose father, John Weld, Wylde or Weald, had died in 1571. He was a mariner who had died in Ramsey, but his children had his body brought to Little Oakley for burial, as the parish register records. Evidently his home was Little Oakley, and he made his will there, with John Blosse – Cecily Cartwrite's first husband – among his witnesses.

Godlife Weld Osborne's brother Richard had died aged eleven in 1572, and her sister Dorothie Weld, by then the wife of John Cressie, had died in 1573. Her surviving, elder, sister was Anne Weld West, the wife of Andrew West. Godlife had spent the early 1570s as Andrew's ward, custody of her and her siblings having been given to him. Anne West, Dorothie Cressie and Godlife were their brother Richard's co-heirs. They inherited on his death the leases of a tenement and five acres called Heathes, a two acre croft known as Alcottland, one to two acres called Sigges, a two and a half acre croft called Partriches, and a croft of one and a half acres with the unpromising name of Tarepightle (small, weedy field – maybe Annis Herd's jibe about Anne West's weeders was based on an inconvenient truth). Dorothie and Godlife also inherited jointly from their father a messuage and garden called Penters or Wardes as well as land in Ramsey (two pightles called Glovers and Grene Pightell, and Monks and Monks' Acre in the former chapel lands), land at Bradfield called Britts and in Little Oakley called Styles and Symsons. All this was Godlife's after Dorothie's death. That their land was valuable to Godlife, Anne and their husbands – both actual and future – is clear from an attempt to broker an unusual settlement with their baby nephew, Dorothie's son, who was six months old when his teenaged mother died in 1573. Dying intestate, Dorothie had said she wished to leave her land to her son rather than her co-heir sisters and Dorothie's husband John Cressie wanted her verbal legacy honoured.

The late sixteenth century was a time of consolidation of landholdings in Little Oakley, with farmers attempting to pull together third and half shares of properties and strips and pightles adjoining each other in the old open fields of the manors of Little Oakley, Beaumont, Moze, New Hall and Old Hall. The Wests and Godlife Weld did not want to lose the parts of their family land that would go to their nephew if Dorothie's instruction was followed. There was thus some contestation of Dorothie's right to will land verbally to her son. The manorial court records show the Little Oakley community struggling to resolve this issue of family tragedy and material practicality in a way that would not offend either the living or the dead: in fact, jurors said that they could not decide what was the right outcome, and had to be steered by the steward, Geoffrey Nightingale who, as we already know from Chapter 2, had a legal training and practised at Gray's Inn.[17] His solution, 'intending

[17] Will of John Wylde, TNA PROB11/53/554, and for the Ramsey land and a Herd connection see also ERO D/DRc B10 (c.1542); burial Little Oakley Parish Register 24 February 1571; Little Oakley parish register: Godlife and Edmund's marriage 20 May 1575; Richard's baptism 14 November 1560, burial 28 February 1572; Dorothie's marriage 6 September 1571, burial 2 February 1573; Fletcher, ed., *The Pension Book of Gray's Inn* 30.

Justice should be done', was to grant the boy the land as his mother's heir, and to give his father custody of him until he attained his majority. Thus in 1574 the Wests and Godlife gallingly lost control of a third part of their land. Its effective possessor John Cressie remarried and moved to Great Oakley. In 1596, young John would also get Godlife's third to join to his own when after Edmund's death she married John Stevens and let go her holding.

The Weld family, with their Osborne and West husbands, seems to have reached a point of economic stasis in the 1570s. Their landholdings were piecemeal and did not increase – unlike, for example, those of their neighbours John Wade, Thomas Cartwrite, John Herd or John Aldus, who inherited, bought and leased parcel after parcel of land, growing holdings over several decades. The Weld male line more or less died out: John's brother Richard Weld had daughters (Anne and Alice who died young, Joane, Margaret and Dorothie), and their lands frittered away into other families. Richard left his properties Paynetts and Gardelers to his surviving three daughters. Inference from the manorial record, based on the names of the three sisters who control Paynetts and Gardelers, shows that Joane married Robert Anwick and Margaret married John Haukyns. The parish register tells us that Dorothie married the son of her guardian, the churchwarden John Wood and, after his death in 1584, the manorial record shows she married Thomas Crosse.

Robert and Joan Anwick, who will be important later in our story, spent the 1570s and 1580s waiting to get possession from the other Weld sisters of all the shares of Paynetts (a tenement and fifteen acres) and Gardelers (three acres) and they finally achieved it (Paynetts in 1582,

Gardelers in 1587). They were the most successful of the Weld children. Meanwhile, Richard and John Weld's brother Thomas's male children fared rather worse. Thomas's eldest son Walter died in 1562, only four years after his father. Thomas's younger son, John, was brought up by his uncle John alongside his own children Richard, Godlife, Anne and Dorothie. When Richard died in 1572 that left John junior the only surviving boy of his generation of Welds. He and his wife Margaret later sold half their land – Aylwyns and Trumpers, six acres – to John Aldus, keeping only the seven acre Harts.[18] Whilst the Welds were not as stretched as some others, they had slipped from success in the 1540s and 1550s, when the brothers Richard, John and Thomas had acquired most of their leases, into financial strain. Every acre mattered symbolically and actually to the Welds, and their relations the Wests and Osbornes.

Bearing in mind the family's multiple accusation of Annis Herd, we can speculate about their wider life beyond the economic, too, although more tentatively. Godlife's name perhaps hints at the Welds' religious orientation, although she was actually named Goodlie, as

---

[18] ERO D/DEl M76 1546, 1551 (acquisition of Paynetts and Gardelers), 1558, 1572, 1578, 1582, 1586 (Paynetts in the Weld family), and 1587 (Gardelers); Little Oakley parish register: Dorothie's marriage 4 July 1573, John buried 28 March 1584 (he is listed as a churchwarden in LMA DL/B/A/002/MS09537/004; will of John Wood, Emmison, ed., *Essex Wills … Archdeaconry Courts 1583–1592* 172, naming his wife 'Dorvye' and brother-in-law 'Anwick''s children as beneficiaries and John Wade as executor; TNA PROB 11/53/554; ERO D/DEl M76 1548, 1558, 1573 (acquisition and regrant of Harts), 1572 (death of Walter, Aylwyns and Trumpers to Aldus); Little Oakley parish register 10 August 1572 (marriage of John Weld and Margaret Shemans).

FIGURE 5.2 Little Oakley parish register, baptism of Goodlie Weld.
(Source: Author's photo; reproduced by courtesy of the Essex Record
Office. D/P 388/1/1)
Note: A black and white version of this figure will appear in some
formats. For the colour version, please refer to the plate section.

recorded in the parish register (Figure 5.2). Her father
referred to her in his will as Goodleve, a deed calls her
Goodlief, and later manorial records match *A True and
just Recorde* in referring to her as Godlife. Either way, she
was the first baby to be received into the church after the
commencement of the parish's written register. The register begins with a fanfare welcoming 'ye first yeare of
the reigne of our sovereigne Lady Elizabeth' in 'the yeare
after the creation of the world ffyve Thowsand ffyve hundred, Twenty ffyve', and there is an additional sense of the
specialness of firstborn status preserved in the individual
entry's text too: 'Imprimis Goodlie Weld … Christianed
the first of A[nn]o supradicto'.

Goodlie was a special Christian soul when she was born,
and she strengthened into the even more pious sounding
Godlife as she grew older. She married well, but her life
was saddened by loss. Later parish register entries show
that Godlife had at least two children with Edmund but

their first child, a boy named after his father and born in 1577, died within three months. Susan, a daughter born in 1579, survived.[19] There was no male heir for the Osbornes, as with others of the Weld family. Again the family story is one of bitterly unfulfilled promise. Why, for instance, should Annis Herd – poor and godless as she was – have several thriving children when Godlife Osborne did not?

Godlife's sister Anne and her husband Andrew West leave no noticeably pious record, however. They had a larger family, although by the time of their father's death only three of six or seven children survived: Andrew, born 1573, Thomas, born 1577, and Anne, born April 1582. They had lost several children: Bridget born 1568, a daughter or possibly two with the then-popular, now-extinct name of Rabich, Rabeche or Rabbage, born possibly 1569 and 1571, and Richard born 1579.[20] In this context, it is interesting that the accusations made against Annis by the West–Osborne family are exclusively economic. Despite the repeated deaths that afflicted them, these people do not seem to have believed that a witch could bring about the grand tragedies that had in recent

---

[19] Little Oakley parish register 1558 (date unclear – register begins on accession day, 17 November 1558); ERO D/DRc B10; Edmund's baptism 6 August 1577, burial 20 October 1577; Susan's baptism 5 April 1580.

[20] Little Oakley parish register: Bridget baptised and buried 16 January 1568, confusion about Rabich with the clerk making multiple erasures (she/they was/were born 16 January 1569 or 16 September 1571 and one was buried 3 February 1571/2; their grandfather John named a child Rabeche in his will in December 1571), Richard 14 February 1579–12 June 1581. Andrew was baptised 5 April 1573, Thomas 6 April 1577, Anne 1 April 1582. Another West child, Beatrix, was baptised in 1575, but no parents are named.

times blighted their lives: the death of Dorothie Cressie, say, or of the baby Richard West, lost only a few months before in 1581. Even Annis Herd's more forthright accusers Thomas Cartwrite and John Wade focused on relatively minor harm to their livestock. For Thomas it was his herd of cattle rather than any imagined hurt done to his family. The loss of the Cartwrites' cows was significant, but it would not break them. John Wade's livestock losses appear to have been the worst but his flock was a large one for Essex in this period and, as we have seen, he also farmed extensive holdings elsewhere. He made no reference to worse harms. Annis Herd was perhaps imagined by her farming neighbours as someone who might hurt their cattle, sheep and pigs, their spinning and brewing, but not as someone who would kill their families, immoral as she might be. Either that, or the Assize court process weeded out more serious accusations and these did not proceed to indictment. We know that happened with one murder charge, as we shall see below.

The two richest men of this village group and the two churchwardens of Moze and Little Oakley, John Wade and Thomas Cartwrite, seem to have led the prosecution, if the record of evidence preserved in *A True and Just Recorde* is any guide to the order in which it was given. Other accusers, as we have seen, were more muted in their statements. Little Oakley looks like the Sokens: a community where some of the wealthier tenants, connected by business, family and legal dealings, moved against a suspected witch and pulled in others of moderate or small holdings to add to their collection of evidence against the accused. Yet there is a surprising amount of detail in the records even about the least wealthy and least vocal of Little Oakley's people. Annis Herd's poorest accuser was Bennet Lane. She was less well off than the Wests or Osbornes, much poorer than Thomas Cartwrite or John Wade. It is unlikely that the horseshoe she heated came from a horse that she owned. Bennet had a lease on just two acres and a cottage named Stallwoods with a yard, left to her by her marriage with William Rushe or Rushy, a substantial villager who served on the manor jury. But since his death, her financial situation had worsened.[21]

In 1581 Bennet married William Lane, a widower with several children – one of them servant to John Aldus – but this marriage did not apparently confer any property or benefit upon her. She does not seem to have had children of her own, and William Lane did not bring her anything substantial. So five years after William Lane's death, in 1587 Bennet was obliged to surrender the lease of her cottage and plot to her neighbours George Cowbridge and his wife Christian Herd Cowbridge (as we saw above), retaining for herself only a life interest in the house.[22] Her statement to Annis Herd that she was 'a poore woman'

---

[21] Emmison, *Elizabethan Life: Home* 49; ERO D/DGh M45/16; William and Bennet are referred to as Bushe in the transcribed manorial record ERO D/DEl M76 (c1700), but this does not match her marriage record (Little Oakley parish register, 28 September 1581) and is a misreading; William Rushe was buried 31 July 1578.

[22] Little Oakley parish register, baptisms Anne undated 1560, Thomas 13 April 1571 (buried 7 November), Johane 24 February 1572, William 6 April 1577, to William Lane and his wife Anne, listed as Agnes Lane when buried 27 August 1579 – there are a number of blank years in the 1560s. Johan was left a cow and six ewes in Aldus's will in 1589 (PROB11/74/256); ERO D/DEl M76 1587, see also 1574, 1591 when Bennet and George both died; Little Oakley parish register, burial of William Lane 30 November 1582, burial of George Cowbridge 31 May and Bennet Lane 17 October 1591.

thus seems to have been true. Her concerns are accordingly about matters that seem small – some thread, a little milk – but to her they loomed large. However, as we have seen, Bennet's evidence also has a reluctant quality about it, a sense that she shares the poverty of the woman she is accusing and perhaps had even considered her a friend. And if Annis was a black sheep member of the wealthy herd of Herds, then she might even have been better off than Bennet, at least in her connections.

Perhaps things would have rested there, in an uneasy but workable equilibrium, occasionally troubling the church courts but not the criminal ones, if there had not been a more powerful accuser in Little Oakley. Perhaps his input catalysed others in making their smaller claims. The accusations that John Wade, Thomas Cartwrite, the Wests, Osbornes and Bennet Lane made were minor in comparison to that of the Beaumont rector, Richard Harrison, who lived in Little Oakley and is named third in the header listing accusers in *A True and just Recorde*. The rector was a man of much greater cultural reach and spiritual authority than even the wealthiest farmers, and he exceptionally and bitterly accused Annis of murder, a crime which if proven would see her executed. He spoke out without fear, and violently, accusing her not just of witchcraft but also of sexual sin – which we know was repeatedly dragged to the attention of the church courts, though not in Richard's parish – and theft. Richard disapproved of every aspect of Annis's life, and he did not temper his words to disguise this fact or offer her any Christian charity. Annis was not his parishioner, belonging to Little Oakley parish and being thus the concern of the rector Hugh Branham, but Richard seemed to know a good deal about her and to hate her.

Rector Richard Harrison had arrived in his parish of Beaumont in 1566 to officiate at St Leonard's church at the behest of the patron of the living, John, Lord Darcy, the father of the third baron, Thomas, and he also had the parsonage of Little Oakley 'in farm'. Manor court and parish records tell us about him and his wife Anne. They were married in 1568 when Anne was the widow of Hugh Spencer, who died in 1567. Anne brought Richard some freehold and copyhold property: a tenement and garden called Baldwynn's, about forty square perches of land, a one and a half acre share in a cottage and four acres called Gardelers which Hugh had leased from Richard Weld in 1551. The Harrisons let Baldwynns in 1568. They had five children: Richard born 1570, Mary born 1572, Thomas born 1575, James born 1577 and Anne born 1579. All the children were healthy, and the Harrisons' affairs prospered. But in summer 1581, while her husband was away in London, Anne Harrison fell out with Annis Herd. She accused Annis of stealing some ducklings that Anne's duck was raising in the hedge of the Harrisons' garden. Unlike the carefully articulated accusations made against Annis in the Little Oakley informations that we have seen so far, Anne Harrison's complaint was made directly and furiously to the suspected witch. Her husband told Brian Darcy that 'his said wife went unto the said Annis Herd and rated her and all too chid her ... and was very angry against the said Annis'.[23] Anne Harrison lost her temper and apparently heaped abuse on the suspected thief.

[23] ERO T/Z 590/3; will of Hugh Spenser, ERO D/ABW 34/59; Little Oakley parish register, burial of Hugh Spencer 27 March 1567, baptism of Anne Harrison, 2 August 1579; ERO D/P 285/1/1

But afterwards, for all her material security and happy home circumstances, Anne must have repented and succumbed to anxiety. When Richard returned from London and was busy among his books for several hours one night, he suddenly heard his wife cry out: 'Oh Lord Lorde, helpe me and keepe me'. He ran to her and she told him that 'I am sore afraid, and have bin divers times, but that I would not tell you'. Her fear was that 'yonder wicked harlot Annis Herd doth bewitch me'. Richard was appalled. Like many clergymen, he tended to discount witchcraft beliefs that granted infinite power to the witch. Where, these ministers argued, did that leave God? Surely he could defend his own against the malice of a village woman? And, further, it was not the witch who had the power but the devil. Surely, if so, God would always defeat Satan. Accordingly Richard told Anne 'I pray you be content and thinke not so, but trust in God ... he will defend you from her, and from the Divell himself also'. His concern was not just for the state of his wife's belief, but also for his own reputation. 'What will the people say', he reproached her, 'that I beeing a Preacher shoulde have my wife so weake in faith'?

Anne Harrison was not reassured, however. It was alright for Richard, with his scholarly notions, his cultural world beyond the village. She believed she was doomed. Tensions in the Harrisons' relationship widened. A few

Beaumont parish register, baptisms of Richard Harrison 27 June 1570, Mary 30 May 1572, Thomas 17 July 1575, James 21 April 1577; Little Oakley parish register records that Anne had also lost a child, Hugh Spencer, buried 10 November 1566; another Hugh, born after his father's death, survived (Beaumont parish register 14 November 1567). ERO D/DEl M76 1567–8, see also 1581; *ATAJR* F2v.

months later, Anne told Richard that if he did not do something to save her, she would involve her father in the matter. Desperately, she played on Richard's feelings and his faith: 'as ever there was love betweene us', she begged, '(as I hope there hath been for I have v [five] pretie children by you I thanke God) seeke som remedie for me against yonder wicked beast'. Despite continuing caution, Richard promised help; indeed 'he wold hang her the said Annis Herd if he could prove any such matter'. So one day he confronted Annis at Beaumont parsonage. Richard was picking plums from his tree in the parsonage garden when Annis asked him for some as a gift. Their relative status as rich clergyman and poor spinster is made clear, for she called him 'sir'. But instead of a charitable hand-out, she must have been shocked by his response. 'I am glad you are here you yield strumpet', Richard cried:

I do think you have bewitched my wife, and as truly as God doth live, if I can perceive she be troubled any more as she hath been, I will not leave a whole bone about thee, and besides I will seeke to have thee hanged.

He told Brian that he threatened Annis with his father-in-law's wrath too, and as he was descending the ladder from the plum tree Annis fled.[24] Both the Harrisons had now verbally attacked her, they thought her a thief, harlot and a witch: hurrying away from her powerful neighbours must have seemed the only option.

Just before Christmas, Anne Harrison was 'taken sore sick'. Whatever she had been afraid of before, she was now

---

[24] *ATAJR* F2v–F3v. I have been unable to discover who Anne Harrison's father was (yet).

in mortal danger. She died sometime between Christmas 1581 and late March 1582. Her distraught husband did not record her burial in his parish register. Anne died in fear, asserting to Richard that 'I am now utterly consumed with yonder wicked Creature ... Oh Annis Herd, Annis Herd shee hath consumed me'. Richard brought to Brian Darcy witnesses to these heart-rending last words. They were John Pollin and Johane Brett, and Richard explained that 'Mother' Poppe (probably Johane Poppe) had also heard the accusations. The witnesses were likely nursing Anne and minding the Harrison children. Other sources show us that Johane Brett's husband William had witnessed Hugh Spencer's will in the 1560s, that Johane and William's children had been baptised and buried by Richard throughout the 1560s and 1570s and that William was a churchwarden in the 1580s. The Harrison and Brett families had been friendly for years, and John Pollin was a churchwarden of Little Oakley.[25]

Deathbed words, spoken in trust to pious friends like these, were thought to be particularly potent in witchcraft

[25] Little Oakley parish register: marriage of William Brett and Johane Hayward 26 February 1559; baptisms of their children: Elizabeth 22 September 1560, William 9 January 1570. William was buried 6 June 1572, and daughters Marian, Johane and Margaret were buried 19 August 1567, 22 July 1584 and 1 August 1584. Johane was buried 2 November 1583 and William 10 August 1584; 'Mother Poppe' in the will of Agnes Johnson of Little Oakley, 19 January 1585, which also mentions the Anwicks and Penlys, Emmison, *Essex Wills ... Archdeaconry Courts 1583–1592* 185; see also will of Robert Hickman, same page; burial of Johane Poppe, widow 20 February 1586, Phillice Pollin, wife of John, 23 July 1580 and John Pollin, widower 24 February 1591; ERO D/ABW 34/59, D/ACV 1; LMA DL/B/A/002/ MS09537/004.

accusation. Johane Brett accordingly told Brian Darcy that 'mistres Harrison … cried out upon her [Annis] to the hour of her death'. In echoing this, both Richard Harrison and John Pollin were careful to protect the rector's reputation. Richard said that Anne had died 'in a perfect faith' and the churchwarden John stated that he had given his wife 'good counselling for her salvation'. Neither wanted it to be thought that the Rector of Beaumont was a bad pastor or his wife a weak Christian.[26] Richard had made a good case against Annis, and John Pollin and Johane Brett were effectively character witnesses for him as well as corroborating his claim about his wife's accusations. This was dangerous for Annis: godly officials from two parishes were now accusing her of a capital crime. Her own rector, Hugh Branham, did not speak out against her, however. That may have been significant both at the time and in the longer term, alongside her connections to other Herds and to the Ramsey churchwarden John Aldus. Later we shall see that vicars and churchwardens could make a difference by speaking for and helping those under attack in neighbouring parishes.

So Annis Herd was not friendless. And in addition to the connections already explored, when Richard accused her of witchcraft at Beaumont parsonage, *A True and just Recorde* tells us that she was with 'Anwicks wife': this was

---

[26] Anne Harrison's burial is not recorded. See also Cockburn, *Calendar: Essex: Elizabeth* record 1096: Pollin was accused of the homicide (not murder) of a sixteen-year-old boy during shooting at Little Oakley butts in 1579. The unrecorded verdict was presumably that this was an accident. See also will of Agnes Stowe of Beaumont, which Richard Harrison witnessed on 2 March 1582, Emmison, *Essex Wills … Commissary Court 1578–1588* 190.

Joane Anwick, formerly Weld and the cousin of Godlife Osborne. Robert and Joane Anwick were reasonably well off and their circumstances were improving: by the time of his death in 1593, Robert could afford to give forty shillings to the poor of Little Oakley, in two annual instalments of twenty shillings each. By then the Anwicks held the cottage Gardelers, with three of its four and a bit acres, which Richard Weld's daughter Dorothie Wood had surrendered to Robert as her brother-in-law, and which they shared with the Harrisons who held the final acre. They also had lands at Caselands as well as their 'mansion' with its fifteen acres, Paynetts. By the time of Robert's death, Joane had already died and Robert had remarried. The Anwicks then owned a share of a hoy, *Maygold*, and another ship, *Carnation*. Eleven years before, Robert's former wife Joane had not been afraid to be seen with Annis, although the Anwicks considered themselves comfortable, well-connected and pious. Robert witnessed the will of John Aldus in 1589, and left ten shillings in his own will to Samuel Moore, curate of Little Oakley, and another ten to the rector Hugh Branham to preach a sermon at his burial. John Heard witnessed Robert's will.[27]

So when we see Joane Anwick and Annis Herd walking together at Beaumont, on that day in plum season in 1581, we see incarnated in the two women a number of established interconnections between Annis and her community. Despite having a poor reputation and unreliable finances, Annis was not a total outcast even from the society of respectable wives. She spent time with

---

[27] *ATAJR* F3; ERO D/ACW 3/29; Little Oakley parish register; ERO D/DEl M76 1578, 1582, 1587.

the Anwicks, who had dealings not just with John Herd but also with John Aldus. We also see a Weld walking with Annis Herd, suggesting the warmer relationship that we saw lingering in the stories of Anne Weld West and Godlife Weld Osborne, before witchcraft suspicions intervened. Little Oakley was a small village where it was hard for people to avoid each other, but it also seems likely that Annis had some social capital – inherited from the Herd family and built up during her life. The churchwardens John Wade and Thomas Cartwrite had their suspicions, but the wider group who joined them in accusation were apparently friendly with Annis until the early 1580s. Even Richard and Anne Harrison were not recordedly antagonistic to Annis before 1581, whatever their opinions of her sexual conduct. Annis appears to have been taken aback when Richard not only refused her plums but began to harangue her in the street. Once set against Annis, it seems likely that the Harrisons disturbed the delicate balance of her credit in the community. Anne Harrison's tragic death must have seemed confirmation of vague fears that Annis was a witch, perhaps precipitating her formal accusation and trial.

There was also something else going on in Little Oakley and wider Essex that contextualises the case against Annis Herd. On 22 October 1580 at the archdeaconry court held in St Peter's Church in Colchester, multiple allegations of 'incontinent living', sexual misconduct, began to surface about several villagers in Little Oakley and Ramsey. John, Agnes and Reginald Marven were accused alongside Margaret Seaman and others of Ramsey and Dorothie Weld Wood of Little Oakley, Anne and Godlife's cousin. On 23 and 27 November came more allegations, and some of these concerned Richard Harrison, Joane Weld Anwick and Susan Herd as well as a man from Wix, although they were not explained in full. In August 1581 new accusations were made across a wider group including John Brightwell, Maria Bird, John Seaman and Audrey Cawston of Ramsey, Hugh Bayning and Agnes Cawston of Elmstead, and several others including Widow Herd and Thomas Aldust or Aldus of Dedham. Joane Anwick was mentioned again too. On 9 August at a court held in Little Bromley the Ramsey churchwardens John Aldus and Thomas Herd and vicar John White submitted a statement to the court counter-ing the accusations: 'there is and hath been never' any rumour of 'incontinent lyving' by the accused, they said, adding that 'they cannot tell' whether the present report is true. Evidently they did not make these accusations and were not disposed to believe them.[28] John Seaman then said that a 'lewd person' named Carter was Joane Anwick's accuser, and Joane brought two women to the court on 26 August as compurgators, people who would swear that she was of good character. The case against some of the other accused dragged on well into 1583.

These allegations of were unusual in their scope: around thirty people were drawn in, including leading citizens. Sexual sin was on the minds of easterly Essex

---

[28] In 1583 John White was himself accused of living a 'scandalous life', troubling his neighbours by law, knowing no doctrine and having a 'low voice' which, together with the howl of the wind through a crack in the chancel wall, meant that his parishioners could not hear him – godly complaints? (D/ACA 10–11, D/AZ 1/7). For wider discussion, suggesting that elsewhere such offences were being investigated *less* often, see Higgs, Godliness and Governance 258–63.

villages in 1581–1583, and Annis Herd may have become an epitome of the problem of unchastity in the eyes of Beaumont's rector and his wife. But although sex scandal flooded the church court, it's notable that nothing substantial was proven: the Elmstead couple did confess, Audrey Cawston was shown not to have received Easter communion and so on, but it hardly amounted to proof that the people of Ramsey, Little Oakley and beyond were insatiable swingers. Yet many villagers had been publicly humiliated, with unsavoury stories circulating for months. Snooping watchmen alleged that unmarried men and women had been alone together with candles out, knocks had not been answered although there were people at home, and visitors had been spotted scurrying from back doors. Churchmen had been forced to speak out to defend their flock. Some people refused to cooperate with the court, some cases were dismissed as baseless. The fact that the Alduses, Herds, Marvens, Dorothie Weld Wood, Joane Weld Anwick and others had been investigated during some kind of moral panic must have cast into relief the witchcraft accusations made against one of their wider set, Annis Herd. Annis was a proven incontinent liver: perhaps some people thought that merited further action against her as a witch, thief and undesirable neighbour – concepts bound up in the notion of 'honesty'. But conversely if many of those accused of incontinent living were not guilty, was Annis really a witch?

It must also have been noticed that Richard Harrison was making increasingly frequent appearances in the church court presentments at this time. As well as inspecific accusations connected to the sex scandal, the churchwardens at Beaumont had several times reported him for the common offence of failing to repair the chancel, and by April 1582 the church at Beaumont was said to be in severe decay. This was not uncommon in the region, but it had not been true in the 1570s and something had clearly changed at Beaumont. Meanwhile at Little Oakley, the parsonage that he had had in farm, was described as 'likely to fall' and 'ruinous' when taken over by the vicar Hugh Branham in 1583.[29] As we shall see in Chapter 6, this was not Richard's last brush with ecclesiastical law and eventually he would end up in the criminal courts too. If Richard was thought not to be an exemplary rector or a reliable witness, the whole witchcraft case against Annis might fall apart. There were therefore many factors for accusers to consider in bringing forward stories about Annis to Brian Darcy when he arrived in Little Oakley. There was a complex series of family inter-relationships to negotiate and surely a wider sense of uncertainty about what was truth and what was innuendo. Some people, especially the Moze and Little Oakley churchwardens and Richard Harrison, look to have been agitating for moral reform, while others sought to rebut accusations made against them personally – and this second group also includes Richard. People under such pressure often lash out, but accused women like Joane Anwick might have felt more sympathy for Annis

---

[29] ERO D/ACA 10 and Emmison, *Elizabethan Life: Morals* 274. On honesty see Alexandra Shepard, 'Honesty, Worth and Gender in Early Modern England 1560–1640' in Henry French and Jonathan Barry, eds., *Identity and Agency in England 1500–1800* (Basingstoke: Palgrave Macmillan, 2004) 87–105.

Herd than before if they thought that they too might be targeted by vicious gossip.

Confusedly, Little Oakley teetered towards getting rid of its 'harlot' and 'witch' for good, and Brian Darcy did commit Annis for trial on 17 March 1582. But she was the only person accused in the village and despite Richard Harrison's violent hatred of her, most of the stories about her activities alleged small scale offences. The dynamic of the witch hunt was changing from one community to another, and with Annis Herd at Little Oakley and Joan Robinson at Walton le Soken as its last two accused some of the momentum seems to have ebbed from it. The clarity and focus of Brian's earlier interrogations, with their clever questioning tricks and excited revelations of key admissions were replaced by meandering accusations and refractory suspects. Was Brian losing interest? Becoming bogged down in detail or tired during his travels? Had those questioned about witchcraft in the villages furthest east of St Osyth learned from the experience of Ursley Kempe and Ales Manfielde that confession did not in fact lead to release? Were accusers having second thoughts about turning in their neighbours? Whatever was going on, the witch hunt was over by the end of 25 March. To see how each of the accusations was framed and received by the Assize court, we need to move on to Chelmsford to attend the trial of the St Osyth witches.

6

An Untrue and Unjust Record

~

Once the witchcraft suspects from St Osyth, Little Clacton, Thorpe and Walton le Soken and Little Oakley had been dragged into the structures of Elizabethan justice, they entered a world of bureaucracy and long delays. Their freedom was taken from them and they were kept in filthy, cramped conditions, half-starved and subject to all manner of disease and abuse. Decisions that literally meant life or death for them were taken in minutes by powerful strangers. As we've seen, when they were being questioned by Brian Darcy, the suspects' words were noted down as a formal document, an examination, and this document preceded them in their journey through the system. In the case of the examinations of this group, more than normal attention was initially paid to recording the process of questioning, suggesting that from 19 February onwards, and certainly by the time of Ursley Kempe's first examination on 20 February, Brian was looking to stage something of a show trial. He may have taken especial care to record his questioning because he wanted other magistrates and the Assize judges themselves to reflect on how the English justice system as a whole should deal with witches. After the trial, he and his collaborator(s) planned the publication of a long pamphlet – a 'Recorde' as they would call it – that would display the problem of witchcraft to a wider readership and impart to others the knowledge gained during the pre-trial and trial processes.

It appears that Brian shaped the pamphlet, *A True and just Recorde*, himself. At times he shows his hand with the word 'I' and throughout the text he and whoever was helping him carefully signposted key moments in the interrogations, from which the Assize trial participants and other readers might draw conclusions. But in organising the documents for trial and then publication, Brian and his clerks and collaborators did a rather unsatisfactory editorial job – albeit with complex material. *A True and just Recorde* is structured along chronological lines but also, cutting across this, it attempts to highlight questioning strategies and point to the outcomes of the Assize trial of the witches. A fascinating numeric table of data was drawn up as an appendix, although it is also flawed, perhaps confused during printing. As we saw in previous chapters when reading the evidence of child witnesses and their parents, some informations and examinations have been reassigned more convenient dates, so it would seem that witches were not being framed by leading questions asked of their impressionable children. But this re-dating is unconvincing because the adult suspects echo phrases used only by the children. Some documents are also in a random order: once the reader has learned about Ursley Kempe and the other St Osyth village witches, they move on to the suspects at Thorpe, but then back to Ursley, then on to Little Clacton, then to Ursley again, then back to Thorpe – and so on. Some documents are missing too and some reported facts are incorrect.

However, despite the flaws of *A True and just Recorde*, it is a uniquely valuable and immersive account of a witch trial. Through its pages, we can get as close as we ever will to the people of this sixteenth century witch hunt:

the suspects, their accusers and the team that drew up their trial papers and the published account itself. We can see that in creating *A True and just Recorde* this team was thinking through how to present the witch hunting process as clearly as they could, village by village, and thinking too about it how would look to an impartial observer. Clarity is not the same as transparency, as we've seen. But observing the attempts to present the material engagingly and informatively is important. Another key part of the pamphlet is its preface, which sets up the whole experience of reading the work. *A True and just Recorde*'s preface has a case to make about better legal remedies for combatting witchcraft and a clearer theological underpinning for these remedies and it claims that the factual details that follow support that case. Busy with the continuing witch hunt, Brian Darcy seems to have got someone else to write it and this person, almost certainly male, signed himself with the initials W.W. One of the mysteries that has always surrounded *A True and just Recorde* is the identity of 'W.W.' The best fit, identified during my searches of the remaining archives of the Darcy estates, is a man named William Whetcrofte the younger.

If he was the prefacer, young William continued a family association with the Darcys from previous generations. His father was also named William Whetcrofte and William senior began the family's documented work with Brian Darcy when he represented him in court at Easter 1578. Brian had been in trouble at the Quarter Sessions since the mid-1570s. On 11 January 1576, the Quarter Sessions jury for Chelmsford and Tendring presented to the court a complaint that a bridge near Machyn's Mill was in a ruinous state. They believed that Brian Darcy ought to repair it, in his capacity as lord of the manor of Bentons in Witham, which as we have seen he had inherited from his father in 1559. Presentations of this kind were common at the Quarter Sessions, with those complained against including some of the wealthiest people in the county. Being a Justice of the Peace did not place Brian above the law, at least in principle. He was expected to fulfil the obligations traditionally associated with his landholdings. However, Brian thought otherwise and determined to exempt himself from this community duty. He would do that by retaining a lawyer, William Whetcrofte the elder.

Initially Brian appeared in court himself to contest the claim, at the Quarter Sessions held at Chelmsford on 3 May 1576. He was not able to halt the case, however, and at the Midsummer session a writ was issued, summoning twelve men to try him and determine whether he did have a legal obligation to make the repairs or not. No further progress is recorded, but at the next court, on 1 October 1576, a further presentment repeated the assertion that Brian should repair the bridge. The matter was becoming troublesome.[1] Brian was clearly in an assertive mood about his landholdings at the time, for at the Easter Session of 1578 he and his local agents accused two Maldon fishermen, John and Richard Frye, of forcibly entering onto his

---

[1] J. J. Muskett, 'Suffolk Wills from the Prerogative Court of Canterbury. Whetcrofte of Suffolk' (n.d.) at http://suffolkinstitute.pdfsrv .co.uk/customers/Suffolk%20Institute/2014/01/10/Volume%20 VI%20Part%202%20(1886)_Wills%20Prerogatice%20Ct%20 of%20Canterbury%20Whetcroft%20of%20Suffolk%20J%20J%20 Muskett_94%20to%20104.pdf

104. Bentons is also known as Benningtons in these records, see earlier and ERO Q/SR 56/57, 57/81, 58/5, 59/64.

land at a fish trap called Hellapolle Ware, a flood weir, and there catching fish worth ten shillings. At the same court, his critics advanced their attack, indicting him for not repairing the bridge and a writ was issued distraining him for six shillings and eightpence. Brian, however, had a sharp answer. He employed William Whetcrofte as his attorney and at this court William appeared for him to plead that the indictment brought forward against Brian was insufficient in law and should be rejected.

William was a forceful lawyer. His reputation generally was that of a clever and not wholly fair man, as a case of 1573 shows. In January of that year, William and his wife Alice were involved in a dispute about a tenancy of customary lands that they held of the manor of Witnesham in Suffolk. Their accusers were the Norman family of Witnesham and their descendant Peter Lyvell. Peter alleged that the lands held by the Whetcroftes should be his. His grandfather John Norman had held the lands along with his son and daughter Richard and Elizabeth until his death in about 1520, Peter said. The lands then descended to Richard and after his death should have come to Elizabeth, mother of the complainant Peter. However, at the manorial court held immediately after Richard's death in 1559, Witnesham's rector John More had stated that Richard had not willed his lands to his sister. Instead, he had made a new will which gave the lands to the church, to sell and use the proceeds for the benefit of his soul. The rector then arranged for the lands to be sold to William and Alice Whetcrofte, and he used the proceeds of the sale for poor relief, to repair bridges in the town and 'other goddlie uses'.

Peter Lyvell had been outraged ever since and in 1573 he at last took action. Possibly his mother Alice had died and he felt able to proceed with his festering grievance. The depth of his feeling against William Whetcrofte shows us how such lawyers were disliked. Peter made a direct attack on William's character, alleging that he had 'practised in the courte of the said mannor by sinister and undewe meanes to obscure and darken the true and lawfull title of the said compleynant to his utter undoing'. While Peter was 'very poore', William Whetcrofte was a man 'of welth and learned in the lawes of this Realme ... and greatlie friended with the steward and homage of the said Courte'. The loss of Peter's mother's land was thus part of a conspiracy by rich, wily men to defraud a poor, simple woman and her son – or so he said. Although the homage jury had found the will was a true one and rejected Peter's claim to the land, Peter argued that it must have been a forgery, that Richard would never have left his sister 'destitute of all lyvinge' and given her inheritance to the rector. He also thought that William and Alice knew their possession of the land was fraudulent. They had paid the steward to turn a blind eye, he concluded, and the rector was in on the scam too: an alliance of new money and new religion had triumphed over an older natural justice.[2]

Likely this accusation was false. The steward, rector, the Whetcroftes, representatives of the manorial jury and

[2] ERO Q/SR 61/17, 66/22, 66/81, 66/88; TNA C78/52 no.5 at Anglo American Legal Tradition at the O'Quinn Law Library, University of Houston Law Center (2015) at http://aalt.law.uh.edu/AALT7/C78/C78no52/IMG_0018.htm, https://waalt.uh.edu/index.php/C78_1573 (second case on list).

other Witnesham tenantry all refuted it: they explained that Richard was a regular juror, a pious man who knew what he was doing, and they defended their own honesty. Peter Lyvell accordingly lost his case. But unease remains. The story chimes unpleasantly with Brian Darcy's refusal to pay for the upkeep of a community asset, the bridge at Machyns Mill, and his purposeful attack on vulnerable women and men as witches, lying to them, using their children against them. No doubt he and his attorneys and agents, men like the two William Whetcroftes – felt themselves to be in the right in such actions. Legally, they were: they had the right to do as they did. But their right was in many ways so very clearly wrong. The rising men of the Elizabethan era like the Darcys and Whetcroftes were assertive and self-righteous, but many people saw them as oppressors of the poor, posh insiders reaping the benefits of sharp practice and cronyism. And they got away with it. In 1580, Brian again refused to pay for the repair of a bridge, this time the Abbot's Bridge at Great Waltham, and in 1581 he was presented again for failing to repair the Machyn's Mill bridge. By then, William Whetcrofte the elder had died, with his will being proved on 3 May 1581.[3]

Our William Whetcrofte, putative prefacer, succeeded his father William Whetcrofte in some of his functions in Brian Darcy's world. William senior was primarily Town Clerk of Ipswich. He managed some of the administrative affairs of the city and represented its corporation in

[3] ERO Q/SR74/62 and 63, 77/43; Suffolk Record Office C/2/10/1/25, David Allen, ed., *Ipswich Borough Archives 1255–1835* (Woodbridge: Boydell Press, Suffolk Records Society and the British Library, 2000) 161–2.

litigation locally and in London courts. Beyond this role, he practiced law in his own right. But he had higher ambitions for his four sons. William senior and Alice had at least eight children who lived into adulthood: Richard, Barbara, Henry, Anne, Katherine, Alice and George as well as William junior. The family lived in a townhouse in the parish of St Mary-at-the-Quay and owned the Bull Inn in Ipswich, as well as holding various other properties there and at Witnesham and Wherstead, all in Suffolk. William junior probably went to Ipswich School, whose most distinguished old boy was Thomas Wolsey, and then undertook legal and religious training, although I have as yet found no record of this. His father was educated at both Oxford and Cambridge Universities at the expense of Katherine Brandon, Lady Willoughby de Eresby, and his elder brothers went to Cambridge, so he may have followed them.

The Whetcrofte boys went into legal and ecclesiastical professions: William and Alice's eldest son Richard was Rector of Witnesham in Suffolk from 1577, and their second son Henry was a Doctor of Law in the 1590s and a Master in Chancery by 1607. William was the third of the brothers and on 13 December 1591 he succeeded Richard as Witnesham's rector, upon the presentation of Henry. He signs himself 'clerk and parson' in the Witnesham parish register in 1592. Before that time he is referred to simply as a 'clerk', a term that was used for a range of intersecting roles: cleric, legal official, scribe.[4]

---

[4] Muskett 104; J. Venn and J. A. Venn, *Alumni Cantabrigiensis* (Cambridge: Cambridge University Press, 1922–1954) vol. 4 379. Transcript of Witnesham parish register CUL MS Add 08262/17 11–13 see also burial of Alice in the chancel 10 March 1590, MS Add 08262/18 and William's successor, presumably after his death,

Following in his father's footsteps as Brian Darcy's attorney, William junior was in St Osyth in 1582 and 1583, where he acted in a clerkly role with Brian. Brian and William witnessed the will of Edmund Beamond of St Osyth together on 1 September 1582. Edmund was probably part of Brian's extensive household and administrative staff at St Clere's Hall, since he called Brian his 'master', owed him 'debts' and named him overseer and supervisor of his will, giving Brian a black colt for his pains in that role. Edmund also named Brian's brother Thomas Darcy and beneficiaries in Tolleshunt Darcy and Tollesbury, other parts of the Darcy heartland, suggesting a strong connection with this branch of the family, one that William Whetcrofte likely shared. William also wrote the will of the witches' accuser William Hayward of Frowick on 20 February 1583.[5] Perhaps William

in 1601 MS Add 08262/17 15; for other records relating to William Whetcrofte senior (II), his father William Whetcrofte I (MP and also Ipswich Town Clerk) and Henry Whetcrofte (brother of William Whetcrofte III) see also TNA C3/21/80, C3/114/30, C3/110/42, C3/197/38, C3/195/25, C3/418/143 and 144, C3/478/103, C4/160/197, C5/577/38, C21/F10/3, C142/656/32SC2/204/23, SC2/204/24, STAC 5/G21/2, C2/Jas I/G12/57; Suffolk Record Office v5/14/1/1, C/2/10/1/10, C/3/8/6/28, C/3/10/2/5/1/2, C/3/10/2/11/1 HD36/A/47 and HD 36/A/20; *The House of Commons, 1509–1558*, 3 vols., ed. S. T. Bindoff (London: Secker & Warburg for History of Parliament Trust, 1982), iii, 3: 601. Barbara Whetcrofte married Thomas Sherman of Yaxley (see also Thomas Townsend Sherman, *Sherman Genealogy* (New York: Tobias A Wright, 1920). I have not been able to consult all of these records because of the closures of TNA and Suffolk Record Office, Ipswich branch during the COVID pandemic and SRO's relocation to The Hold; some from TNA and CUL were kindly provided digitally.

5 Emmison, *Essex Wills … Commissary Court 1578–1588* 20 and will of William Hayward (see later) 100.

FIGURE 6.1 Horses by a dead tree at St Osyth. (Source: Adrian Muttitt / Alamy Stock Photo.)
Note: A black and white version of this figure will appear in some formats. For the colour version, please refer to the plate section.

Hayward rode down the muddy track from Frowick to St Clere's Hall on his brown horse Bucke (Figure 6.1), to make his will, or perhaps he was too sick to take the journey and instead William Whetcrofte rode in the other direction, to sit by William Hayward's bedside and carefully note down his bequests. This personal interaction with Brian Darcy, Edmund Beamond and William Hayward is William Whetcrofte's closest proven association with the witch hunt of 1582.

William is therefore quite likely to have worked with Brian Darcy on preparing for publication the paperwork for the Assize trial of the St Osyth witches and it is also likely that he wrote the preface to the documentary part of the pamphlet about their activities. There are few other candidates for this authorship too, however. Barbara Rosen suggested in 1969 that another Darcy connection, William Lowth, may have been W.W. but of course his initials are not right and it has always seemed a stretch to imagine that W.W. might stand for 'well wisher' or a similar pseudonym. Jonathan Durrant plausibly suggests William Webbe, a connection of Brian's brother-in-law Edward Sulyard. But in addition to having the right initials, our man William Whetcrofte has a proven clerical association with Brian Darcy specifically, and also with William Hayward. Finally, his known destination in the clergy and his wider familial and legal connections both make him a likely author of a preface which argues for a change in the law to recognise witchcraft's peculiar status as a crime against God.[6]

W.W. began his preface to *A True and just Recorde* by dedicating the book to Thomas, Lord Darcy. This was in both his own interests and Brian's: both could benefit from being brought to the noble lord's attention in an excellent light. In the preface William (as I shall now call him) likely wanted to demonstrate his own scholarly piety and tie it to Brian's conduct of the pre-trial examinations. He therefore began with a free translation of a passage from Jean Bodin's *De la Daemonomanie des Sorciers*. It was Jean Bodin, remember, whose visit to the Queen in 1581 had been used by Brian Darcy to frighten Elizabeth Bennett into confession, just weeks before William wrote

---

[6] In her edition of *A True and just Recorde* (Rosen, 106 note 4); Durrant, 'A Witch-hunting Magistrate?' 6, 25. We can see Brian working with Edward Sulyard in ERO Q/SR 79/57 in the taking of a recognizance for an alehouse keeper in Messing on 20 November 1581.

his preface. One mention of Bodin may be regarded as incidental: two looks like strategy.

If there hath bin at any time (Right Honorable) any meanes used, to appease the wrath of God, to obtaine his blessing, to terrifie secreete offenders by open transgressors punishments, to withdraw honest natures from the corruption of evil company, to diminish the great multitude of wicked people, to increase the small number of virtuous persons, and to reforme all the detestable abuses, which the perverse witte and will of man doth dayly devise, this doubtlesse is no lesse necessarye then the best, that Sorcerers, Wizzards, or rather Dizzardes, Witches, Wisewomen (for so they will be named), are rygorously punished. Rygorously sayd I? Why it is too milde and gentle a tearme for such a mercilesse generation: I should rather have sayd most cruelly executed; for that no punishment can be thought upon, be it never so high a degree of torment, which may be deemed sufficient for such a divelish and damnable practise. And why? Because al the imaginations, al the consultations, al the conference, al the experimentes, finally the attemptes, proceedinges and conclusions of Sorcerers, Witches, and the rest of that hellish liverie, are meere blasphemers against the person of the most high God …

William's translation is very close to the original:

Or s'il y eut oncques moyen d'appaiser l'ire de Dieu, d'obtenir sa benediction, d'estonner les uns par le punition des autres, de conserver les uns de l'infection des autres, de diminuer le nombre des meschans, d'asseurer la vie des bons, & de punir les meschancetez les plus detestables que l'esprit humain peut imaginer, c'est de chastier a toute rigeur les Sorciers: combien que le mot de Rigeur est mal pris, attendu que il n'y a peine si cruelle qui peust suffire à punir les meschancetez des Sorciers, d'autant que toutes leurs meschancetez, blasphemes, & tous leurs desseings se dressent contre la Majesté de Dieu, pour le despiter & offenser par mille moyens.[7]

However, despite adhering to the French text, William introduced some differences into his translation, some of them reflecting the particular circumstances that he and Brian had found in St Osyth and its surrounding villages.

First of all, he added to the list of magical practitioners whom he wished to be targeted by the English courts for rigorous punishment. Not only sorcerers are mentioned, the English word closest to 'sorciers', but also 'wizards' (with a joke about the word's similarity to 'dizzardes' or fools), 'witches' and 'wisewomen'. This extension to include cunning bodies is in keeping with what contemporary English clergy and demonologists, like the Maldon preacher George Gifford, were saying about 'wisewomen': that despite their pretensions to do good, they were as demonic in their inspiration as maleficent witches. The mention of 'wisewomen' points the reader back to the cunning activities of Ursley Kempe, Mother Barnes and several of the accused, making it clear that cunning folk were seen to be a key feature of the St Osyth witch hunt. The inclusion of the term 'wizards' by William – usually accepted to mean male witches – further gestures toward Henry Selles, the only male suspect that Brian had sent to the Assizes that March. These small but significant alterations show how William modified Jean Bodin's text in ways that include, legitimise and highlight aspects of Brian's practice.

---

[7] *ATAJR* A3–A3v; Bodin, 216v–217r.

William was keen for magistrates like Brian to catch witches and punish them. But what always shocks me about his preface is that he also wanted to kill them cruelly and he was not shy in saying so. He wanted Ursley, Ales, Elizabeth, Cisley, Margaret, Henry, Annis and the others 'most cruelly executed', subjected to 'torment' as they died. He was convinced that they were not just guilty of demonic inspiration and the feeding of a few familiar spirits but that:

they worshippe Sathan, unto whome they have sworne allegiaunce … nay … they are guiltie of apparaunte apostasie, which is more heinous (considering the circumstances of their ordinarie actions), then any trespasse against the seconde table, which ouglye sinnes of blasphemie, and grosse, or rather divelish idolatrie concurring in no malefactor so roundly, as in sorcerers, witches, Inchanters and in whom they meete a million of enormities more; as it were in a centre; the magistrates of forren landes, noted so precisely, that weighing the qualitie of the cryme, they kepte a due analogie and proportion of punishment, burning them with fire, whome the common lawe of Englande (with more measure of mercie then is to be wished) strangleth with a rope.[8]

So William wanted the St Osyth witches burned to death. He wanted the gallows at Chelmsford to be replaced with a roaring fire in which screaming people would be burned. If he and Brian were able to effect such an ambitious legal reform, how pious and influential they would be seen to be. And what a benefit for the people of England they would have achieved!

[8] *A True and just Recorde* A3v.

What was Brian's role in all this? It's plausible that he commissioned or at least assented to William's text: it was conventional to have a preface in a news pamphlet and while hack writers could provide them, Brian would not wish his aims to be misrepresented in the account of his activities. Perhaps he contributed to, or edited, it. But William's own pious future as Rector of Witnesham is also suggested by this particular passage, as well as his understanding of the law. The second table is the commandment against worshipping other gods, so that apostacy and idolatry are relevant terms for William to use against the witches as well as blasphemy. And it is interesting how little this understanding of witchcraft as a heretical crime influenced Brian's questioning of the suspects. In some ways, then, William's preface fits awkwardly with the content of *A True and just Recorde* perhaps marking his own agency in composing it. This mismatch also suggests the evolving nature of English demonological theory. In France and some neighbouring territories, it was thought that witches met in groups for ritualistic sabbaths, abusing religious artefacts, consuming human flesh and so on. Sixteenth-century English witches were not usually suspected of this, partly because they did not live in a Catholic polity: religious rituals and artefacts were not similarly sacred and notions of communion, the consumption of the body of Christ, were metaphorical not actual. What witches might be suspected of inverting or parodying was thus dissimilar and in his questioning Brian had been completely silent about these lurid and recognisably unEnglish aspects of Jean Bodin's demonology.

As we saw in Chapters 1 and 2, Brian did adopt some of the tactics suggested in *De la demonomanie des sorciers*:

specifically, lying to suspects and questioning their children. He thus experimented with practical witch hunting tools offered to him by Jean Bodin.[9] But much of what the preface says is not further explored in *A True and just Recorde*'s main text and this brought trouble to Brian which he may or may not have deserved. The preface's notions of witches as heretics were unfamiliar to most English readers and religiously radical: therefore, they were suspect. The bruising experience with heresy prosecutions during the Reformation – which alternated between killing Catholics and killing Protestants – did not dispose most people towards reopening religious controversies. And, in this context, by failing to make their preface and main text support one another to the fullest extent, William and Brian had made a poor case for any reform. Their pamphlet was probably prepared in haste because it was entered in the Stationers' Register and thus licensed for printing on 6 April, just a week after the trial. It had journeyed from Chelmsford to London in that time, leaving little space for literary crafting. And its scrambled component parts did not stack up a compelling argument. Accordingly, English witchcraft law did not take the route that *A True and just Recorde* proposed. The relatively recent 1563 Witchcraft Act had not conceived of the crime in this way and was not modified on the basis of a single patchwork pamphlet. Instead William and Brian's unsuccessful attempt to alter public

---

[9] See Marion Gibson, 'French Demonology in an English Village: The St. Osyth Experiment of 1582' in Rita Voltmer, Julian Goodare and Liv Helene Willumsen, eds., *Demonology and Witch-hunting in Early Modern Europe* (London: Routledge, 2020) 107–26.

understanding of witchcraft was attacked in 1584 in a widely read and abusive rant.

This attack was scattered throughout *The Discoverie of Witchcraft*, an idiosyncratic demonology by the Kentishman Reginald Scot. His book set out to prove that conventional demonologists had misunderstood the nature of spirits and thus that alleged witches were not guilty of the crimes of which they were accused. He particularly hated (not too strong a word) Jean Bodin as a European Catholic demonologist whom, he felt, was malevolently whipping up feeling against witches. Reginald deeply pitied those dragged into courts across Europe and accused of witchcraft crimes which he thought they could not have committed. Brian Darcy thus came to his notice through *A True and just Recorde* as a similar-looking demonological troublemaker. Reginald may have known of Brian's Catholic connections but, even if he did not, he certainly noticed his adoption of some French demonological ideas and the pamphlet's documentation of a widening witch hunt. In many ways, Brian was Reginald's perfect target: an English magistrate whom Reginald thought ought to know better than to import 'Popish' ideas from *Demonomanie*, a move which should be stopped.

Brian's use of child witnesses, 'of the age of 4. 5. 6. 7. 8. or 9. Yeares' was Reginald's first point of criticism, drawn as it was from *Demonomanie*'s advice on procedure. Reginald rightly loathed the idea that 'the little children of witches, which will not confesse, must be attached; who (if they be craftilie handled saith Bodin) will confesse against their owne mothers'. Then he also objected to the wider dishonesty of Brian's questioning technique:

let anie man with good consideration peruse that booke published by W.W. and it shall suffice to satisfie him in all that may
be required touching the vanities of the witches examinations,
confessions, and executions ... note how and what the witches
confesse, and see of what weight and importance the causes
are; whether their confessions be not woone through hope of
favour, and extorted by flatterie or threats, without proofe.

'There may alwaies be promised impunitie and favour
to witches, that confesse and detect others' Reginald
observed, since 'Bodin saith, that bicause this [witchcraft]
is an extraordinarie matter; there must heerin be extraordinarie dealing: and all maner of waies are to be used,
direct and indirect'. His use of the word 'favour' here
explicitly recalls Brian's phrases: 'she should have favour'
and 'as thou wilt have favour'.[10]

Reginald followed up his observations of Brian's dishonesty with his trademark biting humour: he pointed
out that St Osyth was a small village, and that given the
number of people arrested in 1582 he doubted there were
any witches left in it. But 'if anie be yet behind, I doubt
not, but Brian Darcie will find them out'.[11] Unfortunately
he was probably correct in his belief that Brian would continue his hunt although with apparently reduced vigour.
St Osyth continued to send suspects to court: in 1583 Anne
Swallowe and Margerie Barnes, in 1584 Elizabeth Lumley
and Alice Boulton, all to the Assizes, and also a woman
known only as Cook's wife to the Consistory Court of the
Bishop of London (she died before she could be tried).

[10] Montague Summers, ed., *The Discoverie of Witchcraft* (1930; New York:
Dover, 1972) 10, 11–12, 13.
[11] Brinsley Nicholson, ed., *The Discoverie of Witchcraft* (London, 1886)
455.

It would be surprising if Brian were not the examining magistrate in the Assize cases. And Reginald Scot attacked William Whetcrofte too for the vicious reform of the law on witchcraft that he proposed in his preface:

If you read a foolish pamphlet dedicated to the lord Darcy by W.W. 1582, you shall see that he affirmeth, that all those tortures are farre too light, and their rigor too mild; and in that respect he impudentlie exclameth against our magistrates, who suffer them [witches] but to be hanged.[12]

A foolish pamphlet, unjust and untrue: that was how Reginald Scot saw *A True and just Recorde* and for all its joyous utility to the historian, it is hard to disagree. Indeed, *The Discoverie of Witches'* first editor Brinsley Nicholson suggested that Reginald wrote his book precisely to discredit Brian Darcy and W.W.: for him, Brian's 'pie-crust promises' of favour 'aroused ... compassion and indignation, and made both find vent in printed words'. If *The Discoverie of Witches* was written due to the folly of Brian Darcy and William Whetcrofte, then we owe them a little gratitude. The *Discoverie* put into the public domain the argument that witchcraft suspects should not be lied to and bullied, and should not subsequently face execution for things that they did not do.

This was, however, the situation for the witchcraft suspects committed for trial at the Chelmsford Assizes in

---

[12] The records of Elizabeth Lumley, Alice Boulton and Cook's wife are in LMA DL/C/0301 which I wasn't able to consult because of pandemic restrictions on using microfilm, although I did check the available originals LMA DL/C/0212 and 0629; Alan Macfarlane, *Witchcraft in Tudor and Stuart England* (1970; Prospect Heights, IL: Waveland Press, 1991) 294; Summers, ed., *The Discoverie of Witchcraft* 10, 11, 15–16, 39, 40.

spring 1582. The prisoners were transported from village lock-ups to Colchester Castle, where they were shoved into the dungeons that formed the prison. Then they were prodded out blinking into the chilly daylight and transported to the gaol of the town where the next Assizes would be held. In this case it was Chelmsford, and the date would be 29 March. At the same time as the suspects were making their wretched journey towards Chelmsford, the two judges for this year's spring Assizes on the Home Circuit, John Southcote and Thomas Gawdy, were riding towards their comfortable accommodation in the town's inns. They were preparing to sit in judgement on the suspects assembled: one judge would hear criminal cases, the other civil. The criminal court role would of course include handing down death sentences. Judges were experienced in capital crimes. In the course of their work, they could expect to encounter suspected murderers, thieves, political and religious dissidents and even outright traitors, and they would take thus responsibility for hundreds of deaths by execution. Most felons were hanged – as convicted witches were – but some were disembowelled, burnt or boiled alive. Judges needed tough minds and strong stomachs.

Their work on Assize circuits and other governmental business meant that as well as being hardened law enforcers the judges were learned, powerful and widely experienced men. They presided at state trials and were Members of Parliament, sitting in the House of Lords with the bishops and archbishops. They practised in the diverse legal systems of the London courts, hobnobbed with Privy Councillors and advisors to royalty. They held large country estates. John Southcote was a Devon man who had made a career in the law since the 1530s and now moved between homes in London and Witham, where at Petworths and Witham Place he was a neighbour of Brian Darcy. Thomas Gawdy was from Norfolk, where he lived at Redenhall.[13] In both their London lives and on their travels judges could build networks that allowed them to access new and niche knowledges. They had the disposable income to allow them to read both ephemera, such as witchcraft news pamphlets, and new scholarship, such as demonology and the theology that underpinned it. This gave them at least the opportunity to acquire a fair understanding of witchcraft as a spiritual crime associated with heresy, as well as a practical matter of life and death. They were ideal readers for *A True and just Recorde* as well as being about to judge the people whose true-crime stories it told.

Most of the personnel in Assize courts also had some experience of magical matters. Although much of the work of Justices of the Peace revolved around mundane issues – who was responsible for road mending, whether a servant should or should not have left their employer, or who was the father of an illegitimate child – they were also used to encountering stories of magic. They dealt directly with witchcraft at their county's Quarter Sessions from time to time. A witchcraft accusation could go before a grand jury at the Quarter Sessions if the holding of an Assize court

[13] J. H. Baker, 'John Southcote' *ODNB* (2008): www.oxforddnb .com/view/10.1093/ref:odnb/9780198614128.001.0001/ odnb-9780198614128-e-26049?rskey=ekoQvU&result=1; David Ibbetson, 'Sir Thomas Gawdy' *ODNB* (2008): www .oxforddnb.com/view/10.1093/ref:odnb/9780198614128.001.0001/ odnb-9780198614128-e-10469?rskey=aN7gF6&result=1

was not imminent. The jurors would then rule on the basis of the evidence presented to them whether or not an Assize trial should proceed in due course. In these cases, Justices and jurors would have a close view of the case's content.[14] Justices might also encounter magical practitioners in other forms, such as mystics and fortune tellers. In some cases these would be vagrants, like the band of travellers ('counterfett egypcyans' as the record describes them) who moved through Essex at Michaelmas 1566. The Justices of the Peace would unsympathetically order such people to be whipped and branded, both because they were homeless and likely to be a burden to local taxpayers, but also because they were seen as faking exotic heritage and magical ability.

The notion of counterfeiting a magical identity was important in local justice. If magic was not to be labelled witchcraft, then it might be labelled fraud. In the Essex Quarter Sessions records for Midsummer 1578, for example, Justices heard about Miles Blumfield or Blomefylde. Miles was no poor cunning body: he was a churchwarden, a collector of books and manuscripts on subjects as diverse as alchemy and religious drama. From around 1566 Miles was one of the chief citizens of Chelmsford, where he lived next to the churchyard on the north side. Here he practiced magic to find stolen goods. His accusers had recently consulted him but had found his advice expensive. Sybil Browne, a maidservant, said that linen had been stolen out of her employer Gabriel Poyntz's garden and she had asked a friend, Thomas Lynforde, to consult someone to see if it could be located. So the next

---

[14] E.g. Cockburn, *Calendar: Essex: Elizabeth* record 1063.

time Thomas went to Chelmsford, he went to Miles's house. After some appetite-whetting delay Miles agreed to see him. He brought out a 'looking glass', about seven or eight inches square, and hung it up on a nail over the bench in his hall. He asked Thomas to look into it and, unsurprisingly, Thomas saw a man's face.

Miles asked Thomas if he knew the face. The answer to this was not the obvious one, and the question was a classic opener during scrying activities. Looking glasses were often cloudy and dark, and they were unfamiliar to most ordinary people. They never saw their own faces and did not know what to expect from a mirror. Accordingly, Thomas hedged: it was, he said, 'like unto' Humphrey Barnes of North Ockenden, the village where Gabriel Poyntz' house stood. Miles also hedged. He 'woulde not', he said, 'saye that [Barnes] had yt' (referring to the stolen linen) 'nor accuse him, but as far as he could judge he had yt'. After that, he made Thomas swear that he would not tell anyone about the consultation, and extracted eightpence as his fee. Another informant, George Freeman, added that he had also visited Miles, who told him that he should look for his lost mare in the north-east and within a month she was found. For this more valuable service, Miles charged him twelvepence. His accusers seemed to feel variously that their money had been wasted and that his powers might be frightening. In this way, magical practitioners could not win: if their powers did not work, they were frauds, and if they did work, they were some sort of witch.

That the victim of theft and magical shenanigans in this case, Sybil's employer Gabriel Poyntz, was himself a Justice of the Peace made the story of the Chelmsford seer particularly ironic. Gabriel's fellow Justices were now being asked to rule on his servants' folly and determine the nature of Miles's magical activities. Sybil had taken her concerns not to her employer, but to his friend and fellow Justice Edward Barrett and given a formal state-ment – an information – against Miles and he was now called to the Quarter Sessions court. Magic, then, was an everyday, complex and fascinating, matter that often came to the attention of the Justices of the Peace. The Justices who attended the Chelmsford Assizes in March 1582 would all have encountered it and the court must have been buzzing with anticipation about the appearance of a large group of witches. No doubt Justices discussed their own experiences and their theories about witches over dinner at the town's inns the night before: the White Hart, White Horse and the Crane and Saracen's Head near the market cross in the High Street, the Woolsack and Dolphin by the fishmarket and leather stalls, the Boar's Head and the Lion near the River Can bridge and so on. They would have continued gossiping as they walked to the courtroom.

The courtroom was not in fact a room at all, in the conventional sense. The Chelmsford Assizes were held in the Market Cross House, slightly to the fore of the pres-ent-day Shire Hall. It was, as the town's historian Hilda Grieve describes it:

an open-sided building, with eight oak columns supporting upper galleries and a tiled roof. The galleries, which overlooked the open 'piazza' below, were lit by three dormer windows in the roof ... the magistrates and justices sat in open court, which measured only 26 feet by 24 feet, with the officers of the law, counsel and clerks, plaintiffs and defendants, jurors, sureties, witnesses and prisoners, before and around them, while spectators, hangers-on, and those awaiting their turn, crowded into the galleries above or thronged the street outside.

This was a very unsatisfactory arrangement for all concerned: although the light, open space suited market traders and corn dealers, it made a poor courtroom.[15]

For frightened defendants like our witchcraft suspects, forced to stand and wait in physical discomfort whilst also trying to shelter from the crowd's reaction to them, it must have been hellish. Would they be jeered or targeted with abuse? How would they make themselves heard in this throng? Bewilderingly, normal life would go on around them as they pleaded for their lives. All the court's attendees:

had to contend with the noise of passing wheeled traffic and droves of cattle, the stifling heat of the sun in the summer, the chill draughts of the wind in the winter, and the all-pervasive dust and odours of the street.

Outside, hawkers shouted, street musicians played, shoppers bargained and chatted. Many homeless people begged loudly for work or charity: in the year 1582–1583, fifty four vagrants were arrested in the town. Housewives with pails and bottles came to the nearby conduit head to fetch water. There were multiple-occupancy galleried houses within yards of the open walls of the court, with children playing, dogs barking, people cooking over smoky fires, beating mats, hanging out washing, arguing and slinging muck into the street.

[15] ERO Q/SR 67/44, 45, 46, 19A/24, 30, 34, 61, 76; Hilda Grieve, *The Sleepers and the Shadows* vol. 1 (Chelmsford: Essex Record Office, 1988) 124–7, 155–7.

Along with apprehension, the smell of the Assize court must have made the defendants feel sick. Chelmsford's residents dumped both organic waste and dung close to the Market Cross House. In 1584 there was so much piled against the exterior of the churchyard fence immediately to the north that the pigs who roamed the streets could climb over it and into the churchyard. It was not just animal waste that was a problem: the dung included human faeces and, moreover, passing pedestrians sometimes used the Market Cross House as a urinal. It was little comfort that they could be fined if caught. Meat, fish and other produce from the shambles and shops of the Middle Row – the buildings down the middle of the present-day High Street – would have stunk too, particularly the guts, bones and rotting vegetables that went into the central gutter. Although it was forbidden to slaughter animals in the High Street, some unscrupulous butchers still did it.[16] Chelmsford's Assize court was a noisy, reeking, cramped circus and undoubtedly traumatic for anyone who was there unwillingly, especially someone from a small village out in the vast silence of the marshes. The accused witches were far from home, surrounded by strangers and enemies and they stood accused of a capital crime.

So what were the charges? This part of the book is hard to write. The charges are important, of course, but they

---

[16] Emmison, *Elizabethan Life: Home* 21; Grieve, *Sleepers* vol. 1, 113–14, 116–17, 119, 120, 122, 133–5, 138, 144. On Essex vagrants see also Higgs, Godliness and Governance in Tudor Colchester 266–72 and city smell and noise Peter Burke, 'Urban Sensations: Attractive and Repulsive' in Herman Roodenburg, ed., *A Cultural History of the Senses in the Renaissance* (London: Bloomsbury Academic, 2019) 43–59.

were all of them untrue in fundamental ways. Yet they represent the only event in the lives of the accused witches that historians have known and written about for many centuries. It is an event that tarnishes the reputations of the accused people, one that was unbearably frightening, embarrassing and painful for them. For many of them was a terminal event, in one way or another. This book has spent its first five chapters reconstructing their lives before their deaths in as much detail as possible, imagining the sights and sounds of their homes, the landscapes they mapped in their heads, the paths they walked, the food they ate, the earth they ploughed. But it is now time to move to their trial and in some cases to their deaths. Brian Darcy 'certified' their examinations as well as all the informations accusing them, 'at large unto the Queenes Majesties Justices of Assise of the Countie of Essex, the xxix. Of Marche. 1582' as *A True and just Recorde* tells us, and their trial began that day. Indictments were drawn up based on the examinations and informations, and the suspected witches were arraigned or charged with them.[17]

Ursley Kempe and Ales Newman were charged with killing Elizabeth, daughter of Richard and Annis Letherdall, by bewitching her on 12 February 1582 so that she died on 26 February 1582, with killing Edena, wife of John Stratton, by bewitching her on 30 November 1581 so that she died on 14 February 1582, and finally with killing Joan, daughter of Grace and John Thurlowe by bewitching her on 3 October 1581 so that she died

---

[17] *ATAJR* table. Brian Darcy is not listed among the attendant Justices in Cockburn, *Calendar: Essex: Elizabeth* record 1284 but it is unlikely he was not present in person.

on 6 October 1581.[18] Ales Hunt was charged with killing William Hayward's six cows, worth ten pounds, on 1 January 1582, and with killing Rebecca, daughter of Henry Durrant, by bewitching her on 4 November 1581 so that she died on 24 November 1581.[19] Annis Glascock was charged with killing Martha, the daughter of Michael Stevens, by bewitching her on 20 December 1581 so that she died on 1 February 1582, with killing Abraham Hedg by bewitching him on 20 February 1582 so that he died on 1 March 1582 and with killing Charity, the daughter of William Page, by bewitching her on 1 May 1581 so that she died on 8 May 1581.[20] Cisley Selles and Ales Manfield were charged with burning Richard Rosse's barn on 1st September 1581, and Cisley was also charged with killing John, the young son of Thomas Death on 4 June 1581.[21] Margaret Grevell was charged with killing Robert Cheston by bewitching him on 20 April 1577 so that he died on 20 November 1577.[22] Elizabeth Bennett was charged with killing William and Joan Byatt, by bewitching both of them on 1 August 1581 so that they both died on 10 February 1582.[23] Annis Herd was charged with killing a cow, ten sheep and ten lambs worth four pounds belonging to John Wade, bewitching them on 1 January 1582.[24]

The charges against Ursley Kempe, Ales Newman, Ales Hunt, Annis Glascock, Cysley Selles, Ales Manfield and Margaret Grevell were all submitted to the same twelve men of the jury, along with those against John Carding,

[18] Ibid., record 1300.   [19] Ibid., record 1301.   [20] Ibid., record 1304.
[21] Ibid., record 1302.   [22] Ibid., record 1303.   [23] Ibid., record 1316.
[24] Ibid., record 1312.

a Southchurch husbandman charged with grand larceny. Juries were expected to hear eight or ten cases at a time before being discharged and a new jury chosen and sworn in – a process known as impanelling – for the next set of cases. The jury for these witchcraft charges were John Everly, Thomas Greenforde, Thomas Stewarde, Thomas Oliver, Robert Patten, Thomas Walker, Lancelot Warde, Anthony Brett, Thomas Glover, Simon Dawson, Robert Morgan and Robert Hearde.[25] Ursley was convicted by these men of all three offences with which she was charged, and she was then sentenced by the judge to be hanged. Ales Newman was also found guilty but was remanded, detained in prison until further notice. Ales Hunt was acquitted of both charges. Cisley Selles was found guilty of killing John Death and remanded because there were other charges to answer in relation to the arson attack, of which more in a moment. Ales Manfield was acquitted. Margaret Grevell was acquitted. Annis Glascock was convicted of all three offences, but was remanded. Elizabeth Bennett chose a different path from her fellow accused. She did not contest the indictment against her and was therefore not tried. She was sentenced to be hanged.

You may have noticed that there are several names missing from the list of indicted witches above. Elizabeth Ewstace and Joan Pechey are two of these missing names. Both of them were discharged by proclamation.[26] This meant that no-one had attended the court to give evidence against them and that no other evidence had been brought forward against them either. Margaret Ewstace does not seem to have been tried, just as she was not

[25] Ibid., record 1299.   [26] Ibid., record 1325.

questioned during the pre-trial investigation, and her mother Elizabeth was now in theory also now free – once she had paid her gaol fees. Ales Manfield and Margaret Grevell, having been acquitted, could also leave. Brian Darcy must surely have been disappointed with this outcome. After all his efforts to collect evidence and his presentation of it to the Assize court, it must have looked and felt bad that he had failed to secure these convictions, and *A True and just Recorde* actually describes Elizabeth and Margaret as 'continued in prison' – perhaps as a temporary hold. It is easy to imagine confusion over what to do with so many accused and such a mass of evidence, as well as perhaps a disappointed Justice of the Peace who was concerned that some accused seemed to be being released untried or mistried.

Joan Pechey, however, was certainly kept in gaol for much longer. This was because a discharge by proclamation was not the same as an acquittal, and suspects were sometimes remanded so that anyone who did have evidence against them might be given time to come forward. In effect, the matter was carried over because it was unresolved and possibly subject to further investigation before revisiting. Unlike Elizabeth Ewstace, Joan is listed as a prisoner in the gaol on 2 August 1582, the date of the next Assize court. Elizabeth was gone by then, probably back home since she does not appear on the lists of those who had died in gaol. But, sadly, Joan does. Joan Pechey died in the autumn in Colchester Prison and an inquest was held on her body on 11 October 1582.[27] She never

---

[27] Ibid., record 1334, *Introduction* 146; *ATAJR* E2v and E5 (both Grevell) and E6.

went home to the little house in Nether Hoo, to her pets and to her son Philip.

Ales Newman, Cisley Selles, Annis Glascock and Ales Hunt were also still in gaol on 2 August 1582, as was a new addition: twelve-year-old Robert Selles, the son of Henry and Cisley. Henry Selles may have been there too. He was not apparently charged with any crime at the March Assizes, but we know that he was charged subsequently, as was Robert, and we'll look at those charges later. *A True and just Recorde* also describes Annis Herd as 'continued in prison' but there is no evidence of her presence in August. Instead, the imprisoned group had been joined by Anne Swallowe or Eswell of St Osyth, accused of bewitching John Byrde on 30 April 1582 so that he died on 14 May. Witchcraft accusations on the Darcy lands did not end with the March trial, and – as we've already concluded – Brian Darcy therefore likely continued his witch hunting activities. Anne Swallowe was, however, acquitted at the summer Assizes.[28] Meanwhile, the mercy shown towards Annis Glascock in sparing her from the gallows was to no avail: like Joan, Annis died in gaol in the autumn and an inquest was held on 11 October 1582. It was the same day as the inquest on Joan. Perhaps they died of the same cause: maybe plague or typhus, which spread through insanitary cells carried by lice and fleas.[29]

[28] Cockburn, *Calendar: Essex: Elizabeth* record 1335; *ATAJR* E2v and E5 (both Grevell), F4v. Durrant argues that Brian disengaged from witch hunting in mid-1582 but the evidence of continuing St Osyth prosecutions to me suggests not, although his interest may have slackened (Durrant, 'A Witch-hunting Magistrate?' 26).

[29] Cockburn, *Introduction* 146.

It was a wretched end for the lodging-house keeper, who had once thought that someone else bewitched her for being young and pretty.

There is more misery to come. Henry Selles is listed as a discharged bailee at the end of the March Assizes of 1582, meaning that he had appeared at the court and was in theory free to return home. The reason why he does not seem to have been charged with witchcraft and his status after the March trial are both unclear. Cisley remained in prison having been convicted. On 2 August Henry, Cisley and their son Robert all appeared once again at the Assizes, this time charged with arson. At this Assize the prosecution case against them was better organised in that all three were charged and there were no loose ends. Henry was charged with burning Richard Rosse's granary on 31 August 1581, a day earlier than the last, unsuccessful indictment drawn up against his wife and Ales Manfield. Then Cisley and Robert Selles were jointly charged with Henry with burning another of Richard Rosse's barns on 31 March 1582. This was after the first Assize trial. A good lawyer, had the Selles family been allowed one, would have walked all over this indictment. Cisley had been in gaol at the time of the supposed crime, so how could she have set fire to Richard's barn unless by magic – with which she was not, this time, charged. She, Henry and Robert were acquitted of this new offence, and Richard Rosse should at that point have stopped his pursuit of the family.[30]

Nevertheless, the story of Henry and Cisley Selles has a tragic end. The couple were both remanded in

30 Cockburn, *Calendar: Essex: Elizabeth* record 1327.

gaol after the Assize of August 1582, although this is not recorded in the surviving papers of the trial. Why Henry was remanded is unclear: he had not apparently been convicted of anything so perhaps it was unpaid fees that kept him in Colchester Castle. Cisley could have been executed for her supposed witchcraft crime, but perhaps mercy was being shown or she was being held until sentence could be passed or she and Henry were still being pursued by Richard Rosse with further charges. Either way, the outcome was the deaths of both of them. Cisley died in January and her inquest was held on 31 January 1583. Henry died a few weeks later, and his inquest date was 8 March 1583.[31] Perhaps young Robert made it home to Little Clacton, to care for his orphaned brothers and sister, but if so he would have had to deal with the fact that Henry and John's evidence had killed their parents. The family might have been offered charitable relief, but how grudgingly it would have been given! They might have gone to live with relatives, if there were any, or been dispersed among strangers. Did the children survive to see adulthood – little Joyce, traumatised Henry and John, angry Robert? They disappear from the records and perhaps they left Little Clacton: took ship to London, joined a band of vagrants. They certainly walked out of the history books.

So, and with better hope of survival, did Joan Robinson and Margerie Sammon. Theirs are two other names missing from the records of the March 1582 Assizes. Brian Darcy should have committed Joan and Margerie for

---

[31] Cockburn, *Introduction* 146.

trial at the end of their examinations on 25 March and 25 February 1582, respectively. But there is no record that either woman was tried at the Assizes so perhaps he did not. Perhaps some records are lost, always an alarming thought. There will always be aspects of this and any other witchcraft trial where we do not know all the details, where the records that are left may be misleading or omit key facts. Perhaps Brian did commit Margerie and she escaped from the constable, ran away or otherwise made herself scarce once she realised the mistake she had made in confessing to keeping spirits. Like her fellow servant Margaret Ewstace she disappeared, leaving a hole in the trial record. Joan Robinson was a more substantial householder and would have found flight much more of a sacrifice, but Margerie, like Margaret, looks to have been more mobile.

However, in summer 1583 Brian caught up with Margerie. Just like Anne Swallowe, Elizabeth Lumley and Alice Boulton, Margerie and a woman called Joan Dale were accused of witchcraft in the aftermath of the great trial of 1582. Margerie appeared as Margery Barnes at the spring Assizes of 2 March 1584. She was accused of keeping three spirits called Pygine (like Ursley's familiar two years ago, but a mole not a cat), a grey cat called Rusfott and a brown dog called Dunfutt with the intention of using them for witchcraft. This indictment is an unusual one: while spirit keeping was indeed illegal, it was not usually made a separate matter of indictment. Perhaps the charge reflects Brian's attempt to hold Margerie to account for her previous confession about the spirits that she had supposedly released into the wild in February 1582? Pointedly, the 1584 indictment claimed that she had possessed these new spirits on 1 July 1583 and on 10 July a further indictment alleged that with Joan Dale she had bewitched John Lanne on 1583 so that he died on 20 October. By the time of her trial, Joan Dale had died in prison but Margerie was acquitted.[32] And so she too leaves our story. As far as we know, her sister Ales Hunt also survived the witch trial and presumably went home.

And what about Ales Newman? While we've heard the stories of all the people tried by the first jury at the March Assizes who were convicted or released or who died in prison, a different fate awaited Ales. Even though she had been convicted of all the same crimes as Ursley Kempe, Ales was not sentenced to be hanged with her former friend. Perhaps the judge concluded her guilt was not as great, or was swayed by her refusal to confess. Ales remained in gaol at the time of the August 1582 Assizes and perhaps she heard of, or was present at, the deaths of Joan Pechey and Annis Glascock in October, Cisley Selles in January and Henry Selles in March 1583. She likely saw Margerie Barnes Sammon come to the gaol in July 1583 and then leave for her trial at Chelmsford in March 1584. Perhaps she asked Margerie how her godson Thomas Rabbet was coping with the loss of his mother. Perhaps she asked if her husband William was still alive. Presumably she learned that Margerie had been acquitted: maybe she gave her a message to take back to St Osyth if she survived. Ales might also have seen Elizabeth Lumley and Alice Boulton come and go if they went to Colchester before their 1584 trial at Witham. Alice was hanged, and perhaps Ales Newman worried that she too

---

[32] Cockburn, *Calendar: Essex: Elizabeth* record 1432.

would be hauled off to the gallows. But it appeared she had been forgotten. She is listed as a gaol prisoner in April 1584, April 1586 and March 1587. It was not until 10 February 1588, six years after she had been imprisoned, that Ales was released under a general pardon. With eight other people – a labourer, a husbandman, a cook and several women, at least three of whom had been convicted of witchcraft – she was let go.[33]

The final accused witch to be tried at the March Assizes of 1582 was Annis Herd. She was tried by a different jury from the main group of accused people, and her trial jury were William Andrewes or Peers, Thomas Prentys, William Wortham, Henry Sparrowe, Edmund Harryngton, Richard Ive, William Taynter, Edward Watkynson, James Parker, John Symonds, Edward Hoye and John Porter. Alongside Annis were tried a supposed horse thief, two cattle rustlers, four chicken thieves and a man accused of rape. All the thieves were convicted (one was hanged, two were allowed clergy, and three were whipped) but the supposed rapist and Annis were acquitted.[34] Curiously, despite all the hatred flying around Little Oakley and the deeply serious allegation made against Annis by the Beaumont rector Richard Harrison – that Annis had murdered his wife – Annis had only been charged with a single count of harming the animals belonging to John Wade. Why was this? Was

---

33 Macfarlane, *Witchcraft in Tudor and Stuart England* 273 (Q/SR 88/86, 96a/8, 99/1) and Cockburn, *Calendar: Introduction* 199. She does not appear again in the calendars of gaol prisoners, which she does consistently before February 1588.
34 Cockburn, *Calendar: Essex: Elizabeth* record 1306.

his evidence thought to be unreliable? Did the grand jury look at an indictment for Anne Harrison's murder and reject it so that it was discarded? Even if Annis had been convicted of killing John Wade's sheep she would not have been hanged. Was she in some way protected by some of the wealthy influencers in her community?

The grand jury were Richard Rastall, gentleman, Thomas Sadlington, George Clarke, John Mason, Nicholas Haukine, Richard Campe, Thomas Eve, Anthony Rampton, William Faber, Thomas Godfrye, Philip Harrys, Humphrey Tabor, John Collyn, Edward Same, John Barron, Gilbert Woodwarde, Thomas Clarke, Nicholas Humfrye, John Raven, William Stane, John Hawes, John Freshwater and Edward Baylye. Of these, Philip Harrys may have been the yeoman farmer of that name who held Amperswick in St Osyth, the business partner of Isaac Grene and witness and executor of the will of John Butler. But as far as we know, neither he nor any of the other grand jurors knew Annis. Certainly none of them have any proven feeling about her or any of her accusers (Richard Harrison, for example) which might dispose them to judge Annis one way or the other.[35]

We explored Annis Herd's reputation in her village in Chapter 5, but it was also apparent that something was not quite right in the community's relationship with her accuser. Richard was increasingly often reported to the ecclesiastical court, and he was also named in the

---

[35] Cockburn, *Calendar: Essex: Elizabeth* record 1287; TNA C2/Eliz/ H19/46, PROB 11/65/120, ERO T/B 79/1, D/DB M160; Emmison, *Feet* 3–4; Manningtree parish register burial of Philip Harrys 2nd September 1587.

rumours of sexual scandal that enveloped Ramsey and Little Oakley. This swirl of gossip was unfortunately part of a pattern, and things got worse for him in 1586 when as 'Richard Harrison clerk' of Beaumont he was accused at the Quarter Sessions and then the Assizes, together with 'Richard Harrison, labourer', of stealing a sheep. This ewe was said to be worth five shillings, and to have been rustled from a close belonging to Thomas Warde of Moze. A later Assize record confirms that the second Richard is Richard 'junior', the rector's son, who having been baptised on 27 June 1570 was fifteen at the time of the alleged crime, 21 December 1585.[36] The theft sounds like the playing out of a financial dispute, perhaps over unpaid tithes or debts. But that a rector should be accused of a felony was unusual, even in a period of simmering religious controversies.

Conflict between parishioners and their clerics was not in itself uncommon. In a climate of political tension, flirtation with Presbyterianism and Catholic survivals, it was easy to criticise a churchman for his interpretation of doctrine, or to refuse him support in insidious ways. Equally, it was easy for him to decide that his parishioners were resistant Papists or, worse, amateur theologians setting their judgements against his own. Essex records are spotted with evidence of controversy: accusations that Stephen Beaumont, rector of Easthorpe 1579–1609, was a man of evil conversation, did not wear a surplice, administer sacraments or read from the Prayer Book, that William Pinder, rector of Stock, was a common barrator

[36] Cockburn, *Calendar: Essex: Elizabeth* records 1637, 1818; Little Oakley parish register 27 June 1570.

inciting riot and murder, that Roger Herne or Hieron, vicar of Epping, did not wear a surplice, and so on. In 1591 at Stanford le Hope the rector and two clerks were accused of trading 'lewde and contemptuous jestures' and insults during services, such as 'come downe pratinge Jack, thowe fomest owte thyne owne poyson'. In 1592 a parishioner at Bradwell attacked his rector with a cudgel, alleging that Queen Elizabeth was a usurper and that when she died 'all those that be of this religion now used wilbe pulled out'.[37] Some clergymen, of course, engaged gleefully in controversy. But few were accused of stealing sheep.

The direct action of theft recalls Richard's assertive behaviour with Annis Herd in 1582 when he thought she had stolen from him. We know that he was capable of initiating physical confrontation if he felt the occasion warranted it and he might actually have stolen a sheep from his neighbour if he was enraged enough about some previous quarrel. But if so he had committed grand larceny, theft of an item worth more than twelvepence. It carried the death penalty. Richard was on trial for his life. His plea is not recorded, but he was found guilty. As a literate man, of course, he was lucky. Unlike almost all women of his period, he was offered benefit of clergy and read the neck verse: 'Have mercie upon me, O God,

---

[37] Cockburn, *Calendar: Essex: Elizabeth* records 1006, 1407, 1593, 1640, 1642, 1684–5 etc, and 2257, 2305, 2306, 2364. Beaumont was a Dedham Classis attendee (Janet Cooper, ed., *A History of the County of Essex* vol. 10 (London: Victoria County History, 2001) 203); Venn and Venn, 367; Hieron was the father of the godly lecturer of Modbury and Plympton, Samuel Hieron (Augustus Charles Bickley, 'Samuel Hieron', *DNB* vol 26 (London, 1891) 362–363).

according to thy loving kindness: according to the multitude of thy compassions put away mine iniquities'.[38] He may well have been branded publicly on the thumb with the letter T for theft, although this punishment – ensuring that benefit of clergy could not be applied to a second offence – was sometimes omitted. It is ironic that a story that began with the alleged theft of ducklings by one party should end with a conviction for sheep rustling by the other.

Although Richard had escaped hanging, he was still in an extremely serious situation. And he had dragged his son into it. Young Richard was 'at large' at the time of the 3 March Assizes at which his father appeared: likely he had been sent to live with a relative or schoolmaster, while his father hoped that he could talk the boy out of his mess. A verdict is not recorded against Richard junior, and it appears that no trial occurred, so Richard senior was probably successful. However, it must have been an anxious year before at the 24 July Assizes of 1587, young Richard was discharged along with his father as a bailee. This ended their period on the wrong side of the secular law. Richard had committed a sin as well as a crime, however, and resumed his appearances in the church court records. He was effectively suspended from his post, deprived of his living. By 1587, John Thorpe had replaced him as temporary Rector. John had previously been Rector of St Ethelburga in Bishopsgate and was Rector of St Christopher-le-Stocks on Threadneedle Street, also London, concurrently

---

38 Geneva Bible, Psalms 51:1.

with his new post at Beaumont. Unsurprisingly given his London duties, he was presented to the Colchester archdeaconry court in 1587 for holding no services at Beaumont since Christmas last. There was evidently confusion about who was supposed to be officiating, however, since Richard Harrison was also presented for holding no services. However it was noted simply that 'he is gone'.

Over time the scandal presumably died down, but there were still hurdles to overcome. In mid-March 1588 Richard was named along with others in the Archdeaconry of Colchester as a minister who had not shown his license to preach, and he was again suspended. He presented his credentials – letters of ordination in 1566 and a letter from Edmund Grindal when he was Bishop of London – to the Archdeacon's court, his son Richard acting as his procurator, and was reinstated as Rector of Beaumont. His position in the community of Beaumont and Little Oakley was permanently damaged, however. Not only had his wife died, and his accusation that she had been murdered been rebutted, but now his moral authority was gone and key parochial relationships were in tatters. These must have included relationships with the Wardes, but also likely some of the Herds and their friends, Marvens, Alduses and Anwicks. It is hard to imagine that Richard spent much time in his parish after that. He appeared in the ecclesiastical court several times because of suspected inattention to his duties – for example, to refute an accusation that he had married a couple without banns being read – and he died in Mistley-with-Manningtree parish in 1591. He was buried there, far from home, as

'Richard Harrison preacher and parson of Beamont' on 6 March.[39]

Some of Annis Herd's other accusers fared little better. Shockingly, Anne West died in childbirth just before or on 1 April 1582. Her baby survived and was baptised that day, named after her. When she had given her evidence against Annis on 16 March Anne had just two weeks to live. Andrew West died within a year of his wife. His will is dated 26 January 1583 and was proved in March of that year. Andrew left to his three surviving children his house, to be divided equally. He surrendered his lands to John Wade and this was witnessed by John Heard and Thomas Cartwrite as tenants. There are those complex interconnections again, still operating after Annis's trial. William Lane died a few months before Andrew West. His will was dated 5 November 1582 and it left everything that he had acquired since his marriage to 'Benet my wife', and all previous goods to his surviving children William and Joan at eighteen with Bennet to keep them until then. His witnesses included Andrew West and William's will was proved on 1 January 1583. John Wade son of John – the fourth of that name, and aged nine – died in 1585.[40] It was

---

[39] Cockburn, *Calendar: Essex: Elizabeth* record 1818; ERO D/ACA 14, D/AZ 1/7, 29th March; Peile, 1: 82, 131 although his is not the same Richard Harrison; Mistley parish register 6 March 1590.

[40] Little Oakley parish register, 1 April 1582 baptism and burial; ERO D/ACA 10, court of 5th March and 5th May 1583 and Emmison, ed., *Essex Wills ... Archdeaconry Courts 1577–1584* 175; ERO D/ACA 10, court of 10th January and 18th February 1582/3 and Emmison, ed., *Essex Wills ... Archdeaconry Courts 1577–1584* 171; Little Oakley parish register 18th June 1582, 10 January 1585; John Wade the elder was buried in 1607, Beaumont parish register 25 February 1607. He was presented for not receiving Easter communion at a court of 6th May

just this sort of tragic series of events – deaths that seemed inexplicably early, patterns that looked like revenge – that led to accusations of witchcraft.

And indeed, although she never went back to the Assizes, Annis Herd continued to be presented to the church court. By 3 November 1582 she was back in Little Oakley and being accused with Jocosa or Joyce, the wife of Michael Smyth of Ramsey of witchcraft. Nothing seems to have come of the allegations, to which only Joyce responded. In 1583 Annis is named again and in October 1584 John Wese of Little Oakley was presented for going to Harwich on the Sabbath day to sell pears, by which means he missed the service, but also for 'kepinge' the excommunicated Annis Herd 'all this sommer'. This summer lover of 1584 may be the John Wese or Weese whose daughter Alice was married in Little Oakley in June 1582. In 1587 as 'Agneta' Herd, Annis was presented in April 'to be begetten with childe in adultery or fornication by Robert Churchman of Ramsey'. In June 1592 she appears again as 'suspected of witchcraft' for a 'long tyme'. In mid-1593 she addressed her excommunication, being represented in court by Christopher Cooke. She had stood excommunicated on and off throughout the late 1570s, 1580s and early 1590s and was repeatedly presented for continuing in this state, failing to attend church and receive communion.[41] Annis was still young

---

1583, ERO D/ACA 10. He may also have lived at Wix – see F.G. Emmison, *Elizabethan Life: Morals and the Church Courts* (Chelmsford: Essex County Council, 1973) 14, 279.

[41] ERO D/ACA 10 November–December 1582, August 1583, D/ACA 11, D/ACA 14, D/ACA 19 *passim*, D/ACA 21 May, July, September, October, D/AZ 1/7, 1/8 *passim*). Robert Churchman was also presented

in 1587, likely in her thirties or early forties, given that the poor diet and hard labour of poverty tends to bring on early menopause. Although her children went unbaptised and the pious despised her, nevertheless she had survived her Assize trial. She went home after her acquittal and got on with her life, which included inheriting some land.

In 1586 Annis Herd's mother Charity died. Annis appears in the manorial court book, inheriting Charity's lease on the cottage and three acres called Boroughs or Brymleys, the one that Annis's father Robert had inherited in his turn back in the 1530s. She immediately disposed of the cottage lease to Thomas and Priscilla Whitebread. In 1587 she appears again, coming to the manorial court on 12 September to take possession of Gobyns or Gubbins's Pightell, a piece of ground with a building on it. Given her presentment in April, she was perhaps heavily pregnant or had a new baby with her when she came to the manor house to receive her inheritance. In a delightful irony, Gubbins's Pightell was once leased by Richard Harrison and it was next to land belonging to Beaumont rectory. The pightle was also next to the house and land called Skinners, once leased by John Wade and also by John Herd. Annis paid six-pence admission fine for it. It was a small piece of land and it was only a small victory as Annis asserted her right to stay in her village, to hold land alongside her wealthy accusers, and to succeed one of them, Richard Harrison, as a leaseholder. But it was a victory. Annis went on to

in 1587 though nothing came of this presentment. See Macfarlane, *Witchcraft in Tudor and Stuart England* 287, which lists the Smyths but not Annis, and 291. I suspect we have all missed other illegible entries.

survive her further brush with witchcraft accusation in 1592. She had lived to see her enemy Richard Harrison threatened with the punishment he had held over her: hanging. She saw him humiliated and then farmed land under his nose. She also outlived him and the Wests and Bennet and William Lane and Edmund Osborne. Annis was buried in Little Oakley churchyard on Wednesday, 28 April 1602. She returned in this way to her church community. Ministers were not obliged to bury excommunicated people in consecrated ground, but many did so. Perhaps we see another flicker of Annis's social capital or the charity of some of her neighbours in her funeral, twenty years after her accusation.[42]

In this way Annis Herd was lucky: she's the one that we know definitely got away. In one way or another, Elizabeth Ewstace, Margaret Grevell, Margerie Sammon, Ales Manfielde, Ales Hunt and Joan Robinson probably also survived their accusations, although how far their lives could be repaired afterwards is an open question. Ales Newman also survived, although she spent six years in prison: an unexpected amount of time. But these eight accused women were all luckier than the six people who died as an immediate consequence of being accused of

[42] ERO D/DEl M76 1537, 1568, 1586; D/DGh M5; Little Oakley parish register 28 April 1602; ERO D/DGh M45/1, M45/11. On excommunication see David Cressy, 'Who Buried Mrs Horseman? Excommunication, Accommodation and Silence' in *Travesties and Transgressions in Tudor and Stuart England: Tales of Discord and Dissension* (Oxford: Oxford University Press, 1999) 116–37 especially 117–20

Gubbins Pightell was let to Augustin Holder, then David Turner by 1597 and Joyce Mines by 1603, and after that it went to the Fox and Snowdon families.

witchcraft: Joan Pechey, Annis Glascock, Cisley and Henry Selles, and most obviously the two women who were executed at the end of the Chelmsford Assizes in March 1582, Ursley Kempe and Elizabeth Bennett. It is time to follow them to the end of their journey, and so to Chelmsford gallows. Ironically, the condemned witches were walked or carted past the magician Miles Blumfield's house on their way to die. Perhaps he even attended their trial as an onlooker, or their execution, since it took place a couple of hundred yards from his front door. But while Miles then continued his prosperous career in Chelmsford, being chosen as a churchwarden in 1582, the two convicted women were hauled away to the scaffold on Rainsford Road.[43]

The site of the gallows was intended to be a well-frequented roadside, where people could gather to watch the deaths of criminals. The spectacle was a warning to avoid their fate, but it was also part of the Assize circus, a culminating horror to a day of curiosity and thrill. Ursley and Elizabeth would have been taken to a slight widening of the road just north of the modern Rainsford Lane, where Rainsford Road leads towards Writtle. Here the gallows stood. Now the site is by the busy interchange of the A1060 and A1016 (Figure 6.2). A contemporary map suggests that the execution spot is near the Primrose Hill housing development.

If you walk up Duke Street from the site of the Market Cross House courtroom now, you walk in Ursley and Elizabeth's wake. You pass the railway station, war

---

43 Grieve, *Sleepers* vol. 1, 156, 157.

FIGURE 6.2 Junction of Rainsford Lane and Rainsford Road,
Chelmsford. (Source: Author's photo.)
Note: A black and white version of this figure will appear in some
formats. For the colour version, please refer to the plate section.

memorial and council offices, the Shanghai House takea-
way, Pizza Planet and the Tropiway Continental Grocers,
the GMB and Unison trade union headquarters and
the Co-op, the mid-century modern Trinity Methodist
Church and Quaker Meeting House – all the signs of
a society more mobile, more just and open and yet still
dogged by poverty, prejudice, conflict and exploitation.
Ursley and Elizabeth passed these places when they were
green fields along a muddy track. On Rainsford Road
itself, you'll end up at the Globe Inn and the Esso garage,
and by then you have probably passed the site of the gallows. Pay attention to the grim imaginings in your mind:
the creak of rope and the hush of a savage crowd. It was
here that Ursley and Elizabeth died, and probably where
they were buried. The field next to the gallows, 'Barrow

Fyelde', contained an imposing howe and executed people were often interred in howeland. As we saw in St Osyth, howes were suspect, edge-land places. Here the two convicted witches would join the prehistoric ghosts, the devils and spirit animals that in life both women had imagined frisking beyond the safety of settlements, away from the strictures of the preacher, the chatter of the market, the warm firelight. Among the haunted howes Ursley and Elizabeth found their final home.[44]

Brian Darcy died too, of course, but he died comfortably in bed surrounded by his family on Christmas Day in 1587. He slipped into unconsciousness at St Clere's Hall, the place where he had questioned the accused witches. Did he think about them in the years after their trial, remembering Ales Hunt's tears as he walked on summer evenings in the garden where she had cried? Did he meet Ales or Margerie Sammon in Mill Street sometimes or Elizabeth Ewstace, Ales Manfield or Margaret Grevell at Thorpe if they did get home, or Annis Herd doggedly flaunting her survival at Little Oakley? Did he notice the cottages with new tenants, the bereaved children growing up hungry and bitter? At the time of his final illness Brian was building brilliant futures for his own children. He

[44] As at Sutton Hoo: see Martin Carver, *Sutton Hoo: A Seventh-Century Princely Burial Ground and its Context* (London: British Museum Press and Society of Antiquaries, 2005) chapter 9. Thanks to Neil Wiffen for pointing out the howe on the Walker map and sharing his article 'Favourite ERO Documents: Walker Map of Chelmsford 1591' (19 August 2013) at www.essexrecordofficeblog.co.uk/favourite-ero-documents-walker-map-of-chelmsford-1591/ as well as his brilliant GIS work on the question 'Where Were the Gallows?', and thanks to Simon Coxall for discussing these burials of felons.

263

was negotiating with his neighbour Katherine Awdeley to add land to their holdings, having married his teenage son John – then a student at Caius College, Cambridge – to her daughter Dorothy Awdeley in November 1582. In another move to consolidate the family's resources, his daughter Mary later married Thomas Eden of Sudbury, whose mother Elizabeth was the daughter of Sir John St Clere, formerly of St Clere's Hall. Brian Darcy was the saviour of the St Clere estate, taking it into his family, improving it and making his children's' inheritance double sure with the Darcy–Eden alliance in 1593.

Meanwhile, the Darcy family was also building its reputation in legal circles. After his ambitious performance at the 1582 Assizes, Brian had had *A True and just Recorde* published in London by Thomas Dawson, marking up its contents with the word 'condemned' where he believed – not always accurately – that an execution had been secured, and otherwise with 'continued in prison'. The trial seems to have done his reputation good rather than harm. He was chosen as Sheriff of Essex in 1586, a step up the ladder of county administration that allowed him greater access to the circuit judges and others in organising the Assizes. His eldest son, Thomas, was also progressing. He went to Lincoln's Inn in his father's footsteps in the late 1570s, to be followed by John in the early 1590s, while Brian's youngest son, Robert, followed John to Caius in 1595. John became a Sergeant-at-Law, a member of an exclusive order of barristers working in the Court of Common Pleas and King's Bench, among other courts. Brian would no doubt have been pleased. He had taken every step he could to further his sons' legal careers. His will was overseen by his friend William

Drury of Little Holland and Brett's Hall in Tendring, a Master in Chancery like Henry Whetcrofte and no doubt a great help to the Darcy boys as they made their way at the Inns of Court. Brian provided very handsomely for his girls too. He left £800 to Mary, a sum that allowed her to bring a large dowry to the Edens on her marriage. He also left £700 to his younger daughter Penelope. Each woman inherited their legacy upon attaining the age of twenty-one, and with the condition that if they married before this time that both marry with their mother Brigitt's consent. Brian was buried in the parish church of St Osyth.[45] Perhaps Annis Herd walked over from Little Oakley for his funeral. Poor and pious-looking mourners were often give a few pence, a dole, at the funerals of important people like Brian, which would have come in handy. And Annis might have wanted to make sure that he was dead.

---

[45] TNA PROB 11/51/388; ERO T/A 133/1; Cockburn, *Calendar: Essex: Elizabeth* record 1601; P. O. G. White, 'William Drury' *ODNB* (2008) https://doi.org/10.1093/ref:odnb/8102; Venn and Venn, at: https:// venn.lib.cam.ac.uk/; Thornton and Eiden, eds., *The History of the Couty of Essex* 202.

Conclusion

Once More with Feeling

~

It would be satisfying to conclude this book with a neat explanation for the witchcraft accusations that engulfed St Osyth and its surrounding villages in the spring of 1582. The historiography of witchcraft prosecution is well known, and has examined many economic and social factors that undoubtedly contributed to witch hunting.[1] In particular, Keith Thomas and Alan Macfarlane famously studied the Essex witch trials in some detail in the 1960s and early 1970s, although they were looking for high-level socio-economic patterns instead of more granular accounts of lives. Nevertheless, the new information that I have uncovered about the St Osyth, Little Clacton, Thorpe and Walton le Soken and Little Oakley witchcraft accusers and suspects broadly bears out their contention that relative levels of poverty and wealth often appear to have played a part in the choice of accused, and that conflicts over charity were often flashpoints that triggered a visit to the magistrate. But as I argued in *Reading Witchcraft* in 1999, many of the relationships that are portrayed in pamphlets like *A True*

---

[1] In addition to the discussions that follows see generally Darren Oldridge, ed., *The Witchcraft Reader* 3rd. ed. (London and New York: Routledge, 2019) and Marion Gibson, *Witchcraft: The Basics* (London and New York: Routledge, 2018) chapter 3.

and just Recorde are much more complex than a simple story of charity denied. Some accusers are shown here as well as in *A True and just Recorde*'s testimonies to be the socio-economic equals of those they accuse, and for some accused like Annis Herd a broader definition of social capital is evidently required, although the influence of family and friendly contacts is hard to quantify – see the discussion of histories of kinship and neighbourliness later in this chapter.

Such economic approaches as the 'Thomas–Macfarlane' witchcraft accusation thesis were modified in the 1990s and after by historians such as Malcolm Gaskill, Clive Holmes and Robin Briggs, who asked more socially and culturally focused questions about patterns of accusation, community and gender. Also in the 1990s, literary scholars like Diane Purkiss and Deborah Willis paid attention to the gender dynamics of witchcraft accusation in some of the Essex cases and Willis returned productively to the subject of 'witch families' like the Selleses in 2013. This book demonstrates strongly that gender and particularly certain kinds of gendered reputation were a key factor in the selection of the accused. It is important that all of the accused of 1582 except Henry Selles were female, and Henry was the husband of an accused woman: a family link which has been shown by scholars like Willis to attract accusation by association. Family ties also predisposed the accusation of the daughters and sisters of already-suspected women, and this is borne out particularly well in the case of the Barnes family in Chapters 1 and 2. As discussed later, several of the women who were accused had poor sexual reputations and there were wider concerns about their honesty. Gender is also important to the recent work of Charlotte Rose Millar, which examines a number of themes such as the ways in which demonically inspired emotions like anger were framed as feminine vices in early modern English witchcraft cases including at St Osyth. The suspects discussed in this book were often perceived as unreasonably angry people, echoing her reading.[2]

As this book details, the spread of accusations outwards from St Osyth village itself suggests that once one woman was suspected, witchcraft prosecutions tended to multiply if a magistrate or activist took the lead. Brian Darcy is one such figure, but we might also point to more localised organisers like churchwardens (John Wade, Thomas Cartwrite) or aggrieved farmers (Richard Rosse). Jonathan Durrant has to some extent downplayed the magistrate's role in his recent article on the St Osyth witchcraft case, arguing that 'Darcy was not a zealous witch hunter' and

[2] Marion Gibson, *Reading Witchcraft: Stories of Early English Witches* (London: Routledge, 1999), Malcolm Gaskill, 'Witchcraft and Neighbourliness in Early Modern England' in Steve Hindle, Alexandra Shepard and John D. Walter, eds., *Remaking English Society: Social Relations and Social Change in Early Modern England* (Woodbridge: Boydell Press, 2013) 211–32; Clive Holmes, 'Women: Witnesses and Witches' *Past and Present* 140:1 (1993) 45–78, Robin Briggs, *Witches and Neighbours: The Social and Cultural Context of European Witchcraft* (Oxford: Blackwell, 1996) and the influential 'Many Reasons Why: Witchcraft and the Problem of Multiple Explanation' in Jonathan Barry, Gareth Roberts and Marianne Hester, eds., *Witchcraft in Early Modern Europe: Studies in Culture and Belief* (Cambridge: Cambridge University Press, 1996) 49–63; Diane Purkiss, *The Witch in History* (London and New York: Routledge, 1996); Willis, *Malevolent Nurture* and 'The Witch-Family in Elizabethan and Jacobean Print Culture', *Journal for Early Modern Cultural Studies* 13:1 (2013) 4–31; Charlotte Rose Millar, *Witchcraft, the Devil and Emotions in Early Moden England* (London and New York: Routledge, 2017).

questioning his interest in French demonology.[3] He does not believe that Brian was necessarily a puritanical activist against witches or a man single-mindedly committed to introducing 'Continental' demonological thinking to England, points which are absolutely fair. But despite that, Brian's role was pivotal in the events of 1582, and not just because he was doing his job as a magistrate by questioning the witchcraft suspects. In my view, his role went beyond that. He built a longer list of indictments than was usual for one Assize trial, particularly when the suspects were all presented by one magistrate. He recorded in detail questioning practices and outcomes which are suggestively linked to engagement with Jean Bodin's demonology. He also facilitated the publication of *A True and just Recorde* which further showcased new demonological and legal thinking and, at over one hundred pages, was a witchcraft news pamphlet on an entirely new scale.

The scope and perseverance of all this work is important. To build the list of indictments, Brian had to liaise with other key men in several different communities across his family's estate. The accusations of suspects were brought to him, but the evidence of *A True and just Recorde* suggests he received them enthusiastically. He went quickly from village to village in the month before the Assize deadline – from St Osyth to Little Clacton to Thorpe to Little Oakley to Walton – pursuing his information. He called in witnesses to hear Ursley Kempe's first confession, suggesting it was special, and then with Thomas Tey he followed up further allegations made by Ursley at Colchester. The references to Jean Bodin in *A*

---

[3] Durrant, 'A Witch-hunting Magistrate?' 25–6.

True and Just Recorde show that he and his prefacer were both aware of French demonology and Brian recorded the results he obtained with questioning techniques linked to this reading. He manipulated suspects into confession and misrepresented the sequence of the evidence he received. He then shared his pre-trial paperwork with his prefacer and must surely have approved of its publication. If the prefacer was William Whetcrofte, we know the two men worked together into 1583. Witches continued to be committed for trial on Brian's patch in 1583 and 1584. To my mind, this cumulative evidence makes Brian a fairly zealous witch hunter. He did not create the St Osyth witch hunt alone, of course, but he did turn it from scattered suspicions into a coordinated mass prosecution. He remains ambiguous in his religious views, elusive in his motivation, but he was a man who effortfully did great harm in his desire to prosecute witches.[4]

Being unable to determine Brian's religious standpoint, or those of any of the accusers who gave evidence, does however mean that we can't say for sure whether the 1582 prosecutions might best be labelled a 'Catholic' or a 'godly' episode or neither. There are elements that look like pressure from godly moral reformers of the sort that interested Keith Wrightson, David Underdown, Jim Sharpe and Martin Ingram in the notion that a puritanically inclined middle class might have been bearing down on a lewd, disorderly underclass in some Elizabethan villages, a view still often expressed. If this

[4] See Katie Barclay, 'Falling in Love with the Dead', *Rethinking History* 22:4 (2018) 459–73, 468–9 on disliking a historical individual and attempting a fair portrayal.

was so, then perhaps these reformers might include Brian Darcy, perhaps some of the churchwardens – especially in the better-documented northerly parishes like Little Oakley and Moze. But we can't be sure about their piety or sectarian views: a John Wade, for instance, was presented to the church court for not receiving communion at Little Oakley in November 1582 and in 1584 a John Wade was presented for 'that he fanned corne upon Sondaye' at Beaumont; Thomas and Cecily Cartwrite were presented for not receiving communion in 1588. This might or might not mean that they were not godly. Equally, we know that Brian's wider family was proudly Catholic and he had Catholic friends and advisors, like the jurist William Drury. The Awdeleys or Audleys, into which family he married his most successful son, show – like Brian – indications that might be taken as evidence of godliness *and* Catholicism but Katherine Awdeley was evangelically Catholic.[5] It is perhaps more honest and more interesting if no religious label is attached to the St Osyth witch hunt: sectarian politics are rarely that simple and neither are individual spiritual choices.[6]

---

[5] E.g. N. M. Fuidge, 'John Audley I (d.1588) of Berechurch, Essex' in P. W. Hasler, *The History of Parliament 1558–1603* (Woodbridge, Boydell and Brewer) www.historyofparliamentonline.org/volume/1558-1603/member/audley-john-i-1588; ERO D/ACA 14, D/Z 1/7, 1/8; Higgs, Godliness and Governance in Tudor Colchester 237–40.

[6] See Keith Wrightson, *Poverty and Piety in an English Village: Terling 1525–1700* (1977; Oxford: Oxford University Press, 1995), reflection on the 'poverty and piety' 1970s–1980s debate at 197–211; David Underdown, *Revel, Riot and Rebellion: Popular Culture and Politics in England 1603–1660* (Oxford: Oxford University Press, 1985), James Sharpe, *Crime in Early Modern England* (London and New York: Routledge, 1984), Martin Ingram, *The Church Courts, Sex and Marriage in England 1570–1640* (Cambridge: Cambridge University Press, 1987).

Further, if we are looking for wider cultural patterns in the 1582 stories – economic, social, imaginative, epidemiological – then we can find them but we must also note that they are inferred and debatable rather than the clear causal explanations that we might desire. As Henry French and Jonathan Barry said in 2004 'while we continue to see patterns in behaviour, association, expression or values, painful experience has made us reluctant to weave these into generally applicable hypotheses'.[7] The evidence of some kind of epidemic across some of the villages of the witch hunt in 1580–1581 is really suggestive because it is a specific claim, not a wider theoretical one, and Jonathan Durrant is right to foreground it in his account. But while a number of the deaths of supposed witchcraft victims – like Avis Smith or the St Osyth villagers who died of unexplained causes in February 1582 – could be the result of plague bacillus or a virus of the kind with which we are now familiar, the deaths that sparked the first accusations do not seem to be among them. Joan Thurlowe died as a result of a fall from her cradle, while Elizabeth Letherdall died with symptoms of an inflammation or tumour. A higher level of anxiety about mortality does seem to be the result of prolonged pandemic, as we have all now learned by experience, and these events could be swept together in the minds of depressed and frightened people. But one explanation for the witch hunt does not seem to take obvious precedence over another. Instead, we might point to a generally raised level of anxiety in the emotional temperature of the community of each village,

---

[7] Henry French and Jonathan Barry, eds., *Identity and Agency in England 1500–1800* (Basingstoke: Palgrave Macmillan, 2004) 4.

which had a mix of different causes and expressed itself in different ways. As the witch hunt spread out from St Osyth, the cultural dynamics of witchcraft accusation appear to have changed according to local circumstances and the individuals who were suspected.

In the first accusations at St Osyth there was a notable focus on investment in cunning magic, which has been pursued in my account. Ursley Kempe's healing talent was thought to have been turned against vulnerable children and there was a link with her role in lying in, birth and childcare. To this extent the old stereotype of the midwife/healer witch is absolutely spot on – an insight that causes some discomfort to professional historians because it is so often taken for granted in popular culture and conflated with a supposed proto-feminism among suspects. Diane Purkiss correctly skewered the well-meant stereotype of the healing, feminist witch in 1996 when she wrote about the 'healing hands' of the 'healer and midwife' suspected of witchcraft in stereotyped stories, the woman who 'grew all manner of herbs ... had practical knowledge ... took lovers when she wished' and whose 'independence and freedom threatened men' so that 'she was burned alive by men who hated women'. Despite subsequent attempts to relegate the midwife-witch and healer-witch to the realm of 'myth', this stereotype is not mythic in the case of Ursley.[8] Some of it is an observable, documented reality. Ursley did present herself as having healing skills and a specific knowledge of childbirth and

---

[8] Purkiss, in the still-provocative *The Witch in History* 7; David Harley, 'Historians as Demonologists: The Myth of the Midwife-Witch' *Social History of Medicine* 3:1 (1990) 1–26, and Jane P. Davidson, 'The Myth of the Persecuted Female Healer' *Quidditas* 14 (1993) 115–29.

the care of mothers and infants. She did use herbs in her charms, and she did have practical knowledge of dyes and wool work. She did take at least one lover, and she was hanged for witchcraft.

Beyond the identification of individual healers and references to cunning practices, this book suggests that we might also imagine that competition between cunning bodies was a factor in heightening anxiety about witchcraft. Such competition might have been intensified in St Osyth in the early 1580s, or been a focus of particular concern to those observing it. While the women Ursley named as witches were a random-looking group, not evidently cunning folk, it is plausible that they had cunning connections: two of them were the daughters of the possible cunning woman Mother Barnes and both Joan Pechey and Elizabeth Bennett were accused of saying things that implied some preternatural medical knowledge. Even those who were apparently not suspected of being magical healers themselves, like Annis Glascock, were still questioned in ways that elicited stories of such activities from them. Recently, Laura Kounine has pointed to the ways in which 'the category of "witch" was unstable and porous' so that:

while the interrogators ... wished to create a fixed 'identity' of the witch during confessions, the trials often reveal a far more dynamic process of identifications which could be assimilated or contested.

Suspects like the St Osyth 'witches' could thus move very easily, in their own minds and the perceptions of others, between the identity of victim of witchcraft, cunning person and malevolent witch. We can see this happen with Ursley in particular, but it's also evident with Annis Glascock. Drift from victim to healer to witch was a significant trend in St Osyth in the development of the witch hunt in 1582.[9]

Some of this group of healing and harming women were imagined as working together in limited ways, such as sharing familiar spirits. To me, this suggests a pooling of female-oriented skills and emotions in these villages, a shared world of cunning magic and folkloric belief. But despite the accusation of a mass of women, there were no notions of mass gatherings, no coven or sabbaths. All the stories of accusation were about individual or paired interactions and despite shared interests in cunning folk and familiar spirits they don't fit into a wholly legible pattern. Although Millar has examined English accounts across the sixteenth and seventeenth century and, along with Jim Sharpe, suggested a greater interest in the devil and sabbath attendance than was previously imagined, in the St Osyth case of 1582 there is little evidence of this growing concern. It would be evident by the 1640s when, as part of the 'Witchfinder General' trials, further suspects were identified at St Osyth, but that was half a century later. In 1582, the malleable nature of the familiar spirit is of more interest to Brian Darcy – and apparently also interesting to accusers and accused alike – than the idea of an easily identifiable devil. Spirits

---

[9] Laura Kounine, *Imagining the Witch: Emotions, Gender and Selfhood in Early Modern Germany* (Oxford: Oxford University Press, 2018) 19 and see also Marion Gibson, 'Becoming-Witch: Narrating Witchcraft in Early Modern English News Pamphlets' in Esther Eidinow and Richard Gordon, eds., Special Issue of *Magic, Ritual and Witchcraft* 14:3 (Winter, 2019) 317–35.

are mobile and transferable, flit between definitions of animal and ghost, and are apparently both/either corporeal and insubstantial. Despite emphasising Brian's interest in demonological theory in my account, I'm struck by the confused and elusive working out of certain less-discussed demonological ideas, amongst which the witch's relationship with her or his familiar and the ontology of the creature is a standout.

As Jonathan Durrant has rightly written:

there has been a tendency to tidy up the history of witch-craft and present a uniform, teleological version of events ... but the circumstances in which accusations were made and witch-suspects investigated and prosecuted are far too messy and incompletely understood to suggest that one can see the firm outlines of a political approach to witch-hunting.

Durrant's focus is on whether puritans were driving a coherent political approach in the 1580s, but his point holds good for all factions of the period and for other insights beyond the political into the demonological.[10] Various approaches to witch hunting are possible to discern in this case but the problem is the 'firm' nature of the identification, or lack of it. In the case of the witches of St Osyth village itself, I would suggest that the 'shared world of cunning magic and folkloric belief', which is so evasive in the narrative despite its obvious power, was important in sparking the witch hunt. Cunning magic was a delicate balance of pooled imagination, faith and feeling. Once a woman like Grace Thurlowe had fallen out of trust with someone who was a player in that world, it

---

[10] Durrant, 'A Witch-hunting Magistrate?' 29.

quickly disintegrated into mutual recrimination, perhaps influenced by an ongoing plague and fear of demonic, haunting animals roaming the village. And once Brian Darcy had begun to uncover it, this enspirited world, the community of emotion and the imaginative landscape that it involved, looked secretive and irreligious to the magistrate. However untheorized, it was a way of feeling the world that undercut the rational, monetised and law-abiding construct of the Darcy estates and it sited power in other places than the courtrooms and studies of the Priory and St Clere's Hall. It suggested that power might be accessible instead to women wool-workers living in tumbledown cottages. I suspect this complex of insights was cumulatively intolerable and Brian moved determinedly against the unauthorised holders of magical power.

At Little Clacton, in contrast to the cunning element of St Osyth's stories, there was apparently not much interest in healing magic. Cisley and Henry Selles seem to have been suspected because, like Ursley Kempe, Cisley was said to have given birth to an illegitimate child (although she was married) and the word 'whore' was used about her. Richard Rosse had suffered economic damage to his farm and this was rolled into the other accusations. Just one family was recorded as being suspected, although their story was tacked onto pre-existing suspicions in St Osyth and, like Ursley and Ales Newman there, collaboration was imagined between some of the Little Clacton and Thorpe witches: Cisley Selles and Ales Manfielde. In the Soken accusations, things become vaguer: some of the suspects' ages are given (Ales Manfield, Elizabeth Ewstace and Margaret Grevell) and these are older women than the young women who were first suspected at St Osyth and Little Clacton – Ursley, Ales Hunt and her sister, Cisley. But we do not know the ages of some women – Elizabeth Bennett, Joan Robinson – so again a neat pattern is not traceable. With Annis Herd at Little Oakley, we return however to the notion of the witch as the young mother of an illegitimate child. This is a strong pattern across three villages, and again although the sexually subversive witch is a stereotype, here it is a perfectly demonstrable truth, especially in the case of Annis Herd. Annis was described as a 'harlot' by an accuser and repeatedly presented to the church court for sexual offences ('she took lovers when she wished'?) as my account has revealed. In the case of Little Oakley, we move away from midwife-witches and healer-witches, though: there is no suggestion at all that Annis practiced healing magic.

If the circumstances of each accusation are different, there is however a common thread of feeling running through each story: a mix of fear, grief, anger and worry, occasionally wonder and thrill. These feelings are seen most strongly in accusers' informations. There are haunting fears about illnesses and the safety of family members, there is grief at the loss of loved ones, especially the very young, there is hatred of neighbours, and there is a niggling, tired anxiety about household processes and resources. Some people are therefore seeking others to blame. This sense of a shared complex of feeling among accusers is like the shared world of magical power that intersected with it in the villages, and they are part of same emotional whole. This general concept was described by Barbara Rosenwein in 2006 as an 'emotional community' but I have tried to go beyond that concept in this book to include the wider environment in which suspected people lived, and also to evoke those feelings in the mind of the reader, paying attention to the emotions of the historian and the reader of history as advocated more recently by Katie Barclay and Tanya Evans.[11] If we do not feel or try to feel with the people of the past and walk in their steps where we can then how can we possibly understand, let alone learn from, their stories? A dry history of statistics and jargon does not capture anything of the terror and pain of a witch hunt, and these emotions are important in understanding both the past and the present. It would be nice if a neat theory of economics, class or sect had emerged from the fullest excavation of the St Osyth case to date, but it has not. Although my account is interested in injustice and oppression of the working poor, it is obviously incorrect to imagine that 'class positions' compelled people to act in particular ways, like electric charges motivating an automaton, and it's also unhelpful to minimise their agency in other ways by an excessive focus on social structures or cultural themes at the expense of a creative empathy with individual experiences.[12] That is an important insight in itself.

This book, therefore, emphasises that the history of witchcraft is an evasive history. And it lays particular stress on the history of witchcraft prosecutions as a history of unfeeling, of reducing people to representatives

[11] Barbara H. Rosenwein, *Emotional Communities in the Early Middle Ages* (Ithaca, NY: Cornell University Press, 2006); Barclay, 'Falling in Love with the Dead'; Tanya Evans, 'The Emotions of Family History and the Development of Historical Knowledge', Rethinking History 24:3–4 (2020) 310–31.
[12] French and Barry, eds., *Identity and Agency in England 1500–1800* 8.

of a theory about how the world works. Who the chosen suspects were is perhaps less important than the fact that suspects were chosen for persecution, that injustice was enacted with naming, killings and imprisonments and then the 'witches' individuality was written out of history. It's important not to perpetuate this practice in telling the stories of the accused and their communities. The reduction of people into theories and data does continue today: it is not only past history. Thousands of people are accused of witchcraft every year and that should matter. A witch hunt was and is a gross injustice, and it should feel like that when we think about it. Anger is an acceptable scholarly response, just as it is right to feel anger at the history of the enslavement of Africans, or of antisemitism and the Holocaust, or of histories of discrimination against women or LGBTQ+ people. Part of that permission to feel the past consists of permission to imagine the emotions and suffering of historical subjects. A felt microhistory of the individual lives of an Essex witch hunt can help us to think, for example, about how little the politics of power, gender and wealth have changed in some respects in the last four hundred years. Some members of entitled elites, defined in multiple ways, still believe that those they govern are a 'herd' rather than individuals. Activists and bystanders are arrested and sometimes murdered for protesting violence and injustice. Witch hunters are in important respects paradigmatic of the people that still enact that violence and injustice. It's important not to lose sight of that big picture.

My conviction about the importance of affective history – which I think is more accessibly described as 'feeling history' for the purposes of this book – strengthened over 2020 and 2021. Most obviously, research was interrupted by the COVID pandemic. The shocking eruption of multiple feelings into the rational plod of reading records and forming scholarly conclusions from them was instructive. Not surprisingly, fear, grief, anger and worry were top of my list of new interests, although occasionally wonder and thrill intervened. But I had always intended the project to be felt as well as thought. It was an impulse that seeped into the book partly from experiences with social media and the public history that happens online. For example, on 12 January 2020 I tweeted a photo of the flat fields between St Osyth and Frowick (Figure C.1), captioning it 'Walked a very, very long way in #Essex today on paths that accused #witches and their accusers walked. Makes you feel, as well as know, how far people tramped to ask for or give a little neighbourly help'.

I was recording a significant day for myself, but also trying to articulate accessibly the importance of feeling history, of trying to experience those aspects of the past that remain, especially the ones that are incarnate in landscape. Of course this is limited to what is possible and it's particularly plausible where there has been relatively little change: in the handling of material artefacts, in crafts and processes, the spaces and sights of buildings and farmlands, sensory impressions such as sounds and smells. And it is highly subjective. But I think it is worth the experiment.

In tiring myself out in St Osyth, I was hoping the discomforts of distance, weather, dirt, isolation, anxiety and darkness would help me find the right words to describe the experiences of the people of this book. It was an attempt to find 'kinaesthetic empathy' as Katherine M.

FIGURE C.1 Field path to Frowick. (Source: Author's photo.)
Note: A black and white version of this figure will appear in some formats. For the colour version, please refer to the plate section.

Johnson describes it, a 'theatrical, somatic and affective' connection with the witchcraft suspects of 1582.[13] The distance I walked was nothing compared with that walked by poor people the world over to fetch resources or medical help, however. I wasn't hungry and I could be reasonably sure I wasn't going to be attacked or injure myself. In filmic terms, this experience was no more than 'mild threat', if that. In the end, it was probably more an expression of commitment to the project than anything else, although it gave me an appreciation of the desolate flatness, the loneliness and grim tramping conditions of

[13] Katherine M. Johnson, 'Rethinking (re)doing: Historical Re-enactment and/as Historiography', *Rethinking History* 19:2 (2015) 203, 194.

the villages of the Essex coast. But, importantly for my thinking, the post struck a chord with Twitter users: by 3 April 2020, 13,208 people had seen the tweet and 510 had interacted with it. There were one hundred and thirty two likes, ten retweets and seven comments, far more than the two or three interactions that my tweets normally provoke.

Two of the comments expressed their 'love' for 'this idea' and 'this stuff', reminding me of Katie Barclay's exploration of 'falling in love with the dead' in her 2018 article of that name. Barclay draws on work on archives, sentiment and emotion by Emily Robinson, Mark Salber Phillips and others on the 'affective turn' in popular and academic history and wonders 'whether my emotional engagement with the archive was also a form of love'. She concludes that the engagement of the historian with documents is a relationship with features of both love and mourning.[14] And as well as this love of the historic past, its documents and its dead people, the Twitter response showed there was also a public and academic appetite for reading about feeling outside the archive – an experimental history, re-enactment, a method history of the kind discussed by Johnson. Even if this book only briefly engaged in a kind of re-enactment as part of its research, those few hours were crucial to its development, particularly its tone and vocabulary (emotive at times, accessible), structure (invitation at the start, descriptive

---

[14] Barclay, 'Falling in Love with the Dead' 461; Emily Robinson, 'Touching the Void: Affective History and the Impossible', *Rethinking History* 14:4 (2010) 503–20; Mark Salber Phillips, 'On the Advantage and Disadvantage of Sentimental History for Life', *History Workshop Journal* 65 (2013) 49–64.

inserts, methodology section at the end), authorial voice (use of 'I', a small number of creative interjections) and choices about naming (use of forenames). People other than me also want to feel history, or are pleased with an acknowledgement that they already do feel it.

Alongside an interest in feeling history, the book has also attempted to tell the stories of marginalised people especially women accused of witchcraft and their accusers, as discussed earlier. The focus on marginalised people in history is not, of course, new: Alice Clark, E. P. Thompson, Carlo Ginzburg and Keith Wrightson pioneered attempts to write the histories of 'working class' or 'village' people – in different ways, with various levels of success. This history 'from below' in combination with microhistory attempted to give due attention to those who had left evidence of their lives which could be used to understand the big questions asked by social and then cultural historians. A good example of an Essex microhistory is Henry French and Richard Hoyle's study of Earl's Colne, which focuses on understanding experiences of landholding and tenancy.[15] As part of this

---

[15] Alice Clark, *Working Life of Women in the Seventeenth Century* (London: George Routledge, 1919) and see also The Many-Headed Monster essays at https://manyheadedmonster.com/2019/03/21/alice-clark/; E. P. Thompson, *The Making of the English Working Class* (1963; London: Penguin, 2013); on witches, Carlo Ginzburg, *The Night Battles* trans John and Anne Tedeschi (1966; London: Routledge Kegan Paul, 1983) – Sigurður Gylfi Magnússon and István M. Szilártó, *What is Microhistory* (London: Routledge, 2013) especially 4–7 and Luke Freeman with Etienne Stockland, *An Analysis of Carlo Ginzburg's The Night Battles* (London: Macat, 2017) situate this history; on Essex, Keith Wrightson, *Poverty and Piety in an English Village* see also H. R. French and R. W. Hoyle, *The Character of English Rural Society: Earl's Colne 1550–1750* (Manchester and New York: Manchester University

exploration of the world of early modern people, a focus on identity became important, as explored in French and Jonathan Barry's 2004 *Identity and Agency in English Society 1500–1800*. Such approaches do not deal with all the gaps in history, however, as their highly reflective authors are well aware. They address a particular question and understandably choose their evidence accordingly. Where there are no or very limited sources of information written by or about a person then often no academic history of them ends up being written. When some classes of document are overlooked, it can be assumed that nothing of interest is recorded there. Many of the new histories that I read when I looked for more open research questions and writing practices that I could use to illuminate the lives of obscure Essex villagers were works that dealt with these problems in the context of race-based enslavement, a history of particular violence and silencing.

In this field, scholars such as Marisa J. Fuentes, Sonja Boon and Hazel Carby have noted that histories of enslavement were often written from somewhere close to the point of view of the enslaver because of record-keeping practices and survivals, and that conventional narrative histories did not convey the pain and horror of slavery and racism, or its complexity. Whilst it was understandable that older histories should be based on

Press, 2007); see also the classic Eamon Duffy, *The Voices of Morebath: Reformation and Rebellion in an English Village* (New Haven and London: Yale University Press, 2001) and subsequent scholarship on 'below'-ness such as Brodie Waddell, 'Writing History from Below: Chronicling and Record-Keeping in Early Modern England', *History Workshop Journal* 85 (2018) 239–64.

inventories and account ledgers – given the traditional dependence of historical scholarship on rich archival deposits written by subjects – it was no longer justifiable. The very form of the letters of these colonial documents, English round hand, could be seen as incarnating 'terror and violence camouflaged by this cosmetic beauty' and the neat lines of accounting ledgers practised the 'securing and containing, dividing and subdividing ... colour coding' that constituted enslavement. Alongside an examination of these records, Carby accordingly told her family's story through memories and imaginative creations as a way to explore the complexity of racial designations and their politics from the eighteenth to the twenty-first centuries. Carby uses phrases such as 'I imagine Lilly tossing and turning in his bed' and 'I expect she asked herself what Lilly was thinking' as a means to resist reliance on the tainted 'accounts' of empire.[16] Sonja Boon's work is similar, with more of an element of shamanic creative writing in her rhetoric: 'I needed the silence of the archives, so the ancestors could speak'.[17]

Fuentes also imagines aspects of her story of enslaved women by, for example, describing landscape features they would have encountered and analysing what these meant in the local economy of power:

[16] Hazel Carby, *Imperial Intimacies: A Tale of Two Islands* (London and New York: Verso, 2019) 230, 252–3, 288, 294.

[17] Sonja Boon, *What the Oceans Remember: Searching for Belonging and Home* (Waterloo, ON: Wilfrid Laurier University Press, 2019) 4 and 'Creative Histories: Vulnerability, Emotions and the Undoing of the Self' (2017) at https://storyingthepast.wordpress.com/2017/10/06/creative-histories-vulnerability-emotions-and-the-undoing-of-the-self-by-sonja-boon/

Jane might also have walked close to the careenage ... would smell the seawater, mixed with the sour and dank smells of too many people in too small an area, and if she passed by the Cage, which held captured runaways, she would have seen the sweat and sensed the fear of the occupants inside.

Fuentes argues that there are 'consequences of reproducing indifference to violence against and the silencing of black lives' and that instead a methodology is needed 'by which the archival record is stretched to accentuate the figures of enslaved women' as a means of 'redress'.[18] All sources that might reveal their individual stories should be sought. And if what they had experienced and felt individually was not recorded and could not be reconstructed with certainty from existing paperwork, then it should be imagined as accurately as possible. Fabulation of experiences and feelings became an important strategy designed to represent the histories of enslaved people more fully, to make them mean more to contemporary readers, and to have more impact in prompting better, redressing behaviours in the present. This book has tried to do something similar – though importantly on a very different scale and in very different circumstances – for witches, particularly witches as primarily women, and also for their previously obscure accusers. Witches and their accusers have often been subject to 'the enormous condscencension of posterity' just like Thompson's

---

[18] Marisa J. Fuentes, *Dispossessed Lives: Enslaved Women, Violence and the Archive* (Philadelphia: University of Pennsylvania Press, 2016) 12, 153, drawing on Saidiya V. Hartman, *Scenes of Subjection* (Oxford: Oxford University Press, 1997).

hand-loom weavers and 'deluded followers[s] of Joanna Southcott'.[19]

Witchcraft is not just a matter for the history books, then. But the St Osyth witches have been the subject of histories for a very long time and a brief survey shows why they are owed some respect in current scholarship. In around 1615, elements of the stories of Ursley Kempe and Elizabeth Bennett appeared in mangled form in one version of William Shakespeare's *Macbeth*, a play otherwise about the eleventh-century Scottish king. This version was a rewrite which incorporated material from Thomas Middleton's *The Witch*. In a song, 'Blacke Spirits, &c' in *Macbeth*'s Act Four, Scene One occur names from *A True and Just Recorde*, the familiar spirits of Ursley and Elizabeth:

> Black spirits, and white; Red spirits, and gray;
> Mingle, mingle, mingle, you that mingle may.
> Titty, Tiffin, keepe it stiff in;
> Fire-drake, Puckey, make it luckey;
> Liard, Robin, you must bob in.[20]

---

[19] Thompson, *The Making of the English Working Class* 12. For further discussion of *The Making of the English Working Class* and the book's contemporary utility see especially Dipesh Chakrabarty, 'Fifty Years of E. P. Thompson's *The Making of the English Working Class*' *Economic and Political Weekly* 48:51 (2013) 24–6, Zach Sell, 'Worst Conceivable Form: Race, Global Capital and *The Making of the English Working Class*' and Caroline Bressey, 'Race, Antiracism and the Place of Blackness in the Making and Remaking of the English Working Class', both in *Historical Reflections/Reflexions Historiques* 41:1 (2015) 54–69, and 70–82 as well as French and Barry, eds., *Identity and Agency in England 1500–1800* 4–6 and *passim*.

[20] Thomas Middleton, *The Witch*, from the first printed edition (London, 1778) at www.bl.uk/collection-items/first-edition-of-middletons-the-witch). For the background see Marion Gibson, *Rediscovering Renaissance Witchcraft* (London and New York: Routledge, 2017) 26–33.

Ursley and Elizabeth may be imagined as two of *Macbeth*'s company of potent witches, among the 'secret, black and midnight hags', the 'weird sisters' and the other epithets of what Diane Purkiss once described as an 'exploitative collage'. They have become famous through the process of their inaccurate rewriting, which has profoundly shaped the world beyond the text. In 1921, for example, two skeletons were found in a garden in Mill Street, St Osyth and interpreted as the physical remains of Ursley and Elizabeth. One of skeletons was sold to the Museum of Witchcraft in Boscastle, Cornwall and then to the Plymouth artist Robert Lenkiewicz. Initially displayed as a gruesome curiosity, the man (as he turned out to be) was reburied in St Osyth in 2011, but meantime a house fire in the village in 1932 and other unpleasant incidents had been attributed to the witches' supposedly malign ghosts.[21]

This gothic representation of the witch hunt's victims was established by the mid-twentieth century. In 1945, for example, Batsford Books published the folklorist and Conservative Party organiser Christina Hole's *Witchcraft in England*.[22] To illustrate it Batsford chose Mervyn Peake, who was then writing the first of his *Gormenghast* novels.

---

[21] Purkiss, *The Witch in History* 207; John Worland dir. *Ursula Kemp* (Fade to Black Television, 2012) and 'Ursula Kemp: The Witch Who Wouldn't Stay Buried' (2011) at www.ursulakemp.co.uk/index.html; St Osyth Museum, '1921 – The Witches' Skeletons' (n.d.) at www .stosythmuseum.co.uk/village-tales/1921-the-witches-skeletons

[22] See Gibson, *Rediscovering* for mid-twentieth century politics and witchcraft and K. M. Briggs, 'Christina Hole: An Appreciation' *Folklore* 90:1 (1979) 4–8; H. R. Ellis-Davidson and Theo Brown, 'Christina Hole 1896–1985', *Folklore* 97:1 (1986) 109–10; Alison Petch, 'Christina Hole (1896–1985)', *England: The Other Within* at http://england.prm .ox.ac.uk/englishness-Christina-Hole.html

He produced a series of haunting line drawings and pen and wash paintings responding to the text and the result was a distinctive, influential book. Unfortunately, it also contained some important inaccuracies. Christina Hole wrongly implied, for example, that all the group of suspects confessed to acts of malice:

Elizabeth Bennett confessed to killing two farmers and their wives, Joan Robinson had afflicted men with wasting diseases, Cecilia Celles and Ales Manfield had burnt standing corn and farm buildings, and all had helped at various times to destroy cattle, pigs and horses.

She concluded that 'it seems evident that [the St Osyth witches] were all leagued together and that their enmity was a very dangerous thing to incur'. So Mervyn Peake's cover and illustrations reflected that conclusion: in them, the witches appear predatory and villainous. Peake's portrait of Ursley Kempe, which is the frontispiece of Hole's book, set the tone with its bright, shifty eyes, gnarled, ancient skin, its frown and angry downturned mouth.[23]

Many readers accepted Hole and Peake's book as straightforward fact. It was generally well-received. Reviewers thought Hole's text calm and fluent, presenting its material in a lively anecdotal form. But the premier expert on witchcraft trials in England, Cecil L'Estrange Ewen, was deeply irritated. He wrote that the book's approach was 'slapdash' and full of 'resulting factual error' about the St Osyth trial. He also pronounced with his characteristic mix of fairness and acerbity on the

---

[23] Christina Hole, *Witchcraft in England* (London: Batsford, 1945) 86–7; Chris Beetles, 'Mervyn Peake (1911–1968)', www.chrisbeetles.com/artists/peake-mervyn-1911-1968.html

fifty five illustrations, large and small, no one of which exempli-
fies an historical point or anything but the skill and lively imagination of the artist ... No fewer than eight portraits labelled
with witches' names convey a misleading effect of uniform ugli-
ness and decrepitude.[24]

Ewen was right to be concerned: the influence of the
book, along with other portrayals of witches as genuinely
threatening non-Christians can be seen across fiction
and non-fiction, film and TV, in Britain throughout the
1950s.[25] Hole and Peake had created a lasting impression
of witches as terrifying conspirators, and they had represented named individuals from St Osyth and its sur-
rounds as vicious hags.

To Christina Hole's credit, and that of her publisher,
criticisms of this representation were acted upon for a
second edition, albeit over thirty years later in 1977.
Hole revised her statements.[26] Peake had died in 1968
and the publisher decided not to commission new illustrations from anyone else. Instead, the pictures were
reduced in number, weeding out some of the grotesques.

---

[24] C. L'Estrange Ewen, 'Witchcraft in England', *American Historical
Review* 53:2 (1948) 325–6; see also Harry E. Wedeck, 'Thaumaturgic
Vestiges: *Witchcraft in England*', *The New York Times* (27 July 1947)
BR3; Louis C. Jones, 'Witchcraft in England', *Journal of American
Folklore* 61:242 (1948) 408–9; F. H., '*Witchcraft in England*', *Journal
of the English Folk Dance and Song Society* 4:6 (1945) 255; Norah
Richardson, 'Witchcraft in England', *Journal of the Royal Society of
Arts* 94:4710 (1948) 170–1; Kevin Sullivan, 'Witchcraft in England',
America 77:20 (1947) 555–7.

[25] See Gibson, *Rediscovering* for more on the afterlives of witches in
twentieth century film and fiction.

[26] Hole, *Witchcraft in England* 2nd ed. (1977), 97, 100; J. L. M., review of
Witchcraft in England, *Nature* 156 (1945) 765.

The more libellous aspects of the remaining portrayals were also revised: the frontispiece went from being captioned 'Ursley Kempe' to the more tentative 'Ursley Kempe?' But by then accounts like these had established the St Osyth witches in the minds of readerships across the world. Essex was and is often represented as a superstitious county, haunted by its witchcraft history. Writers of newspaper articles and travelogues in the early years of the twentieth century became fond of asserting that that they had found in Essex a woman who was believed to feed 'niggets' or familiars 'forty miles from London!', or a 'Witch-finder', 'a man who is a direct link with the Middle Ages ... here in the midst of our civilization of which we are so proud and within some thirty miles of London .... He alone can tell us how to find witches'.[27]

Even in 2019–2020, The Cage, a house believed to be the site of St Osyth's lock up, was marketed as a place of paranormal activity with news stories such 'I Bought a Witch's Prison' and 'We Spent a Night in Essex's Most Haunted House' helping to promote its sale. Estate agents featured The Cage's plaque on the Domus agency's website, with its claim that 'St Osyth resident Ursula Kemp was imprisoned here before being hanged as a witch in 1582'. Domus also added:

---

[27] Anonymous, 'Superstition in Essex', *The Times* (3 September 1915) 5; Maxwell, *A Detective in Essex* 13–14, 20. The Wikipedia entry 'St Osyth Witches' was also surprisingly inaccurate when I last looked at it on 5 May 2021; see also St Osyth Museum, '1579 – the St Osyth Witches and Witch Trials' (n.d.) at www.stosythmuseum.co.uk/ village-tales/1579-st-osyth-witches-and-witch-trials which despite giving the wrong dates makes some well-researched points.

The Cage was a medieval prison where thirteen witches were kept in 1582 while awaiting trial. They became known as the Witches of St Osyth, and among them was the notorious Ursula Kemp. At the end of the trial three were found guilty, including Ursula, and were sentenced to death by hanging … Many of the subsequent owners could not handle the paranormal activities and sold on quickly, and in recent years there has been a suicide … Call or email … to register your interest and book your special viewing experience. You will need to sign a disclaimer, and you won't be left alone during the visit.[28]

Whilst it is historically inaccurate, this creative and exciting story about the house provokes a response just as *Macbeth* did in its time, as the comments on Domus's facebook page and the press stories confirm. The representation of the St Osyth suspects as actual, dangerous witches has gained traction in a way that most of the conventional histories of the St Osyth witches have not. Paradoxically, this suggests the power that creative writing has to evoke feeling, and through that to engage readers with the

---

[28] Jeff Maysh, 'I Bought a Witch's Prison' (2020) at https://jeffmaysh .medium.com/i-bought-a-witches-prison-ad2e7cbcecb, Richard Brown and Sophie Finnegan, 'The Cage in St Osyth: We Spent a Night in Essex's Most Haunted House and This is What Happened' *Essex Live* (10 January 2020) at www.essexlive.news/news/essex-news/cage-st-osyth-spent-night-3728934, Elliot Hawkins, 'The Cage St Osyth: The Reality of Living Inside the Haunted Essex House that Took 12 Years to Sell' *Essex Live* (10 January 2020) at www.essexlive.news/news/essex-news/cage-st-osyth-reality-living-3724810, Home Domus 360, 'The Cage in St-Osyth' (10 April 2019) at www.facebook.com/homedomus360/posts/the-cage-in-st-osythbritains-most-haunted-house-is-coming-on-the-market-soon-wit/2135861059862060/ and (n.d.) www .homedomus360.com/property/cage/

stories of witch hunts. Much more is needed than a bare recital of supposed facts, although recapitulating stories of fear and threat is not the best response.

An inspiring move in the direction of writing more creative histories has recently been led by Will Pooley, Anna Kisby Compton and Poppy Corbett at the University of Bristol, in collaboration with other historians and creative writers: Laura Sangha, Mark Hailwood, Sonja Boon and others. In the blog *Storying the Past*, which began in 2017, the group discuss how far historians already use creative writing techniques and how much further they could helpfully go. In a post that chimes with my own practice in this book, Pooley wrote that in his recent academic writing:

> when trying to write a realistic account of an important scene that took place in a tavern, I was struck by the fact that I could not easily say how the men there would have ordered a drink. Was there a bar, or table service? Did the customers pay in cash, or run a debt?

Such interactions, as Pooley notes, are often vital to understanding relationships between individuals or groups who are key players in the events described. Pooley's tavern scene was:

> a crucial turning point in a village conflict over trust, neighbourhood, and community. This was just as much about how men might share a drink with one another as it was about accusations of magical harm.

Pooley's reflections suggest how important it is to be able to imagine the social detail of lives in history, and with it subtleties of feeling that decisively shaped events and also resonate with a contemporary readership.

Similarly, public historians such as David Olusoga have called for a history with 'greater emotion and authenticity ... immersive and inclusive but also rooted in the here and now'.[29]

History with feeling is capable of making a difference to the present and future. People are self-evidently not data units: respecting their humanity and paying attention to their agency in detail is always important as well as noting the larger trends that shaped and constrained their lives. And just as history 'from below' was informed by the politics of its time, so contemporary history-writing must engage with contemporary issues: poverty, discrimination, exploitation, the distortion of narratives and the myths of hierarchy that populists, misogynists, racists and others use to set one group against another.[30] The events of the pandemic have encouraged me to take the opportunity to write a history with which I was better satisfied: a feeling history of those less visible and less valued than others. In particular, 2020–2021 emphasised the importance and human needs of the worst paid workers with fewest rights. It also sharpened perceptions of all people

[29] Will Pooley, 'Creative Writing as a Tool of Sustained Ignorance', *Storying the Past* (5 June 2018) at https://storyingthepast .wordpress.com/2018/06/05/creative-writing-as-a-tool-of-sustained-ignorance-by-will-pooley/; David Olusoga quoted in Stewart Clarke, 'Viacom backs UK indie producer Banjo Television' *Variety* (28 September 2017) at https://variety.com/2017/tv/news/ viacom-backs-uk-indie-producer-banjo-1202575218/

[30] Sebastian Shakespeare, 'Euro-Sceptic M.P. Jacob Rees-Mogg' *Daily Mail* (9 August 2014) 34 which notes Rees Mogg's 2007 marriage to heiress Helena de Chair, daughter of Somerset Struben de Chair of St Osyth's Priory and Lady Juliet Tadgell. Somerset wrote the guide book *St Osyth's Priory* (Derby: English Life Publications, c.1960) among other works detailing his exciting and notorious life.

as suffering individuals: confused, irrational, inconsistent and largely powerless. All were driven hither and thither by circumstances beyond their control, all became victims of the indifference and dishonesty of unworthy governors. These, it seemed to me, were the conditions of much of our history: unrecorded, undervalued but vital. There is a moral imperative to write this history and to hope that, however minimally, it shapes a better future.[31] As George Eliot concluded in *Middlemarch*, 'the growing good of the world is partly dependent on unhistoric acts; and that things are not so ill with you and me as they might have been, is half owing to the number who lived faithfully a hidden life, and rest in unvisited tombs'.[32]

---

[31] On this hope, see Maria Ines La Greca, 'Hayden White and Joan W. Scott's Feminist History: The Practical Past, the Political Present and an Open Future', *Rethinking History* 20: 3 (2016) 395–413 drawing particularly on Joan W. Scott, *Feminism and History* (Oxford: Oxford University Press, 1996) and Hayden White, *The Practical Past* (Evanston, IL: Northwestern University Press, 2014).

[32] George Eliot, *Middlemarch* (1872; London: Penguin, 1987) 896.

BIBLIOGRAPHY

A Rehearsall both straung and true, of heinous and horrible actes. London, 1579.

A True and just Recorde of the Information, Examination, and Confession of All the Witches, Taken at S Oses in the Countie of Essex London, 1582 at https://quod.lib.umich.edu/cgi/t/text/text-idx?c=eebo;idno=A14611.0001.001.

Allen, David, ed., *Ipswich Borough Archives 1255–1835.* Woodbridge: Boydell & Brewer, Suffolk Records Society and the British Library, 2000.

An Archaeological Evaluation of Old School Chase, St Osyth, Essex, CAT Report 43, September, 1999.

Anglo American Legal Tradition at the O'Quinn Law Library, University of Houston Law Center (2015) at www.aalt.law.uh.edu/AALT7/C78/C78n052/IMG_0018.htm.

Anonymous, 'Superstition in Essex', *The Times* (3 September 1915) 5.

Baker, John H., 'John Southcote', *Oxford Dictionary of National Biography* (2008) at www.oxforddnb.com/view/10.1093/ref:odnb/9780198614128.001.0001/odnb-9780198614128-e-26049?rskey=ekoQvU&result=1.

Baldwin, Summerfield, 'Jean Bodin and the League', *Catholic Historical Review* 23:2 (1937–1938) 60–84.

Barclay, Katie, 'Falling in Love with the Dead', *Rethinking History* 22:4 (2018) 459–73.

Beetles, Chris, 'Mervyn Peake (1911–1968)' (n.d.) at www.chrisbeetles.com/artists/peake-mervyn-1911-1968.html.

Benham, Hervey, *Essex Gold: The Fortunes of the Essex Oysterman.* Chelmsford: Essex Record Office, 1993.

Bickley, Augustus Charles, 'Samuel Hieron', *Dictionary of National Biography*, vol. 26 (London, 1891) 362–3.

Bindoff, Stanley Thomas, ed., *The House of Commons, 1509–1558*, 3 vols. London: Secker & Warburg for History of Parliament Trust, 1982.

Bodin, Jean, *De la Démonomanie des Sorciers*. Paris, 1580.

Boon, Sonja, 'Creative Histories: Vulnerability, Emotions and the Undoing of the Self' (2017) at https://storyingthepast.wordpress.com/2017/10/06/creative-histories-vulnerability-emotions-and-the-undoing-of-the-self-by-sonja-boon/.

Boon, Sonja, *What the Oceans Remember: Searching for Belonging and Home*. Waterloo, ON: Wilfrid Laurier University Press, 2019.

Borman, Tracy, *Witches*. London: Jonathan Cape, 2013.

Bressey, Caroline, 'Race, Antracism and the Place of Blackness in the Making and Remaking of the English Working Class', *Historical Reflections/Reflexions Historiques* 41:1 (2015) 70–82.

Briggs, K. M., 'Christina Hole: An Appreciation', *Folklore* 90:1 (1979) 4–8.

Briggs, Robin, 'Many Reasons Why: Witchcraft and the Problem of Multiple Explanation' in Jonathan Barry, Gareth Roberts and Marianne Hester, eds., *Witchcraft in Early Modern Europe: Studies in Culture and Belief*. Cambridge: Cambridge University Press, 1996 49–63.

Briggs, Robin, *Witches and Neighbours: The Social and Cultural Context of European Witchcraft*. Oxford: Blackwell, 1996.

Brown, Richard and Sophie Finnegan, 'The Cage in St Osyth: We Spent a Night in Essex's Most Haunted House and This Is What Happened', *Essex Live* (10 January 2020) at www.essexlive.news/news/essex-news/cage-st-osyth-spent-night-3728934.

Burke, Peter, 'Urban Sensations: Attractive and Repulsive' in Herman Roodenburg, ed., *A Cultural History of the Senses in the Renaissance*. London: Bloomsbury Academic, 2019 43–59.

Caius, Johannes, translated by Abraham Fleming, *Of Englishe dogges*. London, 1576.

Carby, Hazel, *Imperial Intimacies: A Tale of Two Islands*. London and New York: Verso, 2019.

Carr, Victoria, 'Witches and the Dead: The Case for the English Ghost Familiar', *Folklore* 130:3 (2019) 282–99.

Carver, Martin, *Sutton Hoo: A Seventh-Century Princely Burial Ground and its Context*. London: British Museum Press and Society of Antiquaries, 2005.

Chakrabarty, Dipesh, 'Fifty Years of E.P. Thompson's *The Making of the English Working Class*', *Economic and Political Weekly* 48:51 (2013) 24–6.

Chambers, William and Robert Chambers, *Information for the People*. Edinburgh and London: Chambers and Partners, 1849.

Clark, Alice, *Working Life of Women in the Seventeenth Century*. London: George Routledge, 1919.

Clarke, Stewart, 'Viacom backs UK indie producer Banjo Television' *Variety* (28 September 2017) at https://variety .com/2017/tv/news/viacom-backs-uk-indie-producer-banjo-1202575218/

Cockburn, J. S., *Calendar of Assize Records: Essex Indictments: Elizabeth I*. London: HMSO, 1978.

Cockburn, J. S., *Calendar of Assize Records: Introduction*. London: HMSO, 1985.

Cokayne, G. E., *Complete Baronetage*. 5 vols. Exeter: William Pollard, 1900–1906.

Collinson, Patrick, *The Elizabethan Puritan Movement*. London: Jonathan Cape, 1967.

Cooper, Janet ed., *A History of the County of Essex* vol. 10. London: Victoria County History, 2001.

Craig, Geraldine, *St Osyth: A Century of Village Life in Pictures*. Clacton-on-Sea and St Osyth: Guild Press and St Osyth Historical Society, 2003.

Cressy, David, 'Who Buried Mrs Horseman? Excommunication, Accommodation and Silence' in *Travesties and Transgressions in Tudor and Stuart England: Tales of Discord and Dissension* (Oxford: Oxford University Press, 1999) 116–37.

Davidson, Jane P., 'The Myth of the Persecuted Female Healer', *Quidditas* 14 (1993) 115–29.

Davies, Owen, *Cunning Folk: Popular Magic in English History*. Oxford: Blackwell, 2007.

Davies, Owen and Timothy Easton, 'Cunning Folk and the Production of Magical Artefacts' in Ronald Hutton, ed., *Physical Evidence for Ritual Acts, Sorcery and Witchcraft in Christian Britain* (Basingstoke: Palgrave, 2015) 209–31.

Dean, Leonard F., 'Bodin's Methodus in England before 1625', *Studies in Philology* 39:2 (1942) 160–6.

De Chair, Somerset Struben, *St Osyth's Priory*. Derby: English Life Publications, c.1960.

Duffy, Eamon, *The Voices of Morebath: Reformation and Rebellion in an English Village*. New Haven and London: Yale University Press, 2001.

Durrant, Jonathan, 'A Witch-hunting Magistrate? Brian Darcy and the St Osyth Witchcraft Cases of 1582', *The English Historical Review* (2021) 1–29.

Eliot, George, *Middlemarch*. 1872; London: Penguin, 1987.

Ellis-Davidson, H. R. and Theo Brown, 'Christina Hole 1896-1985', *Folklore* 97:1 (1986) 109–10.

Elmer, Peter, *Witchcraft, Witch-Hunting and Politics in Early Modern England*. Oxford: Oxford University Press, 2016.

Emmison, F. G. ed., *Essex Wills: The Bishop of London's Commissary Court 1578–1588*. Chelmsford: Essex Record Office with Friends of Historic Essex, 1995.

Emmison, F. G., ed., *Elizabethan Life: Wills of Essex Gentry and Merchants*. Chelmsford: Essex County Council, 1978.

Emmison, F. G., ed., *Essex Wills: The Archdeaconry Courts 1577–1584*. Chelmsford: Essex Record Office and Friends of Historic Essex, 1987.

Emmison, F. G., ed., *Essex Wills: The Archdeaconry Courts 1583–1592*. Chelmsford: Essex Record Office with Friends of Historic Essex, 1989.

Emmison, F. G., *Elizabethan Life: Disorder*. Chelmsford: Essex County Council, 1970.

Emmison, F. G., *Elizabethan Life: Home, Work and Land*. Chelmsford: Essex County Council, 1976.

Emmison, F. G., *Elizabethan Life: Morals and the Church Courts*. Chelmsford: Essex County Council, 1973.

Emmison, F. G., *Feet of Fines for Essex* vol. 6. Oxford: Leopard's Head, 1993.

Emmison, F. G., *Tudor Food and Pastimes*. London: Ernest Benn, 1964.

Emmison, F. G., *Wills of Essex Gentry and Merchants*. Chelmsford: Essex County Council, 1978.

Emmison, F. G. and Marc Fitch, *Feet of Fines for Essex* vol. 5. Oxford: Leopard's Head, 1991.

Essex and the Sea. Chelmsford: Essex County Council, 1970.

Evans, Tanya, 'The Emotions of Family History and the Development of Historical Knowledge', *Rethinking History* 24:3–4 (2020) 310–31.

Ewen, C. L'Estrange, 'Witchcraft in England', *American Historical Review* 53:2 (1948) 325–6.

Favret-Saada, Jeanne, *Deadly Words: Witchcraft in the Bocage*. Cambridge and Paris: Cambridge University Press and Fondation de la Maison des Sciences de l'Homme, 1981.

Fleming, Abraham, *A straunge and terrible wunder wrought very late in the parish church of Bongay*. London, 1577.

Fletcher, Reginald J. ed., *The Pension Book of Gray's Inn*. London: Chiswick Press, 1891.

Freeman, Luke with Etienne Stockland, *An Analysis of Carlo Ginzburg's The Night Battles*. London: Macat, 2017.

French, H. R. and R. W. Hoyle, *The Character of English Rural Society: Earl's Colne 1550–1750*. Manchester and New York: Manchester University Press, 2007.

Fudge, Erica, 'Counting Chickens in Early Modern Essex: Writing Animals into Early Modern Wills' in *Quick Cattle and Dying Wishes: People and their Animals in Early Modern England*. Ithaca, NY: Cornell University Press, 2018. 21–48.

Fuentes, Marisa J., *Dispossessed Lives: Enslaved Women, Violence and the Archive*. Philadelphia: University of Pennsylvania Press, 2016.

Fuidge, N. M., 'John Audley I (d.1588) of Berechurch, Essex' in P. W. Hasler, *The History of Parliament 1558–1603*. Woodbridge: Boydell and Brewer, n.d. at www.historyofparliamentonline.org/volume/1558-1603/member/audley-john-i-1588

Gaskill, Malcolm, 'Witchcraft and Neighbourliness in Early Modern England' in Steve Hindle, Alexandra Shepard and John D. Walter, eds., *Remaking English Society: Social Relations and Social Change in Early Modern England*. Woodbridge: Boydell Press, 2013 211–32.

Gaskill, Malcolm, 'Witchcraft and Power in Early Modern England: The Case of Margaret Moore' in Jenny Kermode and Garthine Walker, eds., *Women, Crime and the Courts in Early Modern England* London: UCL Press, 1994 125–45.

Germany, Mark, 'A Causewayed Enclosure at St Osyth, Essex', *Past* 44 (July, 2003) at www.le.ac.uk/has/ps/past/past44.html#Osyth

Germany, Mark, Neolithic and Bronze Age Monuments, Middle Iron Age Settlement at Lodge Farm, St Osyth, East Anglian Archaeology report 117. Chelmsford: Essex County Council, 2007.

Gibson, Marion, 'Becoming-Witch: Narrating Witchcraft in Early Modern English News Pamphlets' in Esther Eidinow and Richard Gordon, eds., Special Issue of *Magic, Ritual and Witchcraft* 14:3 (Winter, 2019) 317–35.

Gibson, Marion, ed., *Early English Trial Pamphlets* vol. 2. London: Pickering and Chatto, 2006.

Gibson, Marion, *Early Modern Witches*. London: Routledge, 2000.

Gibson, Marion, 'French Demonology in an English Village: The St. Osyth Experiment of 1582' in Rita Voltmer, Julian Goodare and Liv Helene Willumsen, eds., *Demonology and Witch-hunting in Early Modern Europe*. London: Routledge, 2020, 107–26.

Gibson, Marion, *Possession, Puritanism and Print*. London: Pickering and Chatto, 2006.

Gibson, Marion, *Reading Witchcraft: Stories of Early English Witches*. London: Routledge, 1999.

Gibson, Marion, *Rediscovering Renaissance Witchcraft*. London and New York: Routledge, 2017.

Gibson, Marion, *Witchcraft: The Basics*. London and New York: Routledge, 2018.

Gifford, George, *A Dialogue Concerning Witches and Witchcraftes*. London, 1593.

Ginzburg, Carlo, *The Night Battles* trans John and Anne Tedeschi. 1966; London: Routledge Kegan Paul, 1983.

Goodman, Ruth, *How to Be a Tudor*. London: Penguin, 2016.

Gomulkiewicz, Abigail, 'Religious Materiality in Elizabethan Essex (1558–1603)', *Material Religion* 16:3 (July 2020) 275–97.

Grieve, Hilda, *The Great Tide*. Chelmsford: Essex County Council, 1959.

Grieve, Hilda, *The Sleepers and the Shadows*. 2 vols. Chelmsford: Essex Record Office, 1988–1994.

H. F., 'Witchcraft in England', *Journal of the English Folk Dance and Song Society* 4:6 (1945) 255.

Harding, Phil, Catriona Gibson and Nicholas Cooke, *St Osyth, Essex: An Archaeological Evaluation and Assessment of the Results*. Salisbury: Wessex Archaeology, 2005.

Harley, David, 'Historians as Demonologists: The Myth of the Midwife-Witch', *Social History of Medicine* 3:1 (1990) 1–26.

Harrison, William, *Elizabethan England: From The Description of England* ed. Lothrop Withington. London: Walter Scott, 1876.

Hartman, Saidiya V., *Scenes of Subjection*. Oxford: Oxford University Press, 1997.

Hawkins, Elliot, 'The Cage St Osyth: The Reality of Living Inside the Haunted Essex House that Took 12 Years to Sell', *Essex Live* (10 January 2020) at www.essexlive.news/news/essex-news/cage-st-osyth-reality-living-3724810

Hendy, Phyllis M., *The History of St Osyth: Pubs, Pints and Publicans*. St Osyth: Tooseyprint, 2009.

Hendy, Phyllis M., *St Osyth Parish Council: The First 100 Years*. Clacton-on-Sea: Campwood Press, 1993.

Hendy, Phyl, *The St Osyth Witch Story: 1582 and All That*. St Osyth: n.p., 1993.

Higgs, Laquita M., *Godliness and Governance in Tudor Colchester*. Ann Arbor, MI: University of Michigan Press, 1998.

Historic England, 'St Clere's Hall' (1986) at https://british-listedbuildings.co.uk/101309039-st-cleres-hall-st-osyth#.YJvgcNVKjIU

Historic England, 'St Osyth's Priory' (1987) at https://historicengland.org.uk/listing/the-list/list-entry/1000237

Hole, Christina, *Witchcraft in England*. London: Batsford, 1945.

Hole, Christina, *Witchcraft in England*. 2nd ed. London: Book Club Associates, 1977.

Holmes, Clive, 'Women: Witnesses and Witches', *Past and Present* 140:1 (1993) 45–78.

Home Domus 360, 'The Cage in St-Osyth' (10 April 2019) at www.facebook.com/homedomus360/posts/the-cage-in-st-osythbritains-most-haunted-house-is-coming-on-the-market-soon-wit/2135861059862060/

Home Domus 360, 'The Cage' (n.d.) at www.homedomus360.com/property/cage/

Hope, Robert Charles, *Legendary Lore of the Holy Wells of England*. London: Elliott Stock, 1893.

Hull, M. R., 'Five Bronze Age Beakers from North East Essex', *The Antiquaries Journal* 26:1–2 (Jan–April, 1946) 67–9.

Ibbetson, David, 'Sir Thomas Gawdy', *Oxford Dictionary of National Biography* (2008) at www.oxforddnb.com/view/10.1093/ref:odnb/9780198614128.001.0001/odnb-9780198614128-e-10469?rskey=aN7gF6&result=1

Ingram, Martin, *The Church Courts, Sex and Marriage in England 1570–1640*. Cambridge: Cambridge University Press, 1987.

Jermyn, Stanley T., *Flora of Essex*. Fingeringhoe: Essex Naturalists Trust, 1974.

Johnson, Katherine M., 'Rethinking (re)doing: Historical Re-enactment and/as Historiography', *Rethinking History* 19:2 (2015) 193–206.

Jones, Louis C., 'Witchcraft in England', *Journal of American Folklore* 61:242 (1948) 408–9.

Kounine, Laura, *Imagining the Witch: Emotions, Gender and Selfhood in Early Modern Germany*. Oxford: Oxford University Press, 2018.

La Greca, Maria Ines, 'Hayden White and Joan W. Scott's Feminist History: The Practical Past, the Political Present and an Open Future', *Rethinking History* 20: 3 (2016) 395–413.

M., J. L., 'Witchcraft in England', *Nature* 156 (1945) 765.

Macfarlane, Alan, *Witchcraft in Tudor and Stuart England*. 1970; Prospect Heights, IL: Waveland Press, 1991.

Magnússon, Sigurður Gylfi and István M. Szilártó, *What is Microhistory*. London: Routledge, 2013.

Marvin, William T. R., *The English Ancestry of Reinold and Matthew Marvin of Hartford, CT*. Boston, privately printed, 1900.

Maxwell, Donald, *A Detective in Essex*. London: John Lane, 1933.

Maysh, Jeff, 'I Bought a Witch's Prison' (2020) at https://jeffmaysh.medium.com/i-bought-a-witches-prison-ad2e7cbcecb.

McGinnis, Timothy Scott, *George Gifford and the Reformation of the Common Sort*. Philadelphia: Penn State University Press, 2005.

McIlwaine, H. R., *Minutes of the Council and General Court of Colonial Virginia*. Richmond, VA: Virginia State Library, 1924).

McIntosh, Marjorie Keniston, *Poor Relief in England 1350–1600*. Cambridge: Cambridge University Press, 2012.

Middleton, Thomas, *The Witch*. London, 1778 at www.bl.uk/collection-items/first-edition-of-middletons-the-witch

Millar, Charlotte Rose. *Witchcraft, the Devil and Emotions in Early Moden England*. London and New York: Routledge, 2017.

Morant, Philip, *The History and Antiquities of the County of Essex*. 2 vols. London, 1748.

Muskett, J. J., 'Suffolk Wills from the Prerogative Court of Canterbury. Whetcrofte of Suffolk' (n.d.) at http://suffolkinstitute.pdfsrv.co.uk/customers/Suffolk%20Institute/2014/01/10/Volume%20VI%20Part%202%20(1886)_Wills%20Prerogatice%20Ct%20of%20Canterbury%20Whetcroft%20of%20Suffolk%20J%20J%20Muskett_94%20to%20104.pdf

Nicholson, Brinsley, ed., *The Discoverie of Witchcraft*. London, 1886.

Norman, Tracey, *Witch*, Circle of Spears, 2016–present at www.traceynormanswitch.com

Normand, Lawrence and Gareth Roberts, eds., *Witchcraft in Early Modern Scotland*. Edinburgh: Edinburgh University Press, 2000.

Oldridge, Darren, ed., *The Witchcraft Reader* 3rd. ed. London and New York: Routledge, 2019.

Paphitis, Tina, 'Haunted Landscapes: Place, Past and Presence' *Time and Mind* 13:4 (2020) 341–9.

Peile, John, *Biographical Register of Christ's College 1505–1905*, 2 vols. 1910; Cambridge: Cambridge University Press, 2014.

Pennie, A. R., 'The Evolution of Puritan Mentality in an Essex Cloth Town: Dedham and the Stour Valley 1560–1640' unpublished PhD thesis, University of Sheffield, 1989.

Petch, Alison, 'Christina Hole (1896–1985)', *England: The Other Within* (1985) at http://england.prm.ox.ac.uk/englishness-Christina-Hole.html

Pittman, Susan, 'Elizabethan and Jacobean Deer Parks in Kent' unpublished PhD thesis, University of Kent, 2011.

Pooley, Will, 'Creative Writing as a Tool of Sustained Ignorance', *Storying the Past* (5 June 2018) at https://storyingthepast.wordpress.com/2018/06/05/creative-writing-as-a-tool-of-sustained-ignorance-by-will-pooley/

Poos, L. R., *A Rural Society after the Black Death: Essex 1350–1525*. Cambridge: Cambridge University Press, 1991.

Potts, Thomas, *The Wonderfull Discoverie of Witches in the Countie of Lancaster*. London, 1612.

Purkiss, Diane, *The Witch in History*. London and New York: Routledge, 1996.

Richardson, Norah, 'Witchcraft in England', *Journal of the Royal Society of Arts* 94:4710 (1948) 170–1.

Robinson, Emily, 'Touching the Void: Affective History and the Impossible', *Rethinking History* 14:4 (2010) 503–20.

Rosen, Barbara, *Witchcraft in England 1558–1618*. 1969. Amherst: University of Massachusetts Press, 1991.

Rosenwein, Barbara H., *Emotional Communities in the Early Middle Ages*. Ithaca, NY: Cornell University Press, 2006.

Salber Phillips, Mark, 'On the Advantage and Disadvantage of Sentimental History for Life', *History Workshop Journal* 65 (2013) 49–64.

Scott, Joan W., *Feminism and History*. Oxford: Oxford University Press, 1996.

Scott, Randy A. (translator) and Jonathan L. Pearl, eds., *On the Demon-Mania of Witches by Jean Bodin*. Toronto: Centre for Renaissance and Reformation Studies, 1995.

Scott, Valerie and Libby Brown, *St Osyth: Conservation Area Appraisal and Management Plan*. Tendring: Tendring District Council, 2010.

Sell, Zach, 'Worst Conceivable Form: Race, Global Capital and *The Making of the English Working Class*', *Historical Reflections/Reflexions Historiques* 41:1 (2015) 54–69.

Shakespeare, Sebastian, 'Euro-Sceptic M.P. Jacob Rees-Mogg', *Daily Mail* (9 August 2014) 34.

Sharpe, James, *Crime in Early Modern England*. London and New York: Routledge, 1984.

Sharpe, James, 'The Witch's Familiar in Elizabethan England' in G. W. Bernard and S. J. Gunn, *Authority and Consent in Tudor England*. Aldershot: Ashgate, 2002, 219–32.

Shepard, Alexandra, 'Honesty, Worth and Gender in Early Modern England 1560–1640' in Henry French and Jonathan Barry, eds., *Identity and Agency in England 1500–1800*. Basingstoke: Palgrave Macmillan, 2004, 87–105.

Sherman, Thomas Townsend, *Sherman Genealogy*. New York: Tobias A Wright, 1920.

Simpson, A. W. B., 'The Early Constitution of Gray's Inn', *The Cambridge Law Journal* 34:1 (1975) 131–50.

St James Parish Church, 'Little Clacton' (c. 2007) at www .littleclactonparishchurch.co.uk/Church-History/

St Osyth Museum, '1579 – the St Osyth Witches and Witch *Trials*' (n.d.) at www.stosythmuseum.co.uk/village-tales/ 1579-st-osyth-witches-and-witch-trials

St Osyth Museum, '1921 – The Witches' Skeletons' (n.d.) at www.stosythmuseum.co.uk/village-tales/1921-the-witches-skeletons

Steer, Francis W., *Farm and Cottage Inventories of Mid-Essex 1635–1749*. 1950; Chichester: Phillimore, 1969.

Sullivan, Kevin, 'Witchcraft in England', *America* 77:20 (1947) 555–57.

Summers, Montague, ed., *The Discoverie of Witchcraft*. 1930; New York: Dover, 1972.

The Apprehension and Confession of Three Notorious Witches. London, 1589.

The Examination and Confession of a notorious Witch named Mother Arnold. London, 1595.

The Examination and Confession of certaine Wytches. London, 1566.

The Many-Headed Monster, '#Alice Clark 100' reading group, 21 March 2019–5 November 2019) at https:// manyheadedmonster.com/2019/03/21/alice-clark/

The Wonderful Discovery of the Witchcrafts of Margaret and Phillip Flower. London, 1619.

Thompson, E. P., *The Making of the English Working Classes*. 1963; London: Penguin, 2013.

Thornton, Christopher, 'Before the Resorts' (n.d.) www .tendringcoastalheritage.org.uk/wp-content/uploads/ 2019/06/Tendring-Before-the-Resorts-.pdf

Thornton, Christopher, 'Land Ownership; Kirby-le-Soken', 'Land Ownership: Thorpe-le-Soken' and 'Land Ownership: Walton-le-Soken' (n.d.) at Victoria County History: Work in Progress at www.history.ac.uk/research/

victoria-county-history/county-histories-progress/essex/
essex-xii-part

Thornton, Christopher and Herbert Eiden, eds., *The History of the County of Essex (Victoria County History)* volume XII. London and Woodbridge: IHR/Boydell and Brewer, 2020.

Underdown, David, *Revel, Riot and Rebellion: Popular Culture and Politics in England 1603–1660*. Oxford: Oxford University Press, 1985.

Ursula Kemp, dir. John Worland, Fade to Black Television, 2012.

Venn, J. and J. A. Venn, Alumni Cantabrigiensis. 10 vols. Cambridge: Cambridge University Press, 1922–1954 at https://venn.lib.cam.ac.uk/

Waddell, Brodie. 'Writing History from Below: Chronicling and Record-Keeping in Early Modern England' *History Workshop Journal* 85 (2018) 239–64.

Wales, Tim, 'Living at Their Own Hands: Policing Poor Households and the Young in Early Modern Rural England' *The Agricultural History Review* 61:1 (2013) 19–39.

Walker, Kenneth, *The Story of Little Clacton*. Little Clacton: Little Clacton Parish Council, 1958 at https://littleclacton-pc.org.uk/village-life/local-history/the-story-of-little-clacton-an-essex-village-1958/

Walsham, Alexandra, *The Reformation of the Landscape*. Oxford: Oxford University Press, 2011.

Wedeck, Harry E., 'Thaumaturgic Vestiges: Witchcraft in England', *The New York Times* (27 July 1947) BR3.

White, Hayden, *The Practical Past*. Evanston, IL: Northwestern University Press, 2014.

White, P. O. G., 'William Drury' *Oxford Dictionary of National Biography* (2008) at https://doi.org/10.1093/ref:odnb/8102

Whyte, Nicola, *Inhabiting the Landscape: Place, Custom and Memory 1500–1800*. Oxford: Windgather Press/Oxbow Books, 2009.

Wiffen, Neil. 'Favourite ERO Documents: Walker Map of Chelmsford 1591' (19 August 2013) at www.essexrecordofficeblog.co.uk/favourite-ero-documents-walker-map-of-chelmsford-1591/

Wilby, Emma, *Cunning Folk and Familiar Spirits*. Brighton: Sussex Academic Press, 2005.

Willis, Deborah, *Malevolent Nurture: Witch Hunting and Maternal Power in Early Modern England*. Ithaca, NY: Cornell University Press, 1995.

Willis, Deborah, 'The Witch-Family in Elizabethan and Jacobean Print Culture', *Journal for Early Modern Cultural Studies* 13:1 (2013) 4–31.

Witches Apprehended. London, 1613.

Worland, John, 'Ursula Kemp: The Witch Who Wouldn't Stay Buried' (2011) at www.ursulakemp.co.uk/index.html; www.stosythmuseum.co.uk/village-tales/1921-the-witches-skeletons

Wrightson, Keith, *Poverty and Piety in an English Village: Terling 1525–1700*. 1977; Oxford: Oxford University Press, 1995.

INDEX